MATT CLOUGH

LOFTY

NAT LOFTHOUSE, ENGLAND'S LION OF VIENNA

Cover illustrations: front: Nat Lofthouse in August 1955. (Barratts/S&G and Barratts/EMPICS Sport/PA Images) *Back:* Nat leads out teammate Bryan Edwards as Bolton Wanderers captain. (*Bolton News*)

First published 2019

The History Press
97 St George's Place, Cheltenham, GL50 3QB
www.thehistorypress.co.uk

British Library Cataloguing in Publication Data.
A catalogue record for this book is available from the British Library.

ISBN 978 0 7509 8889 6

Typesetting and origination by The History Press
Printed and bound in Great Britain by TJ International Ltd

CONTENTS

FOREWORD
BY JOHN MCGINLAY

BOLTON IS SPECIAL, and what makes it special is the people. They made me so welcome on the day I signed, 30 September 1992, and even now, almost 30 years later, I'm still treated the same way. When the team does well, the town does well. When they're winning, there's a buzz. They're proud of their football club, so it's important that it's protected, successful and run well.

Nobody did more to make that happen than Nat. I first met him the day I signed for the club. I was in awe of him. I knew his history, I knew what he meant to the football club. But what really struck me was that he was so down to earth. He was such a gentleman – just a fantastic man.

Coming into the football club as a striker, with all Nat had achieved, could have been a bit intimidating, but I never felt that with Nat. He was always approachable, someone that you could talk to and bounce things off, and it helped me greatly. And not just me – all of the players. If you were going through a bad time, maybe hadn't scored for a few games, maybe a loss of form, he'd quietly put his arm around you and take you for a little walk.

He'd always just say 'keep going cocker, keep playing cocker, things will turn out right'. It was just such a boost for someone like that to take the time to do that. He'd never growl 'come on' or anything – he'd just speak to you, and nobody would want to let him down, because everybody knew what it meant to him. In fact, he was the type of guy who would encourage you to beat his records, without any remorse, because it would have meant you'd be doing well for his football club. That was all that mattered to Nat – it was his football club and he wanted to see it do well.

And we saw him every day. At training, the big matches, and the big moments of my time at the football club. The Play-Off Final in 1995 was an unbelievable day. There was an interview with myself and Owen Coyle and Sir Nat, and he kissed me on the cheek! The delight in his eyes that day – this was his club getting back in the big time. He was skipping around Wembley like a 20-year-old.

The nights at Liverpool, the nights at Highbury – he was at all of them. You could look up from the pitch into the director's box, and he'd be there, beaming. When I was called up to Scotland, there was nobody prouder than Nat. He came in and shook my hand and said, 'I'm chuffed for you, cocker, magnificent.' He was proud as punch, as much as if I'd been going to play for England.

He never mentioned that I was making my debut in the same stadium where he scored his famous goals against Austria. That was the thing – when he talked to you it was always about you. He never mentioned playing for England or anything like that. He could have had us in awe, but he never spoke about himself. That was the difference with Nat.

I suppose that, in a way, I'm a bit like Nat was when I first joined the team. If anyone says a bad word about Bolton, I've got to have a go! I love this football club, and I feel like if I don't defend the club, I'm letting Nat down.

He would have done anything for Bolton Wanderers. It was his football club, and he was the heart of this football club. I hope nobody ever forgets that.

John McGinlay
2019

INTRODUCTION

IT WAS ONE of those moments that seemed to happen in slow motion, yet all at once. As soon as Gil Merrick had the ball in his hands, he couldn't get rid of it fast enough, flinging it to the first red-shirted England player free from the attentions of an Austrian opponent that he saw. To the Three Lions' good fortune, the player he found was Tom Finney, Preston North End's brilliant, electric winger, midway inside England's half. As quick of mind as he was of foot, Finney was already renowned in 1952 as one of the most incisive, exceptional players that his country had ever produced. On this occasion, under leaden skies on a warm, muggy day in Vienna, in front of more than 65,000 hysterical fans, he needed but a pinch of his usual passing acumen to know what to do as he brought the ball down and spun towards the Austrian goal. Ahead of him was only one England player, and Finney wouldn't have wanted anyone else there, even allowing for the fact that the man in the number nine shirt was his best mate.

Nat Lofthouse didn't need to stop and think about what to do as Finney laced the ball through to him. It was the same thing he'd been doing for the past two years for his country, for eleven for his beloved hometown club Bolton Wanderers, and for as long as he could remember before that: scoring goals. 'I could hear the hounds setting off after me but I knew it was basically down to me and [Austrian goalkeeper Josef] Musil,' Nat remembered. His face, which usually wore a beaming, slightly lopsided grin, was set in an expression of grim determination. Using his deceptive speed, he began to race toward Musil's goal. Such was the distance he had to cover that various thoughts had time to flash through his mind. The prospect of scoring the winning goal against the fearsome Austrian team, without doubt his most significant contribution to England in his seventh cap. The opportunity to make some of Britain's leading sportswriters, who had called for 'Lofty' to be replaced by Newcastle United's Jackie Milburn, eat their words. With his heart racing, he noted Musil seemed caught in two minds, not knowing whether to rush out to meet Nat or stay on his line and take his chances.

After some hesitation, Musil did advance. Nat sensed an Austrian defender gaining on him, but kept his cool. He and Musil were now steps away from one another but still he kept the ball. Just as he, Musil, and the defender all converged, he calmly picked his spot and shot, sliding the ball past the onrushing keeper and into the net. As the small pockets of British servicemen in the crowd, many of whom had staked an unwise amount of pay on the dim prospect of an England victory, went into a frenzy, Lofthouse and Musil crunched into one another with a sickening thud. It would take several moments for Nat to come to. When he did, he was met by his massed teammates, their faces a mixture of concern for their stricken ally and ecstasy at what his sacrifice had earned. It was then that he learned he'd just scored the most significant goal of his career, one that would enshrine him for evermore in football folklore as 'The Lion of Vienna'.

It was a goal that typified everything Nat Lofthouse was as a player. Surprisingly fleet of foot despite his muscular frame, he had a composure in front of goal that one simply couldn't learn. The lethal, predatory instincts that saw him score 315 goals in 536 league and cup appearances for club and country (every single one he considered himself 'fortunate' to have scored) were allied with an incredible strength that earned him a reputation as an often unstoppable aerial threat. Nat was rarely more than self-deprecating about his abilities, never tiring of repeating what his coach George Taylor had told him: that he could do only 'three things –

run, shoot and head'. While characteristically humble, this analysis of his game left out one potent part of the Lofthouse formula, one that set him apart from his peers even in an age when football was at best rugged, and at worst downright brutal. Nat was utterly fearless, almost to the point of foolhardiness, an irresistible force of nature. In the words of Tommy Banks, another legendary Bolton Wanderer who too enjoys a reputation based on his otherworldly bravery on the pitch, Nat 'never shirked 'owt'. By the end of Lofty's career, he'd have the souvenirs – gruesome scars, reset bones, bloodied shirts – to prove it.

Not only did the goal in Vienna demonstrate exactly what made Nat Lofthouse great, but also what he has come to represent as one of the standard-bearers of his era of football. Indeed, many of the features we traditionally associate with players of his day – the tough upbringing, the undying loyalty to their club, the down-to-earth humility, the 'man of the people' status – undoubtedly borrow from Nat's own story.

With his achievements slowly fading into the mists of time, he, like so many of his contemporaries, has been venerated to such an extent that he is closer to a *Roy of the Rovers* caricature than a real player. Delving into the story behind the legend reveals a more complex, yet no less remarkable, story. Nat Lofthouse was a man who reached the pinnacle of the game not through raw ability alone but with remarkable grit and determination; whose famous loyalty to his club was put to the test and, at times, stretched to breaking point; whose fearsome nature on the pitch belied a friendly, approachable demeanour; and who, perhaps more so than any other sole person, played a pivotal role in shaping one of English football's great clubs. Tom Finney hailed him as 'the King of Bolton', a man who he was 'proud' to call a friend.[*] Tommy Banks calls him 'magic'. Dougie Holden, another member of the famous 1958 FA Cup team, describes him as a 'powerhouse' and 'a great man'. Stan Matthews called him a 'lionheart'.[**]

[*]   Nat Lofthouse & Andrew Collomosse, *Nat Lofthouse: The Lion of Vienna*, pp. v–vi.

[**] 'With Lofthouse at his best we slammed the Scots 7-2', *South China Sunday Post Herald*, 1965.

Gordon Taylor, now head of the PFA, watched Lofty from the Burnden Park stands as a boy and had 'never seen anything like him'. Thousands of Wanderers fans who watched Nat play or had the good fortune to meet him off the pitch describe him, simply, as 'the greatest'. This is the story of Nat Lofthouse, the man they called the Lion of Vienna.

1

BOLTON, LANCASHIRE

QUITE WHAT COCKTAIL of emotions was swilling around Nat Lofthouse's head as he walked out on to the Burnden Park pitch on a cold, damp March day in 1941 only he knew. The fact that this was the first time he was wearing the famous white shirt of the club he'd supported fanatically since childhood would have been enough to have even the hardiest soul balancing a mix of ebullience and sheer, unadulterated terror. But these were exceptional circumstances.

Unlike many modern players, mollycoddled through years within academies and gentle loan spells before being gradually eased into the first team, Nat's situation was very much a case of being thrown in at the deep end. He had signed his amateur papers with Bolton Wanderers the day after Britain had entered the Second World War, eighteen months earlier, and had learned of his imminent first-team call up not on the training pitch, but on the factory floor where he was working. Though already in possession of the robust frame that would serve him well for years of bone-jangling tackles and wince-inducing head clashes, he was still a boy of only 15. As he plodded across Burnden Park's gravel track and on to the pitch, the thick cotton shirt bearing the club's red crest hanging loose on his body, the players surrounding him weren't the heroes he'd grown up watching. Instead, they were a ragtag group consisting of just about anyone who manager Charles Foweraker could get his hands on.

An unfamiliar name on the blackboard paraded around Burnden Park to display the team was nothing new to the 1,500 fans smattering the ground that day. For those in the know, seeing a local lad make his debut was always a matter of pride, invariably dampened by doubts over whether he could truly make the grade. Bolton fans had a reputation for being harsh yet fair, and as usual there was to be no quarter given or allowances made for the 15-year-old's rawness and lack of experience. The world was at war, and many of those in the stands that had yet to be called up knew plenty who had and that their time may well soon come. The local economy, which had been slowly decaying for years, was in danger of falling apart. Those that would still have jobs when the conflict ended could look forward to dangerous, back-breaking work that paid barely enough to survive. Quite simply, they *needed* Bolton Wanderers, one of their only forms of escape, to give them something to cheer about.

To tell the story of Nat Lofthouse is to tell the story of Bolton Wanderers, and to tell that story, it's vital to understand the town and those who inhabited it. The game of football has been called many things over the years – a passion, a devotion, a religion – and rarely have these epithets more readily applied than to those in the North of England during the dark, desperate years of the early 1940s.

History favours periods of extremity. It is for this reason that we know all about the 1920s and '30s in the USA – the former a period of exuberant, opulent wealth, the latter of devastating, previously unfathomable desperation – but less of the state of Britain, which followed a similar, albeit less severe trajectory. The 'Roaring '20s' were more of a tepid mewling, while the Great Depression merely exacerbated many of the country's pre-existing ills. Lancashire's economic bedrock, coal mining and cotton production, was relatively insulated from the collapse of the world's financial institutions in October 1929, but their stability during these years doesn't tell the whole story.

The textile industry was the county's most critical, effectively employing entire towns. As late as the end of the nineteenth century, Lancashire held a virtual monopoly on cotton production. The Empire had an unrivalled expanse, trade relations with key markets were good, and the technological advances of the Industrial Revolution made transporting the goods spun in the mills of towns such as Bolton, Preston, Oldham and Rochdale a simple task. It seemed like nothing would be able to topple Lancashire as the best cotton-manufacturing region in the world. But all that was to change. A combination of mill owners' reticence to modernise their methods and invest in new machinery (after all, if it wasn't broken, why try to fix it?) and the inability to export during the First World War ultimately set Lancashire's most valuable industry on the road to ruin. In the lull created by the Great War, two of Lancashire cotton's biggest markets, India and China, moved to plug the gap by manufacturing raw cotton themselves. By the time the conflict was over, so was the North-west's dominance.

Mining was a similar story, although one playing out on the national stage rather than just the local one. It remained, as it always had been, a remarkably treacherous way of earning a living, with numerous respiratory problems and physical injuries awaiting those who survived long enough to retire. As with the mills, enough technological innovations had arrived to put men out of work, but had failed to make mining any less gruelling or more immune to shifts in the world economy. The speed with which new drills were able to cut through the shelf was such that the age-old technique of propping the ceiling up every few feet was abandoned in the name of penny-pinching efficiency. Both the noise and the vibration generated by the machinery exacerbated the already very real risk of cave-ins and other disasters. In 1910, 344 men were killed in an explosion at the Pretoria Pit in Westhoughton, 4 miles from Bolton, after a cavity filled with gas was ignited by a faulty headlamp.

Most pits were organised into three distinct shifts per day, usually around eight hours in length, not including the time it took the miners to creep down the narrow passages from the main shaft to the coalface, which could easily add another hour either side of the shift. If this wasn't hard work enough, most did it largely on an empty stomach; food had to be taken to the coalface, and so tended to get ruined almost as soon as it was unwrapped. After finishing and returning to the surface, the miner went home with about 9 shillings in his pocket and the promise of a wash in a tub of cold water. And, as unfathomably exhausting, financially miserly and generally nightmarish as this sounds, the one worry that trumped all others in each man's mind as he tried to sleep was whether the colliery would have enough work to give him the chance to do it again the next day.

By the twentieth century, the pattern was virtually set in stone. Men went down the mines or, if they were lucky, had factory work. Women either stayed at home or worked as spinners in the mills depending on how hard up the family was (for many, it was usually a case of somewhere between 'badly' and 'unbearably'). Down the cobbled streets, trodden by milk girls in wooden clogs and on which scruffy kids kicked a ball made from whatever they could find, row upon row of houses were packed tightly. In Bolton, it wasn't unusual to find these already modest homes subdivided into tiny rooms by unscrupulous, uncaring landlords determined to eke out every last penny from the squalid, claustrophobic conditions as they could. Frequently, multiple houses shared the same toilet. With so many families and lodgers crammed into a space meant for a comparative few, it was all too familiar to encounter a queue for the facilities in the dead of a bitter winter night.

For some, the remnants of the Industrial Revolution – the rows of houses, the towering factories, the billowing chimneys – that had once represented hope and ambition became merely another tool of the gloom. Not only were they reminders of the broken promises of prosperity, but they brought with them illness and disease, exacerbated by the cramped living conditions. Any potential industrial investors in the North-west only needed to enter the labyrinth of sorry lodgings surrounding their prospective factory and cast their gaze on the sickly, broken workforce to quickly take their business elsewhere. One prospective player for the Bolton Wanderers football team, George Eccles, was warned by a doctor not to sign for the club lest he wish to jeopardise his health. The Bolton climate, the physician declared, was 'lethal'.*

In 1936, a writer was commissioned to travel to Lancashire and Yorkshire to document the lives of the most impoverished. A keen analyst of people, their characters and conditions, and already in possession of an innate sense of social justice, the journey was a sobering and formative experience for the young man. The resulting account of his journey, *The Road to Wigan Pier*, talked at length about the lamentable, squalid conditions that many working-class families found themselves in. The meagre portions of flavourless food totalled an 'appalling diet'. The mines were his 'own mental picture of hell. Most of the things one imagines in hell are in there – heat, noise, confusion, darkness, foul air, and, above all, unbearably cramped space.' Living arrangements bred disease and homes were infested with insects. While some contemporary critics suggested that the account was sensationalised, there's no doubt that life in 1930s Lancashire was almost unimaginable by modern standards. Twelve years after *The Road to Wigan Pier* was published, George Orwell published another work, *Nineteen Eighty-Four*. In its dystopian view of the future of Britain, a tiny elite have engineered a totalitarian system that keeps the working classes in a constant state of economic and social depression. It isn't difficult to see from where he took inspiration.

Another bastion of early twentieth-century British culture, acclaimed artist L.S. Lowry, spent much of his professional life living and painting Pendlebury, a small town less than 6 miles outside Bolton. His body of work remains a fascinating glimpse into not only the world that the people of Lancashire lived in during the early 1900s, but of the people themselves. Invariably, his paintings were dominated by the industrial landscape, with the people depicted as wraithlike shadows, victims of their often shattering circumstances.

However, despite the almost irresistibly grim situation many had to contend with, an unbreakable spirit prevailed. Although many thousands

---

★   Percy M. Young, *Bolton Wanderers*, p. 68.

abandoned the North-west in search of better prospects in the 1920s and '30s, rather than splintering communities, it only served to drive those who remained closer together. With so many crushed into a tiny area, inevitably you got to know just about every face that you saw on a regular basis. The lack of diversity in employment meant that if a man didn't work with another at Mosley Common Colliery or one of the other nearby pits, their wives may well have been sat at neighbouring spinning machines at the Bolton Union cotton mill. There was scarce money for recreational activities, so children had to make do by getting together in large groups and inventing games on the street. Even holidaying was a communal activity for those lucky families able to afford an annual trip. Blackpool's Pleasure Beach, just a short train ride from Bolton, was the destination of choice. With the pits generally shutting down for the same two weeks in the summer, it was like the whole town upped sticks for a jolly.

With the pits taking lives on a regular, indiscriminate basis, malnutrition and disease quickly robbing communities of some they'd known for years, and infant mortality rates in some areas of Lancashire rivalling those of Victorian times, the people of Bolton had little choice but to try to make the best of things. Orwell noted a common practice of families squirreling away some of their meagre food budget in order to buy something sweet to break the dietary monotony. Pubs were crammed to the rafters on the weekends, offering a brief chance to forget the dire straits of modern living and catch up with colleagues without having to yell over the din of the mining equipment or the weaving machinery. Dances and music shows were held at places like the Palais de Danse and the Empress Dance Hall in the town centre, giving the younger generation a furtive glimpse of a more glamorous lifestyle, as well as the opportunity for some dalliances of a romantic nature. The football pools, which involved predicting the outcome of matches to win a substantial prize, offered working men and their families a weekly source of hope that maybe, just maybe, this time it would be them. And, of course, there was football itself. While it may seem trite to suggest that the sport cured any of society's ills, the fact that the dawning realisation of the cotton and mining industries' inevitable demise in the '20s coincided with the white-shirted Bolton Wanderers becoming one of the country's most successful sides undoubtedly kept spirits up among the tens of thousands of people who crammed themselves into the paddocks at Burnden Park on Saturdays.

Like most major teams across the country, Bolton Wanderers could trace their origins back to the previous century when rapidly growing interest in football, buoyed by a countrywide desire to cast off the shackles of working during the Industrial Revolution, saw the number of clubs explode. One of the trailblazing teams in the Bolton area were a church side from Deane Road. Christ Church FC appeared nomadically on the shrubland and fields around the town during the mid-1870s before eventually settling on a rented field off Pikes Lane. Frequent meetings between those with a stake in the club demonstrated an increasing level of professionalism, and the club began to accept those beyond Christ Church's traditional congregation. However, there was a sticking point. The vicar's autocratic temperament was, in the opinion of the others involved in the team's business, becoming something of an issue. On 28 August 1877, the committee members took the decision to rename the team and cut ties with the church, at once increasing their catchment area of potential players and fans and ridding themselves of a nuisance that could hinder the progress of the club. Bolton Wanderers Football Club – so named because of the team's lack of fixed abode – was born.

Progress was rapid. The team remained on the rented pitch, but crowds swelled considerably from a few stragglers to thousands. By the early 1890s, the team was attracting gates of almost 15,000 for local derby fixtures and collecting hundreds of pounds in ticket revenue. The popularity of the team reflected the growing profile of the sport across the nation. The Trotters began meeting local rivals in the FA Lancashire Cup in the 1879/80 season, and took their game to teams from up and down the country when they first entered the newly anointed FA Cup in 1882. The early years of the Cup were riddled with numerous replays due to countless appeals and counter-appeals between teams accusing one another of having forbidden paid professionals playing for them. Wanderers themselves weren't particularly subtle about flaunting the rules on professionalism. Local businesses had been running adverts in Scottish and Welsh newspapers advertising 'jobs' for men who would also be willing to turn out for the club. Finally, in 1885, the FA decided to make paying players a wage legal after several clubs, including Bolton, seceded to a rival football association where professionalism was permitted.

With the advent of professionalism came a new standard of quality.* No longer did players see club affiliations and playing overall as trifling matters. Now they could make decent money in football, it paid to settle down at one club and work hard. As play improved, demand for the sport continued to snowball, with games being organised on Christmas Day. On 17 April 1888, the Football League was formed, ensuring standard-ised, competitive football for all participating clubs for the entire season. Bolton Wanderers was a founding member.

Bolton's early years in English football's first official league system were highly promising. Wanderers, in their new strips of white tops with navy shorts (they'd previously experimented with pink, red and even polka-dotted kits) narrowly missed out on a league championship in 1892, the final year before tiered divisions were introduced. Two years later, the club had its first experience of an FA Cup Final, where they earned the dubious honour of becoming the first top-flight team to lose the showpiece match to lower league opposition. Chagrined by the rising rent on Pikes Lane, the club's key players – among them J.J. Bentley, a visionary who foresaw both the communal and commercial possibili-ties of the team – decided to move. A substantial area by the railway had been bought with the intention of building a gasworks. However, when the venture became financially unviable, the club was offered the land at

---

* The game still had some way to go to considering itself refined. A report from the *Football Field* newspaper in 1890 offers this account of one of Bolton's goals against the visiting Belfast Distillery team: 'A shot came into goal and was well caught by Galbraith, the visiting goalkeeper, who fell to the ground. Thereupon, all the Wanderers attempted to roll him through the posts, whilst the visitors manfully strove to prevent them … More than half the players were struggling in the mud, but eventually the Wanderers managed to drag custodian, backs, and the others through the coveted space, and thereby registered their third point [goal].'

a discounted rate. The team issued shares and, having swiftly raised the required capital, began construction on the ground that became known as Burnden Park, opening in time for the 1895 season. Boasting room for over 50,000, Burnden would go on to become one of the iconic pieces of English football stadia. Trains moving along the lines that ran beside the ground would often slow to a crawl to allow passengers to take in some of the game. For big games, the Railway Embankment end would become a heaving mass of bodies, a huge crashing wave constantly threatening to engulf the pitch. The freezing winters did little to deter the punters, and as the nights drew in, the ground would become engulfed in pipe smoke during matches. The turf did a fine job of retaining much of the Lancashire drizzle deposited upon it (the *Sports Argus* wrote that, at Burnden, 'the mud always seems to be thicker and blacker than anywhere else'*), and the result was a pitch that suited the robust play style of the Wanderers to a tee. A drop of several feet awaited any player who lost his footing on the touchline – a threat made all the more real during the 1950s when Tommy Banks and Roy Hartle ruled the flanks.

For the first decade and a half at Burnden Park, Wanderers lived up to their name by never truly establishing themselves in either the First or the Second Division, which they bounced between no fewer than eight times. The chief cause of their failings tended to be their inability to forge an effective (or at least consistent) strike force. When they finally did, things changed. Under the stewardship of secretary-manager Charles Foweraker, who had first joined the club in 1895 as a turnstile operator** and was promoted from the assistant manager role after Tom Mather left to join the navy in 1915, Bolton became a force to be reckoned with, thanks largely to the spectacular play of their forwards.

Two of the mainstays, Ted Vizard and Joe Smith, had been with the club for some time, but the end of the First World War finally afforded them the opportunity to develop an understanding between one another. Vizard was a sublime outside left who played for the club for over

---

★   *Sports Argus*, 5 January 1952.

★★   Foweraker's father had done the same at Pikes Lane.

twenty years, blessed with a rare, visionary ability to sense his teammates' movements and create opportunities for them. The true focal point of the attack was Smith, who ended his career with more goals for Bolton Wanderers than any other player and who remains eleventh on the all-time English First Division goal scorers list. Having been at the club since 1908, he was already a veteran by the time he captained the team at the first ever FA Cup Final played at the brand new national Wembley Stadium in 1923. It was here, in front of an estimated 300,000 spectators, that Bolton finally broke their hoodoo and collected a major piece of silverware by beating West Ham United 2-0. Two more Finals, in 1926 and 1929, brought two further titles.

The unprecedented success of the club during the 1920s was a huge boon for the town, a welcome distraction from the growing concerns about the economic climate. The team had everything: flair, a never-say-die attitude that made them a fantastic cup side, and a combination of local lads and some of the best stars sourced from elsewhere in the United Kingdom. It was impossible for any young boys from the town to resist the pull of the glamour, the idolatry and the dizzying amounts of financial remuneration that the players of Bolton Wanderers enjoyed.

Lowry's paintings may have dehumanised the figures depicted in his landscapes to an extent, but one marked feature of many of his works was the sheer multitude of people, hinting at a collective social spirit that defied economic realities. One of his most memorable pieces, *Going to the Match*, depicts fans heading into Burnden Park. The stick-thin bodies of men and women, young and old, are bent head-first toward the welcoming turnstiles, bottlenecks before which the concentration of punters naturally swells, a testament to the unifying, intoxicating power of football. Like a visit to the pictures, going to the match offered pure escapism, a chance to forget about the trials and monotony of life, and gave entire communities a common goal to pull for. It was a social event. In *The Road to Wigan Pier*, Orwell wrote of miners 'riding off to a football match dressed up to the nines' together, relishing a chance to laugh and cheer along with their co-workers. Football may not have promised any long-term cures for the troubles faced by those in Bolton during the first half of the twentieth century, but its role as the lifeblood of the town cannot be overstated.

This was the world into which Nathaniel Lofthouse was born on 27 August 1925 at his parents' home, 80 Willows Lane, close enough to the terraces of Burnden Park for the roar of the crowd on match days to be heard.

2

EARLY YEARS

THE STATE OF life in Bolton had an effect on everyone who experienced it, even just for a passing moment like George Orwell had. For Nat Lofthouse, the town was in his veins, interwoven with his DNA, forming an indelible part of his character long before he was old enough to comprehend the grand, neoclassical town hall, Ye Olde Man and Scythe pub or Burnden Park. His family's Lancashire connections stretched back hundreds of years, and since the turn of the nineteenth century, Nat's ancestors had been born, lived, loved and died in the town, rarely living more than 5 miles apart from each other. It's little surprise that despite all the remarkable, extraordinary adventures that his career would take him on, he would always call Bolton home. Nat 'had two families', he said, 'the people of Bolton and the Lofthouse family'.

Nat's paternal great-great-grandfather, and with him the Lofthouse name, had arrived in Bolton permanently in the early 1800s from nearby Ribchester. His great-grandfather, Thomas, was the first of the Lofthouse line born in the town, and spent most of his life as a bricklayer, helping to build the factories, mills and houses that would come to define Bolton's landscape. Thomas settled down and by the 1880s had his wife, Susannah, a brood of eight as well as a lodger stuffed into 289 Derby Street, a four-roomed Victorian terrace. Thomas' eldest son, Andrew, was the first in the family not to enter the mining industry, escaping the hellish pits for work as a carter, tramping the streets with a horse and cart, hauling the mineral carved from the ground around Bolton to the homes and businesses that relied on it for warmth and fuel. It was tough, tiring work, but it provided a steady income away from the ever-present dangers of the pits.

One of the men who was toiling in the depths of the mine shaft was William Powell, born the year before Andrew in 1857, who had travelled to Lancashire in the hope of more steady work than was available in his native North Wales. In the late 1880s, both William and Andrew tied the knot, the former to a widow, Sarah Griffiths, and the latter to a local girl named Elizabeth. Marriage was quickly followed in both cases by children. The Powells would have two daughters and three sons by 1901, as well as Sarah's two daughters from her previous marriage; the Lofthouses had a more modest two sons and two daughters. Although working class, the Daubhill area in which the Lofthouses lived on Willows Lane was prosperous and boasted all the amenities of a well-to-do community. At the turn of the century, tracks were laid on the street for a new electric tramway, run by the Bolton Corporation. The sight of these double-decker marvels of modern science was a rousing statement of intent, demonstrating in no uncertain terms that the North-west remained a thriving economic power – a jewel in the crown of one of the most powerful empires in history – as the Victorian era drew to a close.

One of the Lofthouse boys, Richard, had been born on 24 October 1889, around the time of the Powells' first daughter together, Sarah. The Lofthouse's second eldest son followed his father into the carting trade after leaving school, reassured of the occupation's stability and constant need for workers. More ore was being mined than ever; 1907 saw a yield of 26 million tonnes, the biggest year of production ever. When Sarah went to work in a mill and with Dick carting, their paths eventually crossed. It could have been as simple as her mill being on his rounds. Another possible meeting point was a local dance. 'Mill dances' grew in popularity throughout the first half of the twentieth century. Held locally for the workers of multiple mills, the dances were a chance for some much-needed revelry to break up the drudgery of factory work.

The high proportion of young women working in the mills was all the encouragement many young men needed to attend, too.

Sarah was a straight-talking, pragmatic young woman with a quick wit and a readily apparent maternal instinct. In Richard, she found a driven, ambitious man whose career in the carting profession had bestowed upon his 5ft 6in frame a tough, hardy physique. On 30 August 1913 they were married at St Anne's Church in Hindsford. Their marriage certificate lists both living at 27 West Bank Street in Atherton, suggesting that they'd been cohabiting prior to marriage, perhaps with Richard living with the Powell family as a lodger. Although marrying at 24 was fairly typical, Dick and Sarah's courtship may have been expedited by the massing dark clouds on the horizon. Relations between the Russian and Austro-Hungarian empires were strained, and across Europe the rumblings of a wider conflict were beginning to be felt.

It wasn't long before the newly-weds bade farewell to Atherton and moved nearer to Bolton's centre, just across the way from Dick's parents on Willows Lane. Dick kept up his tireless work and earned a respectable £2 10s a week. While many couples immediately looked to start families after marriage, the Lofthouses heeded the increasingly fraught signs from the continent, with Sarah's pragmatic streak dictating that they should wait for the troubles to pass before trying for children.

Sure enough, on 4 August 1914, war was declared when Britain responded to the German invasion of Belgium. Both sides provided assertions that the war would be over by Christmas. In reality, the resulting conflict lasted four long years and became the bloodiest in human history. In typically British fashion, the attitude adopted was one of stoic bullishness. The call for 100,000 volunteers was surpassed almost five times over within two months of the declaration, with Bolton contributing more than its fair share of men. One of those was a carter, who strode confidently into the station in Nelson on 14 September to offer his services for King and country, perhaps inspired by the iconic poster of Lord Kitchener telling each and every man who saw it that the country wanted him specifically. Dick may well have escaped conscription when it was introduced in 1916 due to various jobs in the coal industry being classed as 'starred occupations', important enough to the war effort that the country was best served by keeping those men where they were. The fact he signed up just a month after the declaration speaks volumes about his character. The Bolton regiments would go on to face some of the worst fighting of the Great War. The Lancashire Fusiliers and Loyal North Lancashire Regiment both fought heroically at Gallipoli; the Manchester Regiment spent the first year on the Western Front before being dispatched to the Middle East. However, Dick was destined not to be with them.

After just over a month of training, an army doctor ruled that Dick simply wouldn't be able to 'become an efficient soldier'. The root of this assessment wasn't his overall fitness or his mental aptitude but an old injury he had sustained to his hand while completing his rounds one day. The injury prevented him from holding a rifle for a prolonged period of time, and this, combined with the importance of his trade, led to his discharge. The absence of many miners and other carters as part of the war effort meant Dick's job security was better than it ever had been. Despite the war still casting a fearful gloom over Lancashire – never more so than when a Zeppelin mistook Bolton for Derby and unleashed a payload that killed thirteen and demolished homes on Kirk Street and Derby Street, just yards from where Dick's father Andrew had grown up – the Lofthouses decided to start a family. Almost exactly nine months after Dick's army reprieve, the couple had a son, Edward, and another, named for his father, followed just over a year later.

After four years, the German armistice was signed on 11 November 1918, and the Treaty of Versailles some seven months later brought a formal end to the war. Over 16 million had died, roughly 3,300 of whom were from Bolton. As life returned to normal in one respect, it was becoming clear that the Lancashire economic machine was ailing, the competitive advantage that the region held in cotton and coal being eroded by increasing foreign competition combined with local greed and apathy. Dick was one of the fortunate ones in that his years of tireless service for the Bolton Corporation had stood him in good stead and he was never wanting for work. This continued security eventually meant he and Sarah had two more boys: Thomas, born in 1923, and, on a dull, cool summer's day – 27 August 1925 – Nathaniel. Their youngest son was baptised in the idyllic St Anne's Church, where his parents had been married twelve years earlier.

The Lofthouses were, like so many families at the time had to be, a tightly knit unit. St Anne's Church, the site of Nat's baptism and Dick and Sarah's marriage, was less than half a mile from where Sarah had grown up and where her parents still lived. Nat's home, 80 Willows Lane, a modest yet comfortable two up, two down, was just a few doors down from his paternal grandparents. This proximity to the previous generations of the family ensured that Nat and his older brothers* grew up with a strong sense of family and a constant reminder of the virtues of a hard day's work. Nat's father's long-standing occupation kept him insulated from the gradual suffocation of Lancashire's industries and the creeping unemployment that came with it, but he never failed to impress upon his boys the importance of an unbending work ethic. Though such an upbringing could have verged on stiflingly authoritarian, it was also a house filled with love, and even before he began his first years of education, the Lofthouse's youngest son was already demonstrating the happy-go-lucky confidence that so many would remark upon after meeting him as an adult. Already, the beaming, slightly lopsided grin was being worn at regular intervals. Looking back on his earliest years, Nat reflected that 'although life was not always easy … I enjoyed [it] thoroughly'.

Dick's wages covered the basics and a few luxuries like the occasional pint or a family trip to the pictures. The latter pursuit was particularly of interest to the young Nat, who grew up spoiled for choice by the countless yarns of heroes and villains, adventures, and damsels in distress from Hollywood's 'Golden Age' that graced the silver screen. Even when he was performing feats worthy of their own big-screen treatment, Nat would always have a love of the pictures (particularly those of John Wayne), just as he would for so many pivotal parts of his childhood. Besides Hollywood, the other pastime of choice in Bolton in the

---

* Edward, Nat's eldest brother, passed away in 1927.

1920s had a distinctly more British feel, imbued with grit and bullishness. Willows Lane was about 2 miles away from the concrete and steel that made up the home of Bolton Wanderers Football Club, Burnden Park. On match days, when a westerly wind blew, the chants and the roars of often more than 50,000 people supporting manager Charles Foweraker's men drifted right to the family's front door. Dick had resisted the overtures, regarding the idea that men could earn more by kicking some cowhide around a park than by toiling down the mine for hours with suspicion. However, the cheers and shouts floating over the terraced roofs proved irresistible for Nat and older brother Tom. The guttural, primal noise had the same effect on them as the Pied Piper's tune had on the children of Hamelin.

Even without the presence of one of the defining monuments to British football just down the road, football as a sport had already got its hooks into the two youngest Lofthouse boys, with neither needing any encouragement to join in the impromptu street games among neighbouring children. These games were basic to say the least. There was no council spending on local pitches for youths, and little disposable income to pay for specialised boots or even balls. England star Tommy Lawton, six years Nat's senior and also from Bolton, would remember the pitches of his formative years being the cobbled streets or unoccupied pieces of scrubland, on the days when the weather hadn't transformed them into mud baths. Some of Nat's earliest memories would echo Lawton's: playing with Tom and other local kids with items of clothing for goalposts and old newspaper stuffed down their socks as rudimentary shin pads; 'We could never afford a proper football, of course, so whoever had the nearest thing was the most important kid around.'

Aged 5, Nat began attending Brandwood Primary School, where his immediate preoccupation was not academics, but rather how to stop them from interfering with his desire to spend every waking moment playing the sport that had captured the imaginations of so many boys of his generation. It's extremely telling that, when recounting his school days, Nat suggests the most crucial pearl of wisdom he gleaned was that 'it was impossible to learn all there was to know about football'. He was never short of a self-effacing observation about his lack of aptitude when it came to education, but it's hard to imagine that his cheeky sense of humour and willingness to try his best had anything other than an endearing effect upon the teachers at Brandwood.

With his decidedly lackadaisical attitude to formal schooling and his insatiable appetite for the game, it was only natural that the thronging crowds headed towards Burnden Park would eventually prove too much for young Nat to resist. Despite being expected at school on Saturday, 18 February 1933, Nat headed east rather than west from Willows Lane, walking down the fabled Manchester Road that ran alongside the Main Stand of the club's home ground. The fixture that day was an FA Cup derby against Manchester City. Given the geographical proximity of the teams, Bolton's recent success in the competition and both teams' league campaigns comprising worried glances toward the relegation zone rather than hopeful looks to the top, it was little surprise that 69,912 supporters, Burnden's biggest ever crowd, packed themselves on to the terraces on this mild winter's day.

Despite this being his first ever experience of live football at Burnden, Nat was not among the recorded number of patrons. With even the 1d programme too expensive for him, there was no chance he'd be able to afford the price of admittance through the turnstiles. Schoolboy rates were threepence for the northerly Embankment terrace, sixpence in the paddocks and a dizzying sum of one and threepence for a seat. However, just as his expected attendance at school hadn't stopped him, nor did this minor inconvenience. Evading the attentions of policemen, club officials and pedantic fans who would have objected to having paid while he watched for free, Nat shinned up a drainpipe and clambered on to one of the lower sections of corrugated roofing before dropping down to join the crowd.

At this point, so embroiled in the game was Nat that even the dourest of 0–0 stalemates would have been unlikely to dim his enthusiasm as he first laid eyes on the mighty 'Whites', about whom he'd heard so much in the Brandwood schoolyard and on the street. As it was, he witnessed an exciting, pulsating encounter, albeit one that saw the Wanderers eventually succumb to a 4-2 scoreline. As well as representing the watershed moment of the young Lofthouse's first time seeing the club that he would eventually become synonymous with (and it him), Nat also had the delight of seeing the team's electric winger Ray Westwood score one of his 144 goals for the club.

Nat idolised the hard-heading Tommy Lawton, but the fact that Lawton would never play for Bolton excluded him from the very highest levels of hero worship (although Nat would occasionally make the relatively short trip to Liverpool to watch Lawton in the flesh from the terraces at Everton's Goodison Park). Ray Westwood, on the other hand, fit the criteria of schoolboy icon perfectly. Though a native of Brierley Hill in Staffordshire, Westwood had been with the club since the age of 16, graduating through the ranks to become the undisputed star of the early 1930s team. An outside left who later moved inside, Westwood was, along with centre forward Jack Milsom, one of the goal-scoring heirs apparent of FA Cup-winning heroes from the 1920s, David Jack and Joe Smith. Westwood was not just an outstanding attacking threat but an entertainer, delighting in not just beating defenders but humiliating them with a dazzling array of skills. 'He was an idol of mine,' Nat would recall decades later. 'A brilliant player, who knew he was a good player, but wasn't big-headed. Over ten, fifteen, twenty yards he was electric. He mesmerised me as a boy, and I wanted to be like him.' Even before he was ten, Nat's dream of emulating his hero appeared unlikely, with his stocky build already resembling that of his father and making him ill-suited for the wide role typically occupied by lithe, speedy players.

Not only did Westwood live out the dreams of the town's boys on the pitch, but off it he gave them a tantalising glimpse of the status, glamour and luxury that being a footballer could afford a young man. Long before the age of astronomical wages, Westwood was a rare example of a bona fide celebrity footballer, a regular at popular Bolton night spots such as the Palais de Danse and appearing in advertisements for Brylcreem. Nat's most vivid memory of Westwood's embodiment of this side of footballing life came one Friday at the ODEON picture house. Before the feature began, it was announced that Westwood had overcome an injury and would be playing the next day. The crowd's reaction bordered on hysteria.

It was in his last year at Brandwood, 1936, that Nat's hours of practising with Tom and the other kids on the street first began to bear fruit, albeit in a somewhat inauspicious and unexpected manner – a 'sheer accident', in fact. Tom, then at Castle Hill senior school, had broken into the school's team as a centre half, thanks in no small part to Nat's insistence on playing as a centre forward (if he couldn't be a winger like Westwood, he could at least score as many goals as him!) and thus needing a natural foil. Not wanting to test his luck by risking the ire of paying patrons at Burnden too regularly by sneaking into matches, Nat sated his passion for the game by watching the older boys – including Tom – pit themselves against the teams from schools in the local area. While taken seriously by the players and schoolmasters alike, team selection was inevitably ruled by fairness and other extracurricular activities taking priority. Such was the case when, one day, Castle Hill found themselves without a goalkeeper. The teacher in charge of the team had no doubt registered Nat's enthusiastic and consistent support of his brother from the sidelines, and seeing no other option, recruited the youngster as the team's custodian.

Immediately, Nat was faced with a dilemma. On his feet were a pair of brand new patent leather school shoes – a substantial expense for the Lofthouse family even with a recent promotion for Dick to the role of the Bolton Corporation's head horsekeeper allaying some of their financial fears. Well aware of Nat's fanatical penchant for football, his mother Sarah had implored him not to 'kick holes' in the shoes, at the very least not on their first day of wear. However, despite not being one to go against the word of his parents, the pull of the pitch was too great. Nat took up his position between the posts against a school from Bury. Although just two years younger than the rest of the players, Nat was a fair shade shorter than the others, which was a notable disadvantage given his newly adopted position. The result – a 7-1 humbling – was hardly the most promising start to a career in organised football, but at least it quickly ruled out the possibility of Nat playing anywhere but outfield. To add insult to injury, the state of Nat's brand new school shoes after the match earned him a scolding from Sarah when he returned home. 'I've a hunch that when she left me and went back to her kitchen, Mother permitted herself a smile,' Nat later said. 'She knew I couldn't resist kicking whether it was a stone, tin can, or ball in the street. Kicking was as natural to me as it is to a mule.' Even such a chastening margin of defeat did nothing to dampen Nat's endeavour; instead, it merely steeled his resolve to show what he could truly do.

In 1937, just after his 12th birthday, Nat joined brother Tom and followed in the footsteps of Tommy Lawton,* now playing for Everton (where he'd been signed as a replacement for the club's legendary striker Dixie Dean), in attending Castle Hill. Despite his baptism of fire the year before, his brother's ability and glowing reports of Nat's talent saw the younger Lofthouse given an immediate trial for the school team by the coach, schoolmaster Willy Hardy. By the end of the school year, he was a fixture in the side that competed on two fronts annually, for the Morris Shield and the Stanley Shield. This formal acknowledgement of his skills served only to further his devotion to playing, and saw him consciously begin to practise rather than simply playing whenever he could. Nat's hours of relentlessly drilling himself, even without instruction, helped him develop basic ball control and passing skills, while watching the ball clip and spin off the cobbles gave him an appreciation for the importance of anticipation. And of course, wanting to be like Ray Westwood meant his shooting skills received an awful lot of practice.

Nat's form for Castle Hill quickly led to him becoming the team's first-choice centre forward, with him reflecting later, 'I suppose I didn't have the brain to be an inside forward or a wing half. We had boys who could win the ball, boys who could use it, boys who could beat a man and cross it … and me in the middle. Scoring was always important to me.' Already in ownership of the relentless determination that would enable him to bulldoze First Division defences in the future, he began immediately scoring goals regularly and catching the eye of spectators.

---

* Contrary to popular belief, although Lawton did attend Castle Hill, it was only briefly; he made his name in the school team of Folds Road Central School.

One such onlooker was Bert Cole, a friend of Nat's father and an amateur coach who 'got a great kick out of helping schoolboy footballers make the grade'. With Dick's lack of interest in the sport, Nat had had few formal mentors, and Cole's impact upon his game was profound. Cole had known Lawton at a similar age and possibly coached him, and he introduced Nat and Tom to a regime that involved practising shooting and heading against the wall of the stables that adjoined the family home. While monotonous and physically exhausting, Cole's enthusiasm kept the Sunday morning exercise interesting, and the repetitive act not only honed Nat's abilities (he later confirmed that 'this form of practice was the basis of the heading technique I later developed with Bolton') but also further impressed upon him the principles of hard work and application that his parents had instilled in him.

Cole wasn't the only one to have noticed Nat's obvious natural abilities. By the end of 1937, Nat received a call up to the Bolton Schools team, with his first game to be against the equivalent team from nearby Bury. Although he needed very little motivation to go out and show what he could do in the biggest match yet of his fledgling football life, Cole promised Nat a brand new bike if he was able to score a hat-trick. Despite his exemplary form for Castle Hill, this would be no mean feat. Nat would now be playing against a carefully selected group of players rather than a cobbled together school team. Quite what Cole's motivation for making such a deal was, we will never know. He may have done so in the belief that he would be giving Nat an added incentive without truly risking having to shell out for the bike, or he may have had faith that Nat would be able to net three goals and deserved a reward for his efforts. The fact he volunteered so much time in nurturing Nat's abilities suggests the latter is more likely than the former. As it transpired, Nat could count himself unfortunate not to have checked prior to the game whether the bargain extended beyond a mere hat-trick. Bolton ran out 7-1 winners, and Nat scored all seven. Though the Bury team were of a higher quality than those found competing in the school league, Nat's precision in striking for goal, allied with the power of both his shots and his style of play in general were far beyond what was typically expected of players of his age. The similarities between Nat's all-round skill and powerhouse tendencies and those possessed by Lawton were lost on none of the onlookers that day.

Preoccupied by his new bike, something that simply wouldn't have been affordable within the strict confines of the family budget, Nat thought little of the ramifications that his glut of goals had had. Unbeknownst to him, the name 'Lofthouse' was being jotted down in a scout's notebook and kept in a musty office, deep in the bowels of Burnden Park, as one that Bolton Wanderers should be keeping an eye on.

Nat's goal scoring kept on apace throughout his school days, although he was only once given the opportunity to turn out for Lancashire Schoolboys. It's entirely possible that given his utilisation of his physicality – by his teenage years, Nat described himself as 'solid', 5ft 7in and 11 stone – the men in charge of selecting county and even national schoolboy teams wrote him off, feeling he was merely more physically advanced than the boys he was wreaking havoc against, which was an advantage that would eventually dwindle. Any disappointment Nat felt for his inability to break into the more advanced teams was offset by his continued enjoyment of what he was able to do with Castle Hill and Bolton's town team, before a chance meeting gave him all the encouragement he would ever need.

As he was travelling to a Bolton Schools fixtures against Burnley, Nat had a chance to meet the hometown hero. Lawton was back in Bolton, visiting his family in Tonge Moor, and as he waited at the bus station, he recognised Bert Cole, who was chaperoning Nat to the game. The trainer introduced Nat, who was 'tongue tied and could only nod like a dim-wit', to Lawton, explaining he was a huge fan and was following the same path that the Everton star had blazed. Even with Nat dumbstruck, Lawton offered up some advice that would stay with Nat for the rest of his life: 'No matter how you play, always try to score. That's the important thing.'* Though simplistic, to hear the art of playing the

---

*   In an interview in the late 1990s, Nat would recall Lawton's exact phrase as being, 'Keep putting t'ball in back of t'net, lad'.

professional game boiled down to such a clear, concise maxim provided enormous motivation for Nat. Although self-deprecating about his lack of guile and finesse when looking back on his career, there's little doubt that these weak points would have played on Nat's mind and made him question whether a professional career was a real possibility for him. If all he needed to worry about was scoring a goal, then that made the path to success appear far less treacherous.

While Nat's burgeoning career was showing nothing but promise, the wider picture wasn't looking quite as trouble-free. The worldwide depression had compounded the issues of unemployment and poverty in Lancashire, and both the coal mining and cotton industries were showing early yet undeniable signs of their irreversible decline. Even more worrisome was the deteriorating situation in Europe. September 1938 saw Prime Minister Neville Chamberlain help to broker the Munich Agreement in an attempt to appease German Chancellor Adolf Hitler. Chamberlain issued his infamous 'Peace for our Time' speech, assuring the British public that the prospect of war on the continent was a distinctly dim one. However, the same month that Chamberlain delivered his edict of peace, gas masks were distributed around the country. Mere weeks later, the *Bolton Evening News* was cautioning readers to memorise the locations of municipal air raid shelters. By late winter, it appeared that war was inevitable.

Government-distributed handbooks on how to prepare for war at home ended any lingering hopes that Chamberlain's words just months before were still the official line. With great uncertainty about how long any potential conflict would last or the number of belligerents that could involve themselves, there was considerable national debate about whether conscription was required for the British Army, or whether the indomitable national spirit would mean that a voluntary force recruited through the Territorial Army would suffice. In April, toward the end of the 1938/39 season, with the Wanderers on their way to recording a respectable eighth-place finish in the First Division, the Football Association requested that players set an example and sign up for the TAs.

It was this request that set in motion the events that would lead to Nat Lofthouse becoming a Bolton Wanderers player. The FA made the call to football clubs as, in the days before radios and televisions were invariably present in every household, there was no better way, other than perhaps through newspapers, to reach vast swathes of the male population than at a match. The reverence in which Westwood and other stars were held added an inspirational element to the message for men to sign up. Prior to the kick-off of a home game against Sunderland on 8 April, club captain Harry Goslin, president and former Member of Parliament for Bolton Sir William Edge and the Mayor of Bolton Cyril Entwistle took to the pitch, with Goslin and Edge delivering rousing speeches encouraging every eligible man in the 22,692-strong crowd to stand up and be counted. After forty-eight hours of anxious debate and soul-searching, the entire Bolton Wanderers team signed up to the 53rd Field Regiment of the Bolton Artillery – one of the few sides to heed the FA's call to a man.

For Nat and his equally football-mad schoolmates, the early summer months of 1939 were a time of uncertainty. The foreboding news emanating from Europe on a daily basis undoubtedly impacted everyone, but he had other things on his mind, too. He was turning 14, the school leaving age for those who weren't destined for further education and beyond. Not only did this mean he'd have to find a vocation, but it also meant an end to his illustrious time in the school football system. There were plenty of amateur teams around that wouldn't have turned their noses up at a youngster who routinely put sides to the sword at the town team level. However, the chances of being spotted by a professional club playing for amateur teams was considerably less than with school teams. With no youth academies and none of the vast scouting networks that exist in the modern game, clubs relied on local schools to separate the wheat from the chaff and showcase the best young talent in the country. If his play at Castle Hill hadn't won him a suitor in the professional game, it was unlikely to ever happen.

He had little inkling that any professional clubs had him on their radar. 'There were no scouts knocking on the door late at night or anything dramatic like that!' Nat recalled. 'Whenever we played there would be a few people standing on the touchline but we always assumed they were parents, teachers, friends and so on. Maybe some of them were scouts but we were too busy playing football to notice.' The steadying pragmatism shared by both his parents kept Nat's feet on the ground in regard to any possibility of him making it as a professional player. Football was all well and good as a pastime, but there wasn't time for him to be frittering away career opportunities once he left school.

Even with Nat's easy-going demeanour, these concerns were swimming around his head when he attended the annual prize-giving event at Castle Hill for the last time. The guest of honour was one of the men who Nat had likely watched take to the field as part of Wanderers' drive to help recruit men to the TAs, Councillor Cyril Entwistle. A second lieutenant during the First World War and, at the time, eight years into a fourteen-year stint as Bolton's Conservative MP, the recently knighted Entwistle was an imposing figure. Unbeknownst to Nat, the mayor also sat on the board of the football club.

As Nat greeted the commendation he received for his outstanding performance on the pitch with delight and the soon-to-be-famous Lofty grin, he noticed Entwistle beckoning him over. The question Entwistle then posed the young boy would change his life forever: 'How would you like to play for Bolton Wanderers?' Nat recalled he 'didn't need to be asked twice'.

It's possible that Nat's break may never had happened had it not been for the impending war, which was becoming more unavoidable with each passing day. Although many of the Bolton players weren't completely sold on enlisting when Goslin gave his speech, the fierce determination in his words left Entwistle, club president Edge and manager Foweraker in no doubt as to their need to secure the future of the club. Thirty-two of the thirty-five Bolton players eventually enlisted. Although the expectations of the war being short were treated as veracious (just as they had been at the beginning of the First World War), the management at Burnden were wary of the fact that if conscription came into effect, the majority of high-quality amateurs could be called into action at a moment's notice. Lofthouse was raw, a promising talent, but his real trump card was his age. Even the worst doom-mongers of the time didn't anticipate a war stretching for four years – the length of time before the 14-year-old Nat would be eligible for conscription. The fact he was a staunch Bolton fan was another feather in his cap, as the club could not afford to spend time developing young players only for them to lose interest or have their head turned by another club before signing professional papers.

With one question, the entire complexion of Nat's life changed. To play for Bolton had been his dream ever since he shinned up that drainpipe at Burnden Park; now, that dream was tantalisingly within reach. Even if Bolton chose not to sign him professionally at 17, he would now at least be able to showcase his talents to other teams, enhancing his prospects of making it in the game. The pressing need for him to choose a trade was suddenly resolved, too. As a way of tying young players to a team, it was common practice for First Division clubs to employ youngsters in a non-playing apprenticeship until they could sign professionally. Clubs treated such employment as a test of character for young players, of their willing-ness to give their all for the cause. After all, as much as youth players may have grumbled about scrubbing the changing rooms and cleaning the boots of the first team, it was a damn sight better than the dangers and the din of the factory floors or the mines.

Nat raced home that day, barely able to contain his excitement as he burst through the door at number 80. As he breathlessly relayed the news to his parents, the reaction was one of cautious optimism. Dick had always been keen for Tom and Nat's love of the game to not interfere with their finding a profession, but now he would have no choice but to at least entertain the notion that Nat could make a real go of it. The money made by a First Division player dwarfed what carting or any other industrial labouring job offered, and even if Nat didn't make the cut, having a steady job through a time of such nearing tumult could only be a good thing. For Sarah, the delight with which young Nat broke the news couldn't fail to warm her heart, and it may have been the moment that she finally completely forgave him for ruining his brand new shoes several years before.

While Nat was coming to terms with his life-altering news, the Territorial Army had mobilised and trained over the summer, with the 53rd Field Regiment that contained the bulk of Charles Foweraker's prized players travelling to the remote village of Trawsfynnydd in north-west Wales for training. Not only had the long-time Wanderers manager lost his captain, now Sergeant Gunner Harry Goslin of the Royal Artillery, but his star player Ray Westwood, who reputedly told anyone who would listen that signing up had been the 'worst decision of my life'.* Even the veteran player-coach George Taylor, who had been with the club since 1926, was recruited as a physical fitness trainer, although he would remain in the country for the duration of the war and would continue to serve the club as loyally as he had done for the previous thirteen years.

Foweraker was determined not to let the loss of the squad that he had meticulously built over numerous seasons dampen his enthusiasm for the club, and the growing certainty of war only increased his resolve to continue getting a team on the pitch every week. In his mid-60s by 1939, Foweraker had been the club's interim manager during the First World War, and knew all too well the importance of maintaining morale and a sense of normality on the home front. To deny the people of Bolton their beloved football team would be a blow equal to nearly anything that the Germans could mete out. Over the course of the summer, he spent countless hours holed up in his office in Burnden Park, trying to find ways to not only file a full team sheet but to keep the lights on, the water running and the crowds coming in. As well as Taylor, Foweraker knew he would be able to count on the services of Goslin's replacement as captain, Harry Hubbick. The left back had followed in his father's footsteps as a miner before football called, and his experience saw him put to work in the collieries to help produce the ore that was so critical to the war effort. He also had, for the meantime at least, George Hunt and Jack Atkinson, the former the club's main goal-getter after Westwood endured a 1938/39 campaign truncated by injury. This age

---

★   Tim Purcell & Mike Gething, *Wartime Wanderers*, p. 38.

and experience was offset by the youthful exuberance of outside left Walter Sidebottom. Just 18 years old, Sidebottom had made his debut during the successful previous season. In him, Foweraker recognised the potential heir to Westwood's throne – someone whose mere presence on the pitch would draw the paying public on to the terraces irrespective of the stature of the opposition. And of course, there was the small matter of the raw, local centre forward who had been making waves at school level that he'd heard so much about.

3

SIGNING FOR BOLTON

IT WAS A curious twist of fate that, just as the opportunity to join Bolton Wanderers was afforded to Nat partly due to the impending war in Europe meaning the team would be stripped of its best players, it was also the war that effectively put the brakes on his career before it had even begun.

On 3 September 1939, the moment that had been fermenting for months happened. Britain had assured the Polish government that what had happened to Czechoslovakia wouldn't happen to them, and the combined might of the British and French militaries would resist any encroachment by Nazi Germany upon Polish independence. When Hitler's forces did just that on 25 August, the Allies mobilised, and despite Germany's offerings of peace following the annexation, there was no turning back. Less than twenty-four hours after Chamberlain had made official the country's position of war, 14-year-old Nat Lofthouse approached Burnden Park. It was a trip that he'd made many times before, but this was without doubt the most momentous, eclipsing even his first time seeing the Wanderers six years earlier. Not only would he be doing his part for the Lofthouse family, chipping in some money to help supplement father Dick's income, but he might actually get paid to play football. Of course, he wouldn't be playing straight away; he'd have a few years of earning his stripes, learning from the same men who he'd idolised from the touchline for so long. In the interim, he'd be a member of the ground staff, helping out with everything from cleaning Ray Westwood's boots to making sure the pitch was in pristine condition in order for his hero to weave his magic. At least, that was the plan. Nat was used to seeing Burnden surrounded by thronging crowds, and this was still the case on this Monday morning, although the atmosphere was entirely alien to that of match days. Hope and excitement had been replaced by panic and nervousness.

The Football Association had sent a memo to all member clubs requesting that any men available to fill the roles of masseurs or physical trainers in the forces be made known to them, immediately quashing any realistic hopes of keeping football running with a semblance of normality. Only three men would remain in the unofficial employ of the club for the duration of the war: Charles Foweraker, George Eccles, the former player who some twenty-five years prior had been warned by a physician not to join Bolton due to the town's lethal climate, and fellow player-turned-coach Walter Rowley, who was made head coach of the first team under Foweraker's management. With money at a premium, these three men would show remarkable dedication to the task of keeping the club alive.

Foweraker, Eccles and Rowley weren't the only faces that Nat recognised from the home dugout as he approached the ground. Many of the players were, to his surprise, also present. He'd followed the stories of the men's Territorial Army travails in the *Bolton Evening News*, and wouldn't have expected to see his heroes back at Burnden. His excitement quickly dissipated when it was explained that the reason the players were there was to get their employment forms in order to become full-time members of the forces, severing their contractual ties with the club. 'I shall never forget the confusion,' recalled Nat a decade and a half later. Among all the turmoil, it was little surprise that nobody was really sure, or particularly cared, why Nat was there. Just as the young man was considering heading home and trying again in a week or two when the drama had died down a touch, Rowley emerged from the crowd. A serious-looking, bespectacled man in his late forties born just south of Bolton, Rowley led

Nat into the offices, a part of the stadium he had never seen before. Sat in Rowley's office, Nat put pen to paper and made official his connection to Bolton Wanderers. With all the uncertainty, Nat wondered, not without reason, if these forms would ever amount to anything. Amateur forms were often little more than a show of faith in a player by the club that didn't translate to professional terms upon his 17th birthday. He could have scarcely imagined that it would be thirty-three years until he would again be without a formal link to the club.

Dick and Sarah were not always the most effusive characters when it came to praise, preferring to keep their boys grounded. Despite their lack of interest in football and worries that their youngest son's preoccupation with the game would dim his prospects in adulthood, however, they couldn't help but swell with pride – and relief – when Nat returned home that day. Despite the seismic news of the day before, the idea that their 14-year-old son may have just set himself up with a well-paying career was a ray of sunshine.

One caveat of signing in such strenuous times was that the club wasn't able to offer Nat a job on the ground staff or a guarantee of employment elsewhere. With this in mind, Dick immediately set about finding his son work. While not boasting the same roster of contacts as the club had, Dick's years of tireless work as a carter and his now elevated position within the Bolton Corporation meant that he was able to quickly pull some strings. Though not quite as glamorous as playing First Division football under a cloud of pipe smoke emanating from the crowd but every bit as evocative of northern towns in the 1930s, Nat got work as a milk boy, walking the labyrinthine streets of Bolton at the crack of dawn for 30 shillings a week. Never one to shirk hard work, Nat set about his new daily routine with the same gusto he had with Bert Cole's gruelling training sessions.

While everything seemed to be falling nicely into place for Lofthouse, Bolton Wanderers remained in turmoil, officially without players. Between Nat's signing and 14 September, there was a period of worrying limbo, with professional football suspended indefinitely and no replacement forthcoming. Long before the days where clubs could draw on countless sources of revenue, the equation for teams in September 1939 was a very simple one: if they didn't play football, they wouldn't survive. Teams were not immune to financial pressures in the manner that most major teams are today, and while fatalities of clubs the Trotters' size were rare, they did happen. Lancashire side Darwen FC had yo-yoed between the First and Second Divisions in the late nineteenth century before disappearing from the professional game, while Glossop, a First Division side at the turn of the twentieth century, had collapsed during the suspension of the Football League during the First World War.

On the 14th, the FA announced the replacement of the Football League with regional leagues that came with a set of stringent regulations. Crowds would be limited to 8,000 in case of air raids, and players would only be permitted to participate provided the game didn't interfere with their national service. Teams could only play opponents from within a 50-mile radius. The FA Cup was also replaced with the War Cup, whose format shifted over the course of its six-season lifespan. As professional contracts had been annulled at the outbreak of the conflict, players were freed to represent any nearby clubs they could – a practical solution to the issue of footballers being stationed all over the country. Ray Westwood and Don Howe both appeared for Newcastle United. Westwood, who was struggling to adapt to regimental life and the relative anonymity that came with it, revelled in the chance to showboat and entertain again. 'Guesting' didn't just bring players a brief moment of respite from the war and a chance to relive what for most seemed like a former life, but it was financially lucrative too: a First Division player's fee was typically equal to two weeks' pay in the forces.

All but two of the Wanderers players in the 53rd Regiment were placed in the British Expeditionary Force that was to travel to Dunkirk and defend strategic points along the France–Belgium border. Vast swathes of men were deployed rapidly, with 158,000 having made their way across the Channel by early October. Among these were Harry Goslin, Ray Westwood and the rest of Nat's childhood heroes. Crossing the water in unstable, nausea-inducing vessels, their minds were elsewhere. Some were fixated on the great number of unknowns that awaited them on the continent, chiefly whether they'd be making the return journey. Others couldn't stop their minds from drifting back to the lives they were leaving behind, possibly forever: thoughts of the comforts of home, warm beds, Lancashire hotpots and of Saturdays spent playing in front of roaring crowds.

Back in Bolton, Nat was making the dreaded adjustment between that last, glorious school summer holiday and the drudgery of work. While he enjoyed being outside and being able to meet and share a joke with people all around Daubhill, the days were beginning to shorten and, faced with the prospect of one of the fearsome northern winters, he wasn't exactly brimming with confidence in his new career path, even if it was to be only temporary. One day, the telephone rang at Willows Lane and Walter Rowley was on the end of the line. True to his word, and in a statement of intent that helped to allay any fears that Nat may have had of his football career being over before it had begun, Rowley informed the young amateur that the club had managed to secure him a job. For an increase in pay, a respite from the increasingly bitter mornings and a career with more future prospects, albeit ones that Nat hoped never to have to explore, the opportunity at reed makers Caffrey & Sons was too good to pass up. Nat quickly struck up a rapport with his fellow workers, who were interested to learn of his connection with their hometown club.

Foweraker and Rowley found that rather than spending their time plotting transfers and ensuring their charges were well drilled, they were instead preoccupied by just securing eleven players for each game. The blackboard that was walked around the pitch before games at Burnden with that day's team written on it bore fewer and fewer recognisable names with every passing match. Harry Hubbick, George Hunt and Jack Atkinson, as well as the young livewire Walter Sidebottom, provided a solid base for the team, but there was a revolving door of players joining them in donning the famous white shirt each week. The crowds that filed through the gates up and down the country in search of a distraction from the excruciating tension of the war found a slower, more disjointed and altogether lower-quality brand of football awaiting them. The last full season of league football had seen an average of over 20,000 watch games at Burnden, with the high-water mark, against Everton, drawing a huge 57,989 punters. The combination of the slower, more pedestrian football, the loss of beloved stars including Ray Westwood and growing fears of gathering in large, open areas saw attendances dwindle. By the end of the season, the Wanderers were playing in front of crowds of fewer than 1,000 – gates that simply could not sustain a club of their size.

Casting his gaze over the pitch on to which he had led teams for twenty years, Charles Foweraker had a heavy heart. Munitions and supplies were stacked high in the stands where once thousands had packed themselves in to roar the team on. If the Phoney War had offered some hope that this conflict may be a brief flashpoint that would barely register as a blip on the radar in the grander scheme of the twentieth century, the retreat from Dunkirk in May 1940 razed those notions. Britain was facing a determined, fierce enemy, and neither side was going to back down in a hurry. What all this meant for Foweraker's beloved club, and other teams across the country, was little short of catastrophic. The joy that football offered simply couldn't be replicated by teams that had been cobbled together. The collective willingness to risk a trip to Burnden Park lessened every time the air raid siren sounded. Germany now had dominion over France after the country surrendered on 22 June, and it was from here that they launched an aerial bombardment on Britain the likes of which had never been seen before. Night after night, the Luftwaffe rained explosives down on the country with the aim of demoralising the British people and hobbling industries vital to the war effort. For the club, the end result was a pitiful yet unavoidable one, despite the best efforts of Foweraker and his loyal staff. For the first time since the Football League was formed in 1888, Bolton Wanderers would not be capable of fielding a team regularly and had no choice but to shut down. The fact that the Burnden turnstiles would remain locked come the autumn of 1940 was just another reminder of the way the war was eating away at the very fabric of what it meant to be from the proud Lancashire town.

‍‍‍‍‍‍‍‍‍‍‌‍‍‍‍‌‍‍‍‍‌‌‍‌‌‍‍‍‍‍‍‍‌‌‍‍‍‍‍‍‍‍‍‍‌‌‍‌‍‍‍‍‍‍‍‍‍‍‍‍‍‍‍‍‍‌‍‌‌‍‍‌‌‌‍‍‌‍‍‍‍‍‍‍‌‍‍‍‍‍‍‍‍‍‍‍‍‍‍‍‍‍‍‍‍‍‍‍‌‍‍‍‍‍‍‍‍‍‌‌‍‌‍‍‍‍‍‍‍‍‍‍‍‍‍‌‍‍‍‍‍‍‍‍‍‍‍‍‍‍‍‍‍‍‌‌‍‌‍‍‍‍‍‍‍‍‍‍‍‍‍‍‍‍‍‍‍‍‍‍‍‍‍‌‍‍‍‍‍‍‍‍‍‍‍‌‍‍‍‍‍‍‍‍‍‍‍‍‍‍‍‍‍‍ ‍‍‍ Although the momentum of the war swung decisively with the Battle of Britain in the summer of 1940, the country was still bearing the brunt of the Blitz. Bolton was spared the worst of it, although there was still extensive damage, and rare was the night that the sky wasn't illuminated a shade of blood red from fires raging in Manchester.

With the prospect of appearing in a white shirt extinguished, Nat was free to find another club to train with and represent, which he did by joining the Bolton Boys' Federation League with Lomax's XI. Still just 15, Nat's natural talent instantly placed him head and shoulders above others in the league, just as it had in the school-level competitions. He also found time to put in some eye-catching performances for Bacup Borough, who were playing friendly games with the Lancashire Combination League suspended. Playing regularly for the first time since leaving Castle Hill, he quickly began to establish a reputation as 'the lad who could "kick" with his head' thanks to the ferocious power with which he directed his headers goalwards.

Football at Burnden Park resumed in a truncated, localised format in January 1941, following a campaign of impassioned lobbying by Foweraker to the board of directors. Wanderers began the shortened programme with six wins from seven games, with pre-war mainstays such as Harry Hubbick and the explosive Walter Sidebottom proving too much for their equally makeshift opposition. By the time March arrived, however, Foweraker was finding guest players harder and harder to come by. A run of three defeats – two in a row to Preston North End in the Football League War Cup and a limp 4-1 battering at Bury's Gigg Lane in the Football League North – led him to previously unexplored avenues to help achieve some semblance of consistency amongst his starting XI.

The din in the Caffrey & Sons factory meant that anyone attempting to reach a worker there by phone had to have a little luck on their side. On Friday, 21 March, Nat was once again throwing himself into a hard day's work, looking forward to the prospect of a brief weekend respite and another chance to showcase his bullish centre forward style for Lomax's XI when he was told there was a call for him. Straining to hear above the racket, he was just able to make out the voice of Foweraker, who explained that, as a result of various absentees for the upcoming fixture against Bury, he was being forced to move George Hunt from the number nine position and they needed someone to fill it. Nat described his response to Foweraker's request as little more than a startled, dumbstruck gurgle. 'I'd have beaten Roger Bannister that afternoon in the race to get home,' Nat remembered. The reaction of Nat's mother Sarah was one of typically understated encouragement, telling her son it was 'lovely – now sit down, get your breath, and enjoy your tea'. Even despite her and Dick's constant desire to keep their son's feet on the ground, they must have shared in his excitement. For a 15-year-old to be asked to play first-class football for Bolton Wanderers – even in such exceptional and mitigating circumstances – was extremely unusual, and hinted at the potential to make a successful career from the game.

In 1954, with his FWA Footballer of the Year award and heroics in Vienna fresh in his memory, Nat recalled that he had still never felt quite so excited as he had the night before his debut. The next day, his excitement gave way to nerves and a nagging disbelief about what was happening. George Hunt, by this stage a veteran who had won the league with Arsenal in 1937/38 and appeared for England, recognised the daze that his young strike partner appeared to be in and attempted to ease his nerves. The Burnden blackboard that day listed Hunt at inside right, Sidebottom at inside left and Lofthouse at centre forward – a seasoned campaigner, a young star, and a complete unknown. Nat knew he would get the requisite service from his teammates; the big question was what he'd be able to do with it.

As the Bolton and Bury players trooped out of the changing rooms, across the gravel and on to the pitch, Nat's heart was in his mouth. A crowd of just 1,587 was in attendance – a far cry from the tens of thousands that he had been a part of as a fan – but to him there may as well have been 100,000 there. To be playing on the hallowed turf in a game that mattered more for local pride than it did for the temporary league format was almost too much for a lad of Nat's age to bear. The superstitious point that he had scored seven against Bury in his first game for Bolton Schools probably never occurred to him. However, Hunt's calming influence and Bury centre half Bill Griffiths, who Nat believed treated him in a gentlemanly fashion after recognising he wasn't ready for the typical treatment meted out by centre halves on their attacking adversaries, helped him play his natural game. Nat, who the *Bolton Evening News*' Tramp match reporter described as being 'well-built and fast', was probably happy with his day's work when he set up fellow debutant Harry Cload for a goal, but he was only getting started. Into the second half, with the score a comfortable 3-1 to Wanderers and the Bury players tiring, Nat, still showing 'plenty of enterprise', scored twice. 'Good God,' Nat remembered thinking, 'I'm in heaven.' An iconic career had begun.

4

THE WAR YEARS

WITH ONE GAME under his belt, the remainder of the 1940/41 season passed in a blur for Lofthouse. He appeared in every game from the Bury match until the end of the season, establishing himself as Charles Foweraker's go-to player in the number nine role. Fellow forward George Hunt's encouragement in Nat's first game quickly extended to a fully fledged paternal relationship, as the veteran took the young striker under his wing and regularly conducted one-on-one training sessions. Hunt had been Tottenham Hotspur's leading goal scorer for five consecutive seasons in the early 1930s and Nat, whose natural humility meant he was never too proud to take the lead from those more experienced than himself, thrived off the attention bestowed upon him.

'Out on the pitch at Burnden Park I learnt more from George in an hour than I could from most people in a year,' he explained. 'Few young footballers have had a better chance to learn their trade. Bolton Wanderers, by playing me alongside George Hunt, made certain that I was given every opportunity of making the grade … I owed much to [his] patience and tact.' While Hunt offered Nat invaluable advice, his fellow inside forward Walter Sidebottom provided a blueprint to follow. Sidebottom had made his debut in 1939, and had played in every fixture the next season after the first team had enlisted him, proving himself a worthy understudy to the absentee Ray Westwood. Despite being four years Nat's senior, the two struck up a rapport thanks to their shared history with the club being relatively unusual among the rag-tag group of players now making up the Wanderers teams on a weekly basis.

After having called the First Division home for all but two of the interwar years, Bolton found themselves in the unfamiliar, complicated and highly congested Wartime League. The loss of their first team meant the 8,000 attendance cap (later raised to 15,000 following the cessation of the most sustained hazard from the Luftwaffe) was rarely threatened by the thinning crowds on the Burnden terraces. Crowds weren't much better for matches that doubled as fixtures in the FA Cup's replacement, the War Cup. The competition was restricted to regional draws until the final, when the winners of the Northern and Southern sections played in a showpiece match.

In the first six games of Nat's Bolton career, he scored seven and Sidebottom three, a testament to their instantly productive partnership. Lofthouse's robust, direct style was the perfect counterpoint for Sidebottom's inventiveness and darting runs. However, a 2-0 success over Blackburn in late April 1941 was to be the last time the two names would ever appear together on the Burnden blackboard, as Sidebottom was conscripted into the navy soon after. Wanderers won only once between Sidebottom's departure and the end of the season. An 8-0 reverse against Chester, who prior to the war had played in Division Three, was a telling reminder of just how times had changed. In their last full season of football, Foweraker's charges had finished a highly respectable eighth place in the top flight with a settled squad of players (just twenty-four players featured during the forty-five-game season). In contrast, forty-eight players were called upon during the twenty-two games of 1940/41. In Lofthouse, Wanderers had at least found a ready source of goals who, due to his youth, was guaranteed to avoid the call from the armed forces for at least a couple of seasons. Even without Sidebottom to aid and abet him, Nat was still finding the net regularly as he benefited from the makeshift defences he was often put up against. Lofthouse was regularly playing against older players whose physical attributes were in decline (and, in some cases, hadn't been particularly great at their peak), meaning his combination of energy, enthusiasm and stamina stood him in great stead. In the five games after Sidebottom's departure, Nat scored four times, taking his total for his debut season to eleven goals in the same number of appearances.

'I remember thinking, "And they pay you for playing, too!"' recalled Nat. Although the 2s 6d match fee was a far cry from what stars such as Westwood and Goslin had been earning on professional contracts prior to the war, it was a welcome addition to the Lofthouse family income, and assuaged any doubts that Nat's parents had about him pursuing football so vigorously. It wasn't enough to live on, but it was a damn sight more than what other 15-year-olds were earning in such lean times, and who knew what it could lead to once life got back to normal? Gilbert Caffrey, Nat's boss at the reed-making firm, recognised the unique opportunity that his young employee had, and was happy to accommodate his afternoon training sessions with Hunt.

Nat began the 1941/42 season with the aim of becoming the team's attacking fulcrum. However, despite the run he had enjoyed in the team at the end of the previous campaign, he found his chances to impress now severely limited. He appeared in four of the opening six games, scoring just once, before being dropped for five months, save for one game in which he scored against Rochdale. In his place came his mentor, George Hunt, as Foweraker desperately sought to arrest a dire run of form that saw Wanderers win just two of their opening seventeen fixtures. Hunt took the opportunity with both hands, winding back the years with twenty goals and offering a lone ray of sunshine in what was a grim season by all accounts. One fixture had to be cancelled when only Lofthouse and Harry Hubbick were available for selection. Under less unusual circumstances, the twelve appearances he did muster were still highly impressive for a 16-year-old. However, the fact he featured in just over a third of Bolton's games and managed just six goals was a demoralising blow for Nat – not least because he would turn 17 at the season's end, the age where the club would have to decide whether he was worthy of a professional contract. With Wanderers still operating on a shoestring budget, Nat was acutely aware that he had to perform to the best of his abilities and demonstrate he was still developing as a player. Even with money tight at Burnden, if he wasn't able to secure a contract in these most trying of times he could never hope to make the grade in peacetime when Wanderers were at full strength. Although rarely failing to outwardly demonstrate an optimistic, carefree disposition, privately Nat was prone to bouts of worry and anxiety. This tendency would surface at several key junctures in his career, and came to the fore when he received a call from manager Foweraker to come in to the club with his father. Nat and Dick approached Burnden Park unsure of whether Nat was about to receive a life-defining offer, or if the veteran manager simply wanted to do the gentlemanly thing in bidding him farewell from the world of professional football.

Their worries proved unfounded. Foweraker immediately reassured Lofthouse senior and junior over a whisky and orangeade, respectively, that while Nat's opportunities had been limited so far, he had demonstrated enough promise that the club were willing to take a substantial gamble by signing him up as a professional. Foweraker regarded the young Lofthouse as the 'jewel in the crown'* of the club's youth policy and he wasn't about to let him escape. Foweraker could not have failed to feel wistful about Nat. He had seen his team, many of whom had trodden the path that Nat followed from boyhood fans to professionals, dismantled after years of careful cultivation. Nat's signing was, in many ways, a reminder of happier times.

In fact, while Nat harboured doubts about his long-term prospects at Bolton following a frustrating second season, Foweraker was more concerned that one of the north-west's many clubs could poach his star talent, something that may have weighed on his decision to limit Nat's playing time before he was able to commit him to a full contract. The manager wasted little time after pouring Dick and Nat's drinks, launching into a full-blown sales pitch, extolling the club's virtues, their rich history and their bright future once the war ended and football got back to normal. Nat needed none of the bravado to be convinced, and would

---

* Tim Purcell & Mike Gething, *Wartime Wanderers*, p. 82.

have put pen to paper without a mention of money, but when Foweraker slid the £10 signing-on bonus in the form of two 'white fivers' across the table, Nat was astonished. 'I'd never seen that much money in my life,' he remembered. 'I felt a little faint.'*

Wishing to repay his parents' faith in his pursuit of what to them must have often seemed to be a naive dream, he immediately offered it to his mother, who politely turned him down, instead insisting that he put it into a savings account lest he fritter it away. Just three years earlier, Nat had been earning 30s a week as a milk boy; now he'd earn the same amount for every ninety minutes he completed for Bolton, with bonuses tied to results and goals. The enormity of the situation didn't sink in until the next morning, when Nat purchased a copy of the *Bolton Evening News* and saw a small piece advising Wanderers' fans that the club had 'added to their staff Nathaniel Lofthouse, a young centre forward'.

Having finished twenty-sixth and thirty-fourth in the previous two campaigns, Foweraker was desperate to arrest the decline and achieve a much-needed morale boost in the 1942/43 season. Even with the mitigating circumstances, for Bolton Wanderers to be performing as they were was an affront to the proud traditions of the club that Foweraker himself had done more than anyone else to forge. Once again, however, the harsh realities facing the club were brought into sharp focus. Nat's hoodoo over Bury, having beaten them in his first game for Bolton Schools and as an amateur for Wanderers, was finally broken in his debut as a professional player, with Wanderers succumbing to a 4-3 defeat at Gigg Lane. Four more defeats followed before the Trotters finally put some points on the board with a win over Manchester City before a return to losing ways. Particularly chastening was a 6-2 defeat away to Southport. Nat scored his first of the season, but it was scant cause for celebration.

---

* In some of his versions of this story, Nat signed without his father's presence. When he returned home, Nat said Dick's immediate response to the £10 his son produced was to ask if he'd 'pinched them'.

Though the team continued to struggle, Nat began to find the scoring touch he'd demonstrated when he'd first graced the team as an amateur. He scored once in a 7-4 rollercoaster win over Burnley, and followed that up by scoring three consecutive braces in a brief upturn of form for the team. In the first of his two-goal games, Nat found himself playing alongside an unfamiliar face at outside right. Although the white shirt with the number seven emblazoned on the back seemed almost natural on his wiry frame, Tom Finney was more accustomed to donning the shirt of Bolton's local neighbours Preston North End than the team from Burnden Park. Finney, who was meeting Nat for the first time, recalled 'an added excitement' for the match, with the crowd eager to see Lofty: 'He looked a superb prospect, scoring a couple of goals and showing great awareness and phenomenal strength.'* Although the two were destined never to play alongside each other in club football again – Finney was called up and served in Egypt and Italy for the remainder of the war – it was to be a different story on the international stage.

As the season wore on, Foweraker increasingly alternated exclusively between George Hunt and Lofthouse as his chosen number nine, and both ultimately enjoyed productive seasons, with the veteran netting seventeen in thirty-one appearances and Nat managing fourteen in twenty-five. With Hunt turning 33 years old at the season's end and the war dragging on with no conclusion in sight, Foweraker was grooming Nat to take Hunt's place in the long term – a development clear to both Hunt and his young protégée, to whom he was still dedicating hours of extra training sessions to a week.

Another glimpse at the future of Bolton Wanderers came in the final game of the season: a 4-0 drubbing by Liverpool at Anfield that consigned the Trotters to an overall record of forty-sixth in the Football League North First Competition and thirty-third in the Second Competition, and their sorriest showing in the war league years yet. This time the number seven shirt was worn by a broad-shouldered Scot three years Nat's senior named Willie Moir. So impressed was Charles Foweraker that, just three weeks later, Moir had signed professional terms at Burnden Park.

★   Tom Finney, *My Autobiography*, p. 59.

As much as Nat's life and Bolton in the 1920s and '30s eschews sepia-tinged visions of the past, there was one moment in 1943 that would have struck even the most soporific of Hollywood writers as being a touch too hackneyed. Walking beneath the wrought-iron girders of Bolton's Trinity Street train station, amidst the bursts of swirling steam emanating from the engine stacks, Nat caught sight of a soft-featured, attractive face, framed with a cut of short, blonde hair, that he dimly recognised.

Racking his memory, he eventually put a name to the face; Alma Foster had been a schoolmate of his, although they'd never really spoken. Having both left Castle Hill at 14, neither had been particularly preoccupied with thoughts of the opposite gender. Now, a couple of years later, Nat was naturally finding the subject jostling for position with football on his list of priorities. Although never the most brash and over-confident lad, Nat had every right to be. Already a strapping young man, his physique had been honed by his twice-weekly training sessions on the unforgiving Burnden gravel track, while his standing in the community – and his bank balance – were both enhanced by his success with the Wanderers. With these reassuring thoughts in mind, Nat resolved to approach Alma. As he began to walk toward her, however, his heart sank. In time-honoured silver-screen fashion, Nat saw she was at the station to bid farewell to a departing soldier.

Despite this setback, something encouraged Nat to keep purposefully striding toward the striking young woman. If, as he anticipated, the soldier she was with was a boyfriend or even fiancé, he'd simply be able to greet her as an old acquaintance. But as they started chatting, a little awkwardly at first, Alma let slip that the soldier was only a friend, and that was all the encouragement that Nat needed. They fixed a date for the coming weekend, at the Empress Dance Hall on Mealhouse Lane. Alma's occupation as a hairdresser meant they weren't automatically invited to the weekly mill dance on Friday nights at the Palais de Danse – a more typical venue for revellers their age – so the 'last-chance saloon' (as the Empress was known because of the higher average age of the patrons) on Saturday it was.

From that moment on, Nat and Alma were virtually inseparable. Away games were accompanied by phone calls; longer trips abroad with England warranted letters. For the next four decades, Alma would be by Nat's side through his triumphs and his lowest moments, a steady hand on the tiller as he navigated the ebullient highs and often heart-breaking lows that those involved in the beautiful game must inevitably endure.

The 1943/44 season was to be pivotal in many ways. At Burnden Park, one half-century-long association was to come to an end, and the beginnings of an even longer one began to take root. While the war swung decisively in the Allies' favour, there were two devastating blows to the Bolton Wanderers family that served as a solemn reminder of the incredible costs that the conflict had borne.

With Hunt restationed away from Bolton, Nat had every reason to expect that the number nine position was now his sole dominion. However, in Hunt's place came Jim Currier, a striker who had been on the club's books before the war and was now serving a stint nearby. Currier, like Hunt, was able to demonstrate more versatility than Nat, switching to inside left when Foweraker opted to play both players. Though his appearances were more limited than he would have liked, Nat still managed a highly respectable sixteen goals – a feat made more impressive as Bolton continued to slide, finishing forty-eighth in the First Competition and thirty-fourth in the Second. Equally worrying for Nat was the emergence of a new talent. Alan Middlebrough's career had followed a similar pattern to Lofty's, though he was only now making his debut, some three seasons after Nat, despite being less than four months younger than him. This may have given Lofthouse some cause for comfort, but the five goals Middlebrough scored in just six games had Lofty looking nervously over his shoulder.

After turning 18 in August 1943, Nat was facing a different sort of pressure than that placed upon him every Saturday in front a set of expectant fans looking for some relief from the grind of the wartime milieu. Now at conscription age, he could expect a call-up letter at any point. Despite Foweraker's assurances, Nat knew that his future career could well hinge on what fate befell him. He would say in later years that 'If I'd signed for Wanderers under normal circumstances in peace-time, there's no way I would have played over 100 games between 1941 and 1946. I would have been making my way up the ladder in the jun-iors and the reserves. Instead I learned my trade in the senior side.' Now, the thing that had afforded him such an exceptional opportunity could easily take it all away.

Even with his fixation on football, Nat understood all too well the dangers he would face if he was to go abroad. Every day news came back from Europe relaying stories of unimaginable horrors and crushing losses. The terrifying, dreadful nature of war was hammered home twice in November of 1943. Having survived Dunkirk and fought in Egypt, the inspirational captain of the Wanderers, Harry Goslin, was killed fighting in Italy as the Allies pushed toward Rome. The second loss hit Nat on a more personal level. Walter Sidebottom, the winger with whom he had shared such a brief yet fruitful partnership and who Foweraker believed to be the future of the club alongside Lofthouse, was killed when his ship was torpedoed in the Channel. These two losses devastated the town, and left no doubt as to the dangers still faced by those going to fight, even with the outlook from the continent becoming more positive.

Many of those from Bolton and the surrounding areas now fighting the Axis powers abroad had been plucked from the mines, a decision made initially in the expectation that the conflict would last no more than a few months. Now, four years after the war began, production shortfalls were beginning to hinder the efforts at home to produce munitions and keep the country moving. With winter looming and coal supplies running low, the Minister of Labour and National Service Ernest Bevin announced an initiative that would see one in ten young men sent into the mines rather than the armed forces. Although some perceived that the 'Bevin Boys' were getting an easy way out of fighting, life in the mines had never been tougher. Fewer men meant longer hours, and this increased fatigue, and an influx of inexperienced men made the already dangerous occupation that bit more treacherous. One of the first to receive the call, in December 1943, was Nat Lofthouse.

Although Nat wished he'd gone to fight – he'd later recall the 'wave of depression' that overcame him when he learned he wouldn't see action – the zeal with which he approached work in the mines was demonstrative of his desire to help his country in whatever manner he could. Mosley Colliery, where he was to be sent, was an imposing pit that stood out even in the Lancashire coal fields for its size and reputation as a tough, unforgiving place to work. Many of those around Nat's age who had followed their fathers into the pits had been conscripted. Others had volunteered to fight in order to escape the mines – an irrefutable counter to those who branded the Bevin Boys derogatorily as 'conchies' for not fighting. Nat arrived to find himself one of the few fresh faces among a workforce of hardened old hands.

Lofthouse's first task spared him the choking, claustrophobic atmos-phere of the below-ground working environment, as he pushed empty tubs to the lift to be returned to the darkness below. While many would have been relieved by being assigned such a simple and safe role, the monotony of the work led Nat to approach his foreman and request a more challenging role. 'I dreamed about getting below ground,' he explained. The same pit tub task, but now underground, did little to dispel his restlessness. Finally, he was transferred back above ground, only now he was to push the full tubs to be unloaded:

> The job proved to be the best I could have possibly had. It made me fitter than ever I had been before. My body became firmer and harder. I learnt to take hard knocks without feeling them. My legs became stronger and when I played football I felt I was shooting with greater power.

As well as added fitness, working in the mines gave Nat an enhanced sense of what a true day's work was for the fans who lined the terraces, conferring on him an appreciation for his lot in life that he would never forget. Nat spoke of his admiration of miners ('they're the best guys in the world') and recalled getting up so early that he walked alongside them as they carried their famous lamps.

Although being fast-tracked into the first team had acclimatised him to footballing life, he had so far missed out on the camaraderie and dressing room banter due to the transient nature of the wartime squads. As well as creating a sense of belonging and togetherness, this raillery also played a crucial role in a player's development mentally. He had to be prepared to take the occasional dig when things weren't going his way, and the criticism meted out by teammates was a diluted brand of what was flung at the players from the stands. Upon starting at Mosley, Nat was immediately recognised as the upstart who fancied himself good enough to fill the boots of Joe Smith and David Jack, and word quickly spread that they had something of a celebrity in their midst. Nat's fellow miners wasted no time in making up for what had been a relatively gentle introduction to the rituals of English male adulthood.

Despite wanting to 'walk home on my knees' after training immediately following another gruelling shift, Nat was enjoying his most successful season in a white shirt. 'I thought nothing of going down the pit at five or six in the morning and then coming up at 11 o'clock and setting off to play football.' By January 1944, when Nat made his first trips to Mosley, he had appeared ten times, scoring seven goals. However, Wanderers' overall results were worse than ever, as they lost fourteen of their first nineteen games, leaving them languishing below teams who hadn't even registered as a blip on their radar prior to the war. Nat's personal success did little to deter the miners, who had cast a critical gaze over countless luminaries in the past and recognised that Nat was not yet at their level – something they weren't shy about telling him. 'Lofty, you'll never make owt,' was one of many catcalls he endured, and although the young Lofthouse recognised the affection in the voices of his fellow miners, he did confide in his mother that the words were having a demoralising effect. As always, Sarah's response was typically reassuring: 'Never mind them, love, just keep on trying and things will work out for you.' In the remaining fifteen games of the season, Nat netted nine times as Wanderers slowly improved.

By the summer of 1944, the future appeared brighter. On 6 June came the D-Day landings and this marked a crucial point in the war. Italy had surrendered in late 1943, and the Soviets were now advancing through Eastern Europe toward Germany. Nonetheless, the war effort was still proving a considerable drain on resources, so Nat and the others in the Bevin Boy scheme continued their daily toil, earning £7 a week. Early in the 1944/45 season, Nat was thankful for the additional income, as he once again found his opportunities to earn playing bonuses limited. Before the season had begun, Foweraker, Wanderers' longest serving and most successful manager, had stepped down from his role, ending a forty-nine-year association with the club. Having battled valiantly against circumstance to keep Bolton Wanderers playing, the effort had taken a toll on Foweraker's health. He knew that the team he had built before the war had lost six years of their careers. Fresh blood would inevitably be needed, and the 67-year-old could no longer summon the energy required to revamp and revitalise the team. In his place came head coach Walter Rowley, the man who had signed Nat to his amateur papers the day after war broke out. Rowley represented continuity from Foweraker in almost every way: he had been signed by, played for and coached under his predecessor – a tenure with the club that stretched all the way back to 1912.

One of Rowley's first major calls as manager was to drop the young man many, himself included, considered the future of the club. Despite his high opinion of Nat's abilities, Rowley had little choice but to replace him with Alan Middlebrough for much of the first half of his first season in charge. Nat failed to register in his first six appearances, which was the worst barren run of his career thus far. In Middlebrough, who scored five in eight appearances, Rowley found a much readier supply of goals. Nat won his place back for the final three games of the Football League North First Competition and repaid Rowley's faith in him by scoring three in three, including two in a 5-0 rout away at Oldham's Boundary Park that led Bolton to by far their best finish in the war leagues: ninth in the First Competition.

Much of Bolton's success was due to fielding a more settled group of players. In Foweraker's final season, he had been forced to pick from a group of forty-nine men. Rowley only needed to utilise thirty-two, nine of whom appeared in thirty games or more. George Hunt, Harry Hubbick, Lol Hamlett and George Taylor, all of whom had been on Wanderers' books before the war, featured extensively. Nat benefited hugely from the experience now surrounding him. Taylor in particular was to have an enormous impact on his development and entire career. Although now nearing the end of his playing days, Taylor's consistency was an inspiration to Nat; he was 'one of those players who never had a bad game'.

With Nat's physical stature and understanding of the game growing with every passing shift in the mines and training session with Hunt and Taylor, Rowley eventually opted to stick with him over Middlebrough, and he was rewarded in spades. 'Things began to go my way,' Nat explained. 'The passes which had failed by inches found their man. Shots which had narrowly missed the post or flown over the crossbar finished in the back of the net.' Nat played in all but one game between December and the end of the campaign and hit a truly remarkable run of form, scoring thirty in just twenty-four games. In February, he scored a hat-trick away at Tranmere and went one better when Rovers came to Bolton a week later, notching four times in front of a delighted Burnden crowd of just over 6,000. Attendances began to increase as word spread of the improved performances of the team, spearheaded by a local lad named Lofty, and Wanderers steadily progressed in the War Cup. The catcalls of Nat's fellow miners gradually became high praise and compliments, albeit some of them backhanded: 'The miners who had been pulling my young leg in good part now told me I'd learned through taking their advice, which was probably true.'

Wanderers' long-held reputation as a 'Cup team' was well deserved, and they proved that even with the fragmented nature of their current squad, the tag still applied. In the biggest game of his career so far, Nat scored all four goals as Wanderers ran rampant at Blackpool's Bloomfield Road in front of 20,000 baying Lancastrians, by far the biggest crowd Lofty had ever played in front of. He netted again in the return leg at Burnden as Bolton advanced and then scored twice against Newcastle United, Rowley's side cruising to a 3-0 success. The semi-final, against Wolverhampton Wanderers, proved to be the first round in which Nat failed to net, but young Scottish inside forward Willie Moir sent the Whites through to the two-legged Northern final. The atmosphere in town reached fever pitch as Wanderers prepared to take on Manchester United.

Before the game took place, however, the news that every Briton had hoped for but had scarcely dared to dream of arrived from mainland Europe. On 7 May 1945, Germany surrendered to the Allies unconditionally. Two weeks later, such was the demand of the townspeople to celebrate the end of the conflict and see their rejuvenated team face off against one of their great rivals, touts outside the ground were able to command almost three times a ticket's face value. For many fans, this was their first trip to their beloved team's ground since the outbreak of war. Such had been the pressures that the conflict had wrought that football had paled into an afterthought. Now, with servicemen beginning to return home for the first time in years, Bolton fans were in the mood for a reminder of normality that was no longer so tinged with melancholy. As Nat left the dressing rooms deep in the bowels of Burnden, he was filled with a mixture of excitement and nervousness. Though it was to be his 104th club appearance, it was the first that was truly representative of what playing for the Trotters was really like. The *Lancashire Evening Post* reported that 'peacetime traffic scenes were seen around the ground. Hundreds of cars were parked in adjoining streets', and the 40,000-strong crowd – Burnden's biggest since 1938 – wasn't left disappointed. Wanderers ran out 1-0 first-leg winners, with Nat giving thousands their first taste of Lofty goal-scoring magic that would become synonymous with the club over the next decade and a half. In a prophecy of future events, the *Bolton Evening News* wrote that '[United keeper Jack] Crompton had scarcely gathered the ball close to the far post when Lofthouse bundled both man and ball into the net'. A last-minute Malcolm Barrass goal secured a 2-2 draw at Maine Road* in the second

---

* Old Trafford was badly damaged by a German bombing raid in 1941 and wouldn't reopen until 1949.

leg, and with it the League North Cup, granting Bolton passage to the War Cup Final and a trip to the capital.

The final, played at Chelsea's Stamford Bridge, was yet another new experience for Nat in a year that had already introduced him to so much that he could expect from life as a professional footballer in peacetime. He had never travelled to London before ('its lights and crowds … an eye-opener'), nor had he played in a match with any sort of silverware or prestige attached to it. Bolton began brightly, with Lofthouse bringing a fine save from Chelsea keeper Ian Black in the first half. Chelsea, who had triumphed over Millwall in the previous round, hit back and made the shift in momentum count when they went 1-0 up before half-time. Nat was finding the Blues' robust defence an effective deterrent to his own goal-scoring attempts, so he deigned to instead use his physicality to aid the endeavours of his teammates. Fittingly, it was Hunt, arguably the star of Bolton's wartime team, who netted the equaliser. The game seemed destined for a stalemate until a late penalty award was converted by Lol Hamlett, winning the final War Cup for the Wanderers. 'You'd have thought we were [the home crowd's] own favourites judged by the ovation given us after the game,' recalled Nat, offering a telling reminder that, while competitive, war football was a far cry from the atmosphere of league football proper – something his mother was quick to remind him when he returned home with his prize of Savings Certificates.

Shortly after his big day in London, Nat was informed that he no longer needed to make the forty-five-minute tram ride to Mosley Colliery as a Bevin Boy. He left the mines with his physique toned and his will and determination imbued with added steel. He had encountered the sort of camaraderie and jestful barbs that he would become accustomed to over the coming years, and there wasn't a centre half in the world who could compare to the oppressive and exhausting work in the mines. Just as he had the day after war was declared, Nat reported to Walter Rowley at Burnden Park the day following his release from duty. This time the atmosphere was not one of panic and fear, but of excitement and hope. Bolton Wanderers were about to become the focal point of the town once again, and they were going to be led by 19-year-old Nat Lofthouse.

5

FIRST TASTE OF THE FIRST DIVISION

WITH THE ROAR of the Stamford Bridge crowd and the revelry of the team's train ride back north still fresh in his mind, Nat was more than ready to meet the new challenge now facing him as a fully fledged professional. The War Cup that Bolton had added to their list of honours was retired on 7 May, the same day the German surrender was signed in Reims. In its place would return the FA Cup, the competition that Charles Foweraker had enjoyed such success in.* New manager Walter Rowley, who had missed the 1923 final due to suspension, was desperate to continue that tradition. Given the disarray many clubs found themselves in regarding playing staff and arrangements off the pitch, the FA held off reintroducing the financially pivotal questions of promotion and relegation so soon, opting for a simplified league format for the 1945/46 season, despite pressure from some clubs who wanted to capitalise on their relative readiness. Guest players would still be permitted, with six allowed until November and three thereafter. Even with their levels of

---

★   In 1945, only three men had won the FA Cup more times: George Ramsey, Thomas
      Mitchell and John Nicholson.

debt lower than many of their competitors, Wanderers were grateful for the reprieve.

Mercifully for Rowley, many of the players he'd called upon regularly in the final season of wartime football were willing to make their temporary commitment to Bolton permanent. Young Malcolm Barrass resisted the call of hometown club Blackpool to remain with Wanderers. New team captain Harry Hubbick, who had worked with Nat in the mines during the war, featured in every single league and cup game at left fullback. Further experience was provided by Messrs Hunt and Taylor, now both in the twilight of their careers but still able to offer leadership on the pitch and encouragement and advice off it. Willie Moir, who had demonstrated considerable attacking verve despite having few appearances to his name, became Rowley's go-to for plugging holes in the attack when the toil of the long season wore others down. Finally, much to the delight of Rowley, who had played alongside him, and the younger players who had grown up idolising him, Ray Westwood returned. Despite being 33 and missing match practice, Westwood re-emerged for the second half of the season and, playing at outside right, once again lit up Burnden Park with a series of effervescent performances.

Despite the return of the crowd's old hero, however, there was no doubting who the weight of expectation now lay with. Though his experience in the wartime leagues hadn't been all plain sailing, beset by false dawns and failures of confidence, Nat Lofthouse now sought to seize his opportunity. He remembered that in the days before the season began:

> I took a careful look at myself. Nature had endowed me with a fine physique. Work in the pits had hardened that physique so that I could give and take hard knocks. I was quite fast, too, and with the experience I had gained in wartime soccer, I felt that I could make the grade providing I was willing to learn my craft.

His record of 100 goals in 139 games in wartime football had fans who had stayed away from games during the conflict buzzing with excitement, and more than 16,000 packed themselves into the Burnden Park paddocks for the home fans' first chance to see Bolton's wonder kid in the new season. Bolton had picked up just one point from their first two games – two away matches on Merseyside, against Everton and Liverpool – but Nat had scored in both. For the fans being introduced for the first time to the name Lofthouse via the pitchside blackboard, Nat ensured they went home unable to forget it, as he produced a stirring performance as Bolton's battering ram, scoring once and running the Everton defence into the ground in a 3-1 victory.

His fine form saw him net in each of the Whites' next three games before injury took him out of the line-up for a home clash against Preston. The fact that this was the first game that Rowley's team failed to find the net was demonstrative of not only Nat's striking prowess, but of his growing influence on the team's style of play. While lacking in some of the guile needed to play at inside or outside forward as Moir did, Nat's ability to compete against towering, hulking centre backs in the air meant that even the most aimless of clearances by the Bolton defence could be transformed into a scoring opportunity. Just as word had spread around the local leagues of the boy who could 'kick with his head', so did Nat's reputation as a fearsome competitor in the air quickly began drawing worrisome glances between centre halves and goalkeepers. Blackpool's great defender, Harry Johnston, remembered, from the safety of a newspaper column, how Nat could 'beat such a master in the air as Billy Wright'[*] and how Bolton's success even at that early stage in Nat's professional career hinged on the young striker. Even the ageless Stanley Matthews, usually the recipient of superlatives rather than the administerer of them, couldn't fail to notice Lofthouse's talent of being 'magnificent in the air'.[**]

With Rowley and his young, raw squad still finding their feet, Bolton soon began to struggle for consistency. A 6-0 victory over Leeds United in which Lofty and Moir both scored twice was followed by four defeats and a draw. Things began to change from December, and it was no coincidence that the upturn in form coincided with the return of Westwood. More than

---

[*]   'Bolton's non-stop brand of football pays dividends', *South China Morning Post*, 1955.

[**] 'With Lofthouse at his best we slammed the Scots 7–2', *South China Sunday Post Herald*, 1965.

17,000 witnessed a triumphant homecoming for the winger, who scored the winner in a 2-1 victory over Middlesbrough. The following month brought with it the return of the FA Cup. With the temporary league arrangement lacking prestige, the FA ruled that every round before the semi-finals of the 1945/46 Cup would be two-legged, so as to enable the fans of both teams in each tie to see their sides in action. Rowley's managerial debut in the competition couldn't have gone better, as Wanderers won 1-0 at home in front of 26,000 against fierce local rivals Blackburn Rovers, before Westwood scored twice and George Hunt once to complete a nostalgia-tinged 3-1 victory in the return leg. The fourth round pitted the Whites against Liverpool. A 5-0 rout, with Lofthouse on the scoresheet twice and Westwood hitting a hat-trick, rendered the 2-0 return defeat at Anfield meaningless. The progress in the Cup combined with vastly improved league form – Bolton lost just three times in the second half of the league season and won fourteen – led to hysteria equal to that which had occurred during Wanderers' run to the War Cup Final the previous season.

During those games, Burnden had been pushed to its limits, with the running track being utilised as a rudimentary spill-over area and one soldier even demanding a refund when he felt unable to enjoy the game due to the claustrophobic conditions. The Burnden Stand remained out of com-mission due to its use as storage for baskets filled with Ministry of Supply goods, which meant a restricted number of tickets. It wasn't simply a lack of preparedness due to the war that was the cause of the sometimes unpleas-antly cramped conditions. As far back as 1929, the *Bolton Evening News* had scornfully pointed out that just 'one means of entrance to the huge railway embankment is tragically inadequate'.[*] Now, with returning soldiers, the ebullient atmosphere of the country as a whole and the prestige of the FA Cup, demand for tickets was higher than ever. Almost 40,000 had seen the thumping of Liverpool and over 43,000 were in attendance as Bolton triumphed over Middlesbrough in the next round. Wanderers faced Stoke City in the quarter-final, and when they returned from the Potteries with a 2-0 aggregate lead courtesy of a Westwood double, the excitement reached

[*]   David Tossell, *The Great English Final*, p. 115.

fever pitch. As if the prospect of seeing the reinvigorated Wanderers roll back the years wasn't enough, the semi-finals were to be played at neutral venues, while the final would be at Wembley, meaning that this would be the last opportunity to see the Trotters in Cup action locally for the season. Yet another factor was the lure of seeing a particular opposition player. Stanley Matthews had already cemented his place in football lore despite not yet being halfway through his illustrious career, and his presence as perhaps the most famous player in the world was enough to attract countless punters who wouldn't have otherwise attended.

With no tickets available prior to the day of the match, eager fans had no choice but to get to the turnstiles as early as possible in order to guarantee a place within Burnden Park's hallowed walls. By midday, three hours before kick-off, long queues of men and women, old and young, were snaking down the Manchester Road and beyond. The baskets occupying the Burnden Stand meant all those wishing to stand in the paddock end needed to go in through the Railway Stand turnstiles, creating a huge concentration of some 37,000 people. With twenty minutes to go until kick-off and both the authorities and club officials beginning to realise that the number of people within the ground was already dangerously high, the decision was taken to shut the gates. However, this did little to stem the tide of people flowing into the ground. Some 2,000 gained entry by walking along the railway lines and vaulting the barriers at the back of the Embankment end or by jumping the turnstiles. More still made it in when a man picked the lock on an exit gate in order to get his son away from the crowding. The desire to watch the game even led some who failed to find a way inside to climb a stationary railway car and watch from its roof. Burnden's previous record attendance was 69,912 (at least one shy of the true total, as that had been Nat's first match, when he'd snuck in). On the day of the Stoke match, the number officially counted was 65,419, with countless thousands more unaccounted for, and, with the limited space in the Burnden Stand, a much lower capacity. 'I have never seen Burnden Park so full,' recalled Nat years later. 'If you'd thrown a golf ball in the air it would have come down on someone's head. There was no space at all.' What should have been one of the proudest moments of Nat's fledgling career was to turn rapidly to tragedy.

As the teams came onto the field just before 3 p.m., the crowd toward the back of the Embankment surged forward, eager to catch a glimpse of their local heroes and of Matthews. The sheer weight of bodies was too much for the barriers to bear, two of which collapsed, sending hundreds to the floor with hundreds more on top of them, crushing those beneath. Excitement turned to panic in the immediate surrounding areas of the paddock, and those still upright began to help those who had fallen. Fan Phyllis Robb commented more than seven decades after the tragedy, 'I don't remember how it started that day but I know they lifted me up and carried me over the top of it all.' By now, the throng of the crowd was so thick that even those mere metres away from the collapsed barriers had little notion of what had happened. The blissful ignorance extended to the players and the referee, George Dutton, who allowed the game to proceed. A brief stoppage was ordered when fans who were being crowded from the stands encroached on the pitch, before at 3.12 a policeman called for Dutton's attention. He informed him of the severity of the situation, which was becoming more apparent with each passing moment, and ordered the players to be taken back to the dressing rooms. As he left the field, Nat recalled seeing people being brought from the crowd on stretchers, their arms hanging limp from the sides, commenting, 'I thought they had fainted.'

Confusion exists to this day about how much the players knew when they emerged from the tunnel some twenty minutes later. Many maintained that they simply had no idea until after the game was finished that there had been deaths. Nat stated his belief that 'I don't think any of the 22 players on that field knew the extent of the disaster'. The early recollections of Stanley Matthews were largely similar, with the only indication being a stray shout from the crowd that it was 'criminal to go on when people are dead'.* In Matthews' 2000 autobiography, his story had changed somewhat, as he reflected on seeing body bags on the touchlines and feeling physically ill. Nat's 1954 memoir, *Goals Galore*, expunged the disaster from history entirely, with the publishers likely deeming the subject too macabre for younger readers.

★   Jon Henderson, *The Wizard: The Life of Stanley Matthews*, p. 153.

What is certain is the devastating effect it had on Bolton as a town and a footballing community. In total, thirty-thee died, while dozens more were treated in hospital and hundreds at the ground. To make the tragedy even more unpalatable, several of those who died had not long demobbed from the armed forces. The very notion that these men had survived the horrors of the most devastating conflict in human history only to die at home, watching a game of football, was beyond the pale for many, including Nat: 'Football was supposed to be one of the ways in which ordinary people could get away from the hardships and the sorrow that War had brought.' The players resumed the match, with the authorities anxious to avoid the potential unrest among the heaving crowd by cancelling the game with no way of communicating the reason to the fans. The gates to the Burnden Stand were opened, allowing some on the Embankment through and relieving some of the pressure on those that remained. Dutton wisely elected to do away with the half-time break, and instead instructed the players to immediately switch ends and continue playing. The final result of 0-0, enough to see Bolton through to the semi-final, scarcely registered with anyone outside the ground, who had heard the harrowing reports via the wireless and faced an anxious wait for their loved ones to return home.

The true magnitude of the event wasn't felt until the next day, when the disaster made national news. Nat, along with other members of Wanderers' playing and coaching staff, returned to survey the scene. 'It was a pitiful sight,' said Lofthouse. 'There were shoes, ties, gloves, hats and other bits of clothing on the running track around the ground. We all felt so helpless.' Despite his occasional crises of confidence, Nat, like so many men of his generation, generally kept his worries and emotions to himself. However, he never shied away from the devastation that he and his fellow players felt when asked to recollect the incident that left a black mark on football. His second memoir, *The Lion of Vienna*, was published months after the Hillsborough Disaster, a tragedy that bore more than a passing resemblance to the events at Burnden over forty years before. While fresh questions were asked about how football could have failed to learn from the Burnden Disaster and later horrors seen at Ibrox in 1971 and Bradford City in 1985, for Nat it reopened old wounds. As well as mourning those lost, Nat's words were laced with anger: 'We thought it could never happen again … we thought our stadiums would be made safer places. But no.' He ridiculed the idea that a perceived loss of atmosphere in seated stadia was worth another potential disaster.

With the harrowing fallout from the tragedy still reverberating around the club, Rowley stoically guided his team through the remainder of their season. The FA Cup semi-final against Charlton Athletic at Villa Park was lost 2-0, but Wanderers ended the campaign in fine form, and finished the final season before the return of league football proper in a highly respectable third place. Nat's twenty goals cemented his status as one of the country's most promising young players. His reward was securing the maximum wage for the following season, the newly raised cap of £12 a week, along with £10 in the off-season and a £2 win bonus. It was more than his father Dick had ever earned, and left him plenty with which to court Alma, taking her to the regular dances at the grand Empress Hall in town. With a vibrant, youthful team still learning their trade, there was scarce indication that the season just passed was to provide Wanderers with their best league position under Rowley's stewardship.

The after-effects of the Burnden Disaster were felt throughout the summer. A relief fund, opened by the Mayor of Bolton, raised almost £40,000 – then an astronomical sum of money. Labour MP Moelwyn Hughes led an inquiry into the disaster, its causes and what actions should be taken to avoid any repetitions. Nat attended the first day of the inquest, solemnly noting 'it seemed the least I could do'. The report found the club and officials had done little wrong in the run up to the game, and that authorities had acted 'appropriately and energetically' when the crisis became apparent. However, Hughes was critical of the speed with which the unexpectedly large crowd was dealt with. The report ultimately decided that the most appropriate action was more stringent control on crowd admittance rather than a wholesale upheaval of stadia, noting 'there was no collapse of structure: it was the first example in the history of football following of serious casualties inflicted by a crowd upon itself'. Despite this, Wanderers spent £5,500 on making improvements to the Embankment end where the disaster had occurred, per the report's recommendations.

Despite anxiousness at board level that the club might yet face financially ruinous legal action, none materialised, and Walter Rowley and his coaches were free to try to focus once again on football. The most pivotal move of the summer was loyal servant George Taylor hanging up his boots, having joined the club as an amateur in 1926, and immediately being tapped for a coaching role. Nat called the decision 'one of the best things they ever did at Burnden Park … He had the gift of making people play for him.' Despite Taylor's career ending just as his own was beginning, Lofty found his and Taylor's attitudes could have scarcely differed less when it came to playing for Bolton Wanderers: 'He preached that the club was always bigger than the individual. We were playing for the club, the town, the people of Bolton.'

Not only were they playing for the people of Bolton, but they were training for them, too. Even allowing for the roughness and aggression of the beautiful game in the 1940s and '50s, the training regimes were often more gruelling than the games themselves. Nat would arrive at the ground at 10 a.m. having caught the bus for the short trip into town. The players would spend half an hour running around the unforgiving cinder track, followed by half an hour's work with a medicine ball, before body exercises. Finally, on the rudimentary pitch behind the Burnden Stand that the players called 'The Gravels', came six-a-sides, in which the players would, in the words of future star Dougie Holden, 'kick the hell out of each other'.* Later, a sand pit with balls suspended from the stand would be installed for brutal heading drills.

Even as the prestige and glamorous status of being a professional First Division footballer was restored, alongside increased pay, the occupation wasn't without its sacrifices. Driven by his insatiable desire to improve, Nat continued to stay behind with Taylor and Hunt after training. The hard leather balls, particularly when combined with some traditional Lancashire drizzle, were rock solid, but Nat would still practise shooting 'for hours at a time'. One exercise saw him don a carpet slipper on his right foot to

---

*   John Gradwell, *Legend: The Life of Roy 'Chopper' Hartle*, p. 71.

encourage him to use his unfavoured left. It didn't take long before his left foot was equally capable of generating cannonball power. 'My friends gave me up for a bad job when I turned down their invitations to visit them – but my conscience told me I was right. I wanted to become a good professional footballer, *not just another player*, and to achieve this end I was prepared to put everything I possessed into the task.'

The next season saw the most welcome return of league football, and with it a crucial sign of life finally returning to normal. Though his confidence wasn't unshakeable, the arrival of full-time football was not a moment that Nat lost much sleep over. The competition would be better and the centre halves he would be pitting his wits against taller, tougher and more street smart, true. However, the sad fact was that many of the great players before the outbreak of conflict were now reaching the end of their truncated careers. Instead, the best players were now, like Nat, those who had never experienced league football, many of whom Nat had faced already. Tom Finney, Jimmy Dickinson, Alf Ramsey, Billy Wright, Jackie Milburn and Stan Mortensen would, along with Lofty, all make their names in the years immediately following the war, and would come to dominate the English footballing landscape for over a decade.

Bolton entered their first season of league football in seven years with mixed expectations. On the one hand, their third-placed finish the previous year equalled their best ever showing, albeit in a diluted competition. Rowley's first season at the helm had also delivered a promising run in the FA Cup. However, there was no escaping the fact that neither he nor many of his young players had experienced an exhausting season of full-blooded English top-flight football. For all his success in the FA Cup, Charles Foweraker's teams had never quite got to grips with league football, despite the side of the 1920s having been capable of a sustained title charge. The 1946/47 season began with the aim of remaining safe enough in the league so as to allow all the focus to be directed to the Cup.

As it was, Wanderers achieved neither of their two objectives. Things started well enough. The Trotters' first engagement was a return trip to the scene of Nat's biggest career success to date, the victory in the 1945

War Cup at Stamford Bridge. Despite a narrow 4–3 defeat (inevitably, Tommy Lawton netted twice for the Blues), there was plenty for Rowley and his players to take heart from as they scored a 'moral victory' in the words of the *Bolton Evening News*' football writer Haydn Berry. Berry singled Lofty out for particular praise, writing: 'Lofthouse was forceful, intelligent in finding the gaps for through passes to Westwood and Moir, scored two good goals and was prevented from scoring a third by Robertson's brilliant late save.' The noted scribe's main criticism was of Bolton's 'tendency to lift the ball … which is bad for a forward line lacking height'. It wouldn't be long before no reporter would ever find such an issue with a forward line containing Nat again.

A run of four wins in their first six games, including a 4-0 rout of Tom Finney's Preston at Deepdale, had Bolton in third. The victory over Portsmouth in the club's opening home game came despite strained circumstances, as Ray Westwood informed Rowley he wouldn't play after learning his wife had been refused entry to the ground. While some of the players, long accustomed to Westwood's prima donna streak, merely smirked, the situation suddenly took a more serious turn when Nat learned that Alma too was being barred entry. Lofty took a stand, wanting both to support Westwood and also understandably irritated by the club's unnecessarily dogmatic application of the rules when the women realised they didn't have their passes. Rowley himself eventually went to set the situation straight.

The bright start didn't last, however. Nine games without victory sent the Whites spiralling into the lower reaches of the table, just three points from the bottom. Their faltering form was largely due to a lack of experience, including Nat's, in Rowley's side. This was particularly problematic given the lack of competition Rowley could call upon in the centre forward role. Age had finally caught up with the 37-year-old George Hunt, who made just three appearances all season. After briefly threatening Nat's place in the team during the war, Alan Middlebrough was found to be nowhere near First Division quality, and would make just five more appearances in a white shirt over the next two seasons before quietly moving on to Bradford City. Nat spoke for Willie Moir, Tom Woodward and the other youngsters when he said that:

Faced by experienced footballers every week my limitations were frequently exposed and there were times when I felt like quitting the game because I was certain I was not good enough. Sometimes only the fact that people would think I was a quitter kept me going. I determined to try still harder, and work harder, to acquire the skill I lacked. Football ceased to become either a game or a job to me. It was almost a religion.

It was another harsh period of acclimatisation, akin to playing his first couple of frustrating seasons of wartime football all over again, only this time with the weight of expectation on his shoulders. That several of Nat's teammates were experiencing the same did have the silver lining of binding them closer together, and occasionally manifested itself in irresistible performances, such as when Wanderers broke their luckless run with a 5-1 defeat of Derby County in which Lofthouse, Moir and Woodward all scored. Rowley's charges continued to limp through the season, and by the time they entered into the FA Cup at the third round to face Stockport County, they were in an alarming sixteenth place, out of the relegation zone by virtue of others' failings more than their successes. More than 30,000 came to sample the first taste of FA Cup action since the Burnden Disaster, and they were treated to an easy 5-1 victory in which Nat scored twice. An unexpected 3-0 league win against eventual champions Liverpool had hopes high for the next round of the Cup against Second Division leaders Manchester City, but Wanderers' interest in the year's contest was ended after they conspired to throw away a two-goal lead before losing in a replay.

Such was the disappointment of exiting the Cup that only 4,280 turned up for the next home game against Leeds – a post-war record low that stood until 1983. Nat overcame his early season woes and eventually finished with a return of twenty-one goals in forty-three appearances – a highly admirable total that made him Bolton's top scorer by a wide margin. However, the club had failed to capitalise on their good previous season, eventually limping to eighteenth. In the off-season, Rowley had the unenviable task of informing George Hunt that there was no future for him at Burnden Park as a player, and the Yorkshireman finished his career in the Second Division before returning to the club as a coach in 1948. With the great forward having played such a pivotal role in the club's pre-war team, Rowley was well within his rights to hope for finances to be made available for a replacement. However, with the renovations to Burnden and other resulting costs of the disaster weighing heavily on the board members' minds and pockets, Rowley was informed he'd simply have to make do.

For a brief moment, Hunt wasn't the only Bolton Wanderers player that was casting his gaze further afield. In January, just as he was beginning to find his feet, Tottenham Hotspur had enquired about the availability of Bolton's young striker Nat Lofthouse. Spurs had spent much of their existence as a Division Two side, playing second fiddle to their illustrious neighbours Arsenal, but in 1947 they were highly ambitious. Like so many clubs, the seven-year hiatus of league football had broken up a promising Spurs side, and they were on the hunt to replace the goals of the retired Johnny Morrison. They also weren't shy about flashing their chequebook around, and with Bolton's finances precarious, their approach wasn't dismissed out of hand, although according to Walter Rowley no bid was ever made.

In the 1940s, transfers were a vastly different business, with the 'retain and transfer' system meaning no freedom of contract and effectively rendering players powerless when it came to deciding their future. As Nat explained:

> If a player wanted to leave and his club said 'No', that was the end of the matter. There was no question of a player being a free agent at the end of his contract; there was no chance of a club cashing in on a prize asset before his contract expired.

Other than in exceptional cases, the power rested almost entirely with the clubs, with players faced with the prospect of being effectively blacklisted should they try to force – or deliberately scupper – a move.

Some newspapers reported Nat had submitted a transfer request – something more commonplace in his era of football due to their largely token nature. A request was little more than a negotiating tactic, lacking almost entirely the power of the same action in the modern game. Nat's openness to the move had nothing to do with money; his wages were already at the £12 ceiling, meaning Spurs could not pay him more had they wanted to. Instead, he was motivated by his recent struggle for consistency. In the pages of the *Bolton Evening News*, Rowley called the speculation 'mischievous'. The Bolton manager elaborated that Nat had 'expressed himself as disappointed at not being amongst the goals as regularly as he would wish and suggested a change [of clubs]',* but that Rowley had reassured him that he would recover his form and Bolton would be patient while he did so. Dropping down a division, even to an upwardly mobile Spurs, would have jarred with Nat's natural competitive streak. Even though his patchy form and difficulties adapting to the rigours of First Division football meant that a period in the Second Division could have seemed appealing, Lofty knew he had got this far; to turn back now would be a betrayal of everything he had worked for.

The 1947/48 campaign began where the previous one had left off, with four consecutive defeats and just a single goal to show for Bolton's efforts. Rowley's paternal style of management made him popular among his younger players, but it did create issues when it came time for more drastic action. In a bid to halt the run, Rowley dropped several players, among them Lofthouse. Both Middlebrough and Ernie Forrest, typically a wing half, were given the chance to prove themselves in the number nine shirt before Nat was recalled – a blow to his still-fragile confidence. However, the trademark Lofty bravery was already in evidence on the field, and he was beginning to develop a mental fortitude to match. Upon his return, he cast aside any self-doubt and hit goals in three games on the bounce. The third match was just Bolton's second win at the thirteenth time of asking, at Burnden against Blackpool in front of 45,000, many of whom were in attendance to once again witness the wizardry of Stanley Matthews rather than out of any belief that Wanderers might secure victory. Despite the win, Wanderers were rooted to the bottom of the table, three points from

---

★   *Bolton Evening News*, 14 January 1947.

safety and the most goal-shy side in the league. Rowley continued to shuf-
fle his pack with ever-increasing urgency, and he appeared to finally hit
upon a winning combination near the end of November, when Wanderers
doubled their paltry number of victories by recording three in a row, all
courtesy of doubles from Lofty. Paradoxically given his occasionally worrisome streak, Nat's improved form seemed to stem directly from more
pressure being heaped upon him. Earlier that season Ray Westwood, still
the town's great hero and fan favourite, had departed the club, meaning the
onus was on Lofty to steer the team's attack. Not for the first time, he rose
to the task. He finished the season with eighteen goals in thirty-one league
games as Wanderers scrambled to safety.

Another possible reason for Nat's resurgence in form was entirely
unrelated to football. Having been with Alma Foster for more than four
years, in early 1947 he decided it was time to do the honourable thing.
In her, Nat had found someone who he not only loved spending time
with, but who he could trust to allay his fears and worries. She would be
sympathetic and encouraging yet also firm, not afraid to tell him to pull
himself together and stop feeling sorry for himself when the circumstances called for it. While he still lacked the belief that he was truly cut
out to be a top-flight footballer, his conscious decision to avoid too much
carousing and socialising in order to further his game had allowed him to
accrue a not-insubstantial nest egg. Though possibly tempted to give it
one more season to ensure he would be able to continue to provide, the
affection that he and Alma shared forced Nat's hand.

The December date of the wedding was, as with so many aspects of
their lives, influenced by football. Preceding Wanderers' involvement in
the FA Cup, it avoided any unforeseen clashes with the competition's
potentially limitless number of replays. However, given Wanderers' packed
schedule, there would inevitably be complications no matter what the
date and so it proved on 6 December 1947. Nat began the day bedecked
in a sharp, wide-lapelled pinstripe suit, complete with a buttonhole
flower, accompanied by his brother, Tom, as best man. Alma looked radi-
ant in a simple white dress. Nuptials completed and photographs taken
on the church steps, one of which was printed on the front page of the

Bolton Evening News, Nat barely had a moment with his new bride before switching into his more familiar attire of a thick cotton white shirt, baggy navy shorts, striped socks and heavy leather boots, postponing his wedding reception for another urgent engagement with Wolverhampton Wanderers. Two goals in a Bolton win was cause for a double celebration that evening. While many women would have baulked at the idea of their husband making a speedy exit from the church on their wedding day, Alma took it all in good humour. She was well aware of the importance of Nat to Bolton, and the importance of Bolton to Nat. The fact that she had to share him with the Wanderers even on her wedding day proved to be a telling sign for their future together.

Following their marriage, the newly-weds moved into a comfortable semi-detached home on Temple Road in the Halliwell area of the town, just over 3 miles from Burnden Park. With attractive gardens at the front and back, and away from the worst of the noise from Bolton's factories, the house would become a sanctuary of sorts over the next few tumultuous years of Nat's career, never failing to provide him respite from the rigours of life as a professional sportsman. Nat's father, Richard, had gone slightly pale when his youngest son told him of the £900 mortgage with £6 monthly repayments, telling him 'you've put a rope round your neck for life', but Nat was quick to allay his fears as best he could, demonstrating some of the bullishness and determination that he was rarely forced to use off the pitch.

Other off-pitch matters weren't quite so wholesome and happy. Long before lurid stories about footballers became commonplace in the tabloid press, the *Daily Dispatch* ran a story alleging that Lofty and Rowley had fallen out over a question of money, complete with quotes from Rowley accusing Lofthouse of financial greed. If this appeared entirely out of keeping with Nat's character, that was because the story was a fabrication. The most likely root of the piece was the *Dispatch* attempting to capitalise upon threatened strike action by the Professional Footballers' Association over wages. With Nat's star rising, plus Bolton's cash-strapped status, he was a decent bet (for someone with no knowledge of Lofty's personality) as a player who may have been agitating for improved wages.

The *Dispatch* also likely reckoned that, with the financial aftershocks of the Burnden Disaster still being felt, Wanderers would have fewer resources than most First Division sides to combat the claims.

Their gamble backfired. Although Bolton's board were having to keep a fastidious eye on the balance sheet, many of them were also native to the town and proud Wanderers fans who had no intention of seeing the name of the club and its star player dragged through the mud. The directors fought for an apology for the inflammatory remarks, which they duly received. To his credit, Nat never stooped to make mention of the unsavoury incident in either of his two autobiographies.

The next two years were ones of consolidation for Bolton. With expectations firmly reset after the previous season's brush with relegation, things got off to a bad start in the 1948/49 campaign when Nat failed to score in the first four games before a rolled ankle kept him out of the team for the best part of three months. Though his eventual tally of seven goals in twenty-two games was acceptable, it did little to help the confidence of a young man who had just months before entertained the idea of quitting the game entirely. Willie Moir came to Rowley's rescue by scoring twenty-five goals in Nat's absence, earning the title of the First Division's top goal scorer in the process, but despite Lofty naturally worrying for his future in the team, his absence ultimately only underlined how crucial he was to the Bolton cause. The only player who came close to offering a viable alternative in Nat's absence was, curiously enough, half back Mal Barrass. Though Barrass was patently just a stopgap, Nat recalled one incident with a fan who felt otherwise. In a reserve game against Chesterfield, as Barrass was turning heads with the first team and Nat was working his way back to fitness, Lofty was repeatedly told by 'a little man in a bowler hat' that he would 'never get back [in the team]!' The man even followed Nat to the team coach while continuing to repeat his grave prophecy. 'Why he had it in for me I shall never know,' pondered Nat, concluding, 'Some football fans have a queer sense of humour!'

Away from the game, Nat had reason to be cheerful. Having settled into comfortable married life with Alma, it was only natural that they took the next step. In 1948, he became a father when his first child, son Jeff, was born. Though his football career kept Nat away from home for stretches of time – Jeff recalls some of the end-of-season tours his father undertook seeming to last all summer – he would always do what he could to involve his son in his hobbies and his life.

The 1949/50 campaign saw a further deterioration in Bolton's form, failing to win away for an entire season for the first time in the club's history. Nat continued to be frustrated in his efforts, managing just thirteen goals, which was still enough to see him finish as the club's top scorer. If he was failing to find the net as often as he had in his early days, he could at least take solace in his contribution to the attacking unit. All of the team's ten league wins that year came with him at centre forward, which made Rowley's occasional meddling (despite his limited crossing ability and trickery, Nat was inexplicably twice played on the wing) all the more aggravating for Lofty. Grumblings from the crowd were common, and while the defence often escaped vitriol barring an unforgivable rick, there was nowhere to hide for the attackers. Nat's fellow forward, Jack Bradley, had a fire at his home during the season, but found sympathetic gestures from the crowd to be hardly forthcoming; Nat recalled one fan shouting, after Bradley had shot narrowly over the bar, 'Never mind Jack, you might put 'em over the top but it's going too far when someone tries to burn tha' house down!' On one bus trip home, Nat overheard a fellow passenger bemoaning his lack of shooting prowess, before remarking, 'I'd like a chance to go down to Burnden Park and show him how it's done.' Unable to keep his mischievous streak in check, Nat sat quietly behind the man until he reached his stop, then tapped him on the shoulder and told him, 'If that offer still stands, I'll be waiting for you at the ground in the morning.' The rest of the passengers saw the funny side, but the gentleman in question, having been confronted with Nat's imposing physical stature, unsurprisingly didn't take the striker up on the offer.

The last two seasons had offered little to cheer about, but Nat at least could take some encouragement from his first pieces of national recognition. In 1949, he was picked to appear for an FA XI side against an army side at Stoke. Not only did the call represent a reward for his often thankless toiling in the blunt Bolton front line, but it gave Nat the opportunity to measure his ability when paired with the inimitable Stanley Matthews. 'I felt like shouting with excitement,' he recalled of his reaction to being picked. Despite the FA side being on the wrong end of a 7-5 scoreline, Nat still had plenty to take from the game:

> The Football Association, in selecting me for that representative match, helped me in more ways than one. I found as a result … a new confidence. I began to introduce more thought into my play. I steadied myself more and made the ball do more of the work. That one game, in short, did me a tremendous amount of good.

He had nothing but praise for Matthews, whose skill and pace dragged defenders out of position time and again, giving Nat far more breathing space than he was accustomed to when playing for Bolton. So good were Matthews' crosses that Nat was sheepish about taking the credit: 'I scored four goals, three of them with my head; at least, Matthews plonked three centres on my head. All I had to do was to nod "How-do" to the goalkeeper, and the ball was in the back of the net.'

One of the most frequently debated topics in football circles over the next ten years would be comparing the relative merits of Matthews' showboating style with the devastating directness of the era's other great winger, Tom Finney. Nat was given a chance to compare the two in quick succession with his next move up the ladder, following a call to play for the Football League side, which was, as Nat put it, 'like a trial run for the England team'. His first game was against the Irish League at Molineux in February 1950. In an imposing team that featured the likes of Bill Nicholson, Wilf Mannion and Finney, Nat maintained his remarkable record of scoring twice on his debut in a variety of competitions as he added the final two strikes to finish off a 7-0 rout. Despite the relatively relaxed nature of the inter-league competition, the Irish would soon be sick to the back teeth of Lofthouse, who repeatedly put their teams to the sword, including a sparkling six-goal performance in 1952. Just seven days after making his Football League bow, he made his debut for the

England B team, filling in for an injured Jackie Milburn at Milburn's home ground, St James' Park in Newcastle. It was another FA test of a player's mettle before deciding whether to give them the honour of a full cap, and Lofty passed with flying colours, scoring the only goal in a 1-0 victory over the Netherlands.

With these confidence-boosting honours offsetting another disappointing campaign with Bolton, Nat went into what was to be a pivotal year in his career determined to drag the club up with him in order to match his lofty ambitions.

6

BECOMING THE MAIN MAN

THE YEAR 1950 proved to be a landmark one for Nat Lofthouse and pivotal in the history of Bolton Wanderers. Having languished in the lower reaches of the First Division since the end of the war and failed to make an impact on the FA Cup since the Burnden Disaster, fears were growing that one of England's most historic clubs was slipping towards obscurity. Although the financial gulfs between teams were nowhere near as pronounced as they are in the modern game, Wanderers fans were already reduced to standing by and watching enviously as other clubs spent sums that the Trotters simply could not sanction.

Thankfully, the club weren't so hard up that they couldn't turn money down when they felt it prudent. Some names were simply non-negotiable. Newly promoted Tottenham Hotspur, one of the country's most liberal spenders, reignited their interest in Lofty. Aston Villa also came in for the striker as they prepared to sell Trevor Ford to Sunderland. On both occasions, newspapers claimed that Nat issued transfer requests, as he reportedly did in 1947 when Spurs first became interested. However, the prospect of him leaving never looked likely. Wanderers may not have been able to compete with the lavish transfer fees that some clubs were doling out, but they understood the precedent that would be set if they were to sell their prolific goal scorer, even after two down years. Neither approach was entertained by the club.

Nat's requests to be placed on the transfer list – of which there were five in all – weren't necessarily motivated by transfer speculation. In the 1949/50 season, he and Mal Barrass had both made their unhappiness known via transfer requests when, for a trip to Sunderland's Roker Park, Nat was moved to the wing and Barrass, who typically played wing or centre half, to centre forward. The club's reasoning was Nat had taken a blow to the face in the previous match, and his injury would make him more reticent to challenge in the air. Nat bullishly responded that he was just as likely to 'get another crack'* playing out wide, and that if the club deemed him unfit to play centre forward, they shouldn't play him at all. Both Lofty and Barrass argued it was unfair on them, their teammates, and the reserves who could have reasonably expected to play in place of an injured first teamer.

Just as with the other requests, this particular example was little more than a headstrong young man making a point, rather than a significant statement of intent to leave. The *Bolton Evening News* explained the token nature of the request, and the scant likelihood that it would lead anywhere: 'If the breach continues to grow and a time should arrive when the Wanderers give way on the transfer list issue, then we can certainly expect them to put up a fee that will stagger any prospective buyer.'** From Nat's perspective, the requests were more of a reminder of his value than the definitive, career-altering statement they would be in the modern game. With the 'retain and transfer' system in place, Bolton held all the cards; if they didn't want to sell, then it would have taken an extraordinary set of circumstances for Lofty to have 'forced through' a move elsewhere.

Though his wages couldn't be increased beyond the limit, he could at least angle for some small increases on his performance bonuses and assurances about his role in the team. Had the club done the unthinkable and acquiesced to one of his transfer requests, it seems highly likely that Nat would have backed down. Rather than calling into question his loyalty to Bolton, this sometimes tumultuous relationship with the club is more indicative of the man Nat was as he entered the prime of his

★   *Bolton Evening News*, 30 December 1949.

★★   *Bolton Evening News*, 6 January 1950.

career: self-assured, assertive, and not afraid to stick his head above the parapet. The same traits were becoming more evident on the pitch with each passing game.

Lofty's continued involvement in the cause could not have come at a more welcome juncture. Fans' fears of what the future held for the club were exacerbated by events off the field that further cut the ties between the Bolton Wanderers of the 1920s and the contemporary team. In July, the club's long-serving former manager Charles Foweraker died following a long illness, as did Dr Cochrane, the team physician who could trace his links with the club back decades. Both were commemorated in the club's annual report as having given 'long and splendid service to the club and their names are indelibly written in the history of the club'. The sense of a changing of the guard was completed when, early in the 1950/51 season, Walter Rowley relinquished his role as the club's manager due to his failing health. Having coached at the club for so long under Foweraker, Rowley's deterioration and resignation was a shock. The pressure of successive scrapes with relegation and battling against the financial odds proved too much to bear and ultimately ended an association that stretched back to 1912, when he had first signed as a player. The ceremonial life membership bestowed upon Rowley did little to quell the impression that, for better or worse, this was now a very different club than the one from before the war.

In his place came Bill Ridding.* At one point a promising young striker with Manchester United before injury ended his career, Ridding had briefly managed Tranmere during the war before becoming part of Rowley's coaching staff. Ridding, who trained as a physiotherapist, was nationally acclaimed as an exceptional trainer, and his final assignment before taking the helm at Burnden was travelling to Brazil with the England national team as their chief coach for the World Cup. He initially worried about his transition to the role of manager 'but gradually I got over the manager's growing pains and in the end I couldn't see myself doing anything else'. Ridding's role was typical of managers at the time. Though he, along with

---

*   Ridding was officially caretaker until February 1951, when he was appointed secretary–manager on a permanent basis.

the board, ultimately had final say on the team sheet, it was down to his coaching team to run training and inform his decisions based on who was fit and performing well. Ridding assumed more administrative tasks such as negotiating contracts, with tactics rarely factoring into discussions. When interviewed, forward Terry Allcock remembered Ridding as a 'very likeable fella', although one that the players 'hardly saw'. Similarly, Dougie Holden recalls a generally friendly presence but one who was not among the small vanguard of managers who dared break from the WM formation* norm: 'from the point of view of tactics he wasn't very up with it'. Tommy Banks, at the time in the Bolton reserves, remembers a tough, somewhat intimidating character who gave no quarter when it came to contract negotiations and who wasn't afraid of forcing out those who he deemed difficult. Banks remembers Ridding, during one particularly fractious contract 'negotiation', likening two players to 'a rotten box of apples in the corner; not wanted'.** The fullback is also similarly dismissive of Ridding as a manager in the modern sense: 'He were alright but he weren't a manager.'

Ridding's ascendency to the manager's position triggered an upward movement in the ranks, and one that no doubt gave some consolation to those worrying that the links to the club's illustrious past had been severed. George Taylor was made head coach, while his long-time teammate George Hunt became assistant coach.*** Taylor and Hunt formed a memorable double act, with Hunt a larger-than-life character who often approached the training drills with more gusto than the players. Taylor, despite being a quieter presence, was extremely well attuned to the players individually, aware of what each man would best respond to. Banks is

---

* In Nat's day, the WM was the dominant formation, with few teams daring to deviate from its tried-and-tested formula. In front of the goalkeeper were three defenders (two wing backs and a centre half). In front of them were two wing halves, similar to modern midfielders. Finally, there were five attackers – two wingers, two inside forwards, and, in the middle, the centre forward.

** Ian Seddon, *Ah'm Tellin' Thee: Tommy Banks, Bolton Wanderers and England*, p. 108.

*** The club's trainer was Bert Sproston, a former England international who joined in 1950 and stayed at the club for more than two decades.

much more forthcoming in his praise for Ridding's head coach, calling him, 'our gaffer – he used to tell us what to do'.

Nat was similarly approving of the appointments. While he had always had the utmost respect for the coaches that had come before, there was always a natural distance between him and them. Hunt and Taylor had both been instrumental in his development when they'd played alongside him, and may well have cited their influence on the young Lofthouse as proof of their credentials when they made their cases to join Ridding's staff. Lofty also couldn't have failed to quietly note his new manager's standing within the national team set-up. Although the board of selectors at the time had absolute dominion over the question of who got to represent their country, Ridding's connection certainly couldn't hurt his chances.

Despite this, and his recent representative honours for the FA team and England B, Nat was still as humble as ever and quick to talk down his international prospects to any fans who suggested the possibility on the bus home after a game. He did have some cause for reticence: the last player to have made his England debut while playing at Burnden Park had been George Eastham, fifteen years beforehand. However, Ridding's emergence as a reminder of Bolton Wanderers' existence to the selectors could not have come at a better time for player or country. Tommy Lawton had received his last call as England's number nine in 1948, and since then the selectors had struggled to find a replacement who could perform with such unerring consistency. Jack Rowley, Stan Mortensen, Jackie Milburn and Jesse Pye were trialled, with varying degrees of success, but none had entirely convinced. England's disastrous maiden World Cup performance would soon underline the need for a true successor to Nat's boyhood hero Lawton.

Nat's rise to prominence continued apace over the summer when he was selected for an FA tour of Canada. While the full England side headed to Brazil for the Three Lions' first taste of World Cup football, the Canadian touring party consisted of an England reserve side. 'I nearly jumped out of my pyjamas,' remembered Lofty, after a large photo of Bolton goalkeeper Stan Hanson, also included on the tour, had first drawn his eye to the article in the *Bolton Evening News* in which he learned of his selection. While Nat's mind was alive with dreams of transatlantic travel, Alma was understandably concerned with the finer details – namely, how long she was to be without her husband. The transatlantic crossing would be made by boat, and with a schedule of games covering more than four weeks, Nat would be gone for the best part of two months.

Lofty's horizons had expanded somewhat since his maiden trip to the capital for the War Cup Final in 1945, as he and Alma had holidayed in the Isle of Man, a relatively luxurious destination compared to the typical Lancastrian holiday in Blackpool. He had still never had call to obtain a passport, which he now did in a hurry, as well as receive the necessary inoculations for international travel. Just three days after the end of the 1949/50 season, Nat and the rest of the party set sail from Liverpool aboard the *Empress of Scotland*. Alongside him were some of the most promising players England had to offer, including Harry Johnston of Blackpool and Johnny Hancocks and Jackie Sewell of Notts County. Perplexingly for all involved, Stanley Matthews was also included, despite the common consensus being that he was a dead certainty to be part of England's full World Cup team.*

After a mercifully gentle crossing, during which the England players trained by jogging around the decks, the party arrived in Canada. Nat was in his element among the new group of players, most of whom he'd only ever encountered as opponents on the pitch. The quiet, unassuming Matthews was in the minority among a set of larger-than-life personalities. Nat struck up a particular rapport with Bert Mozley, a right back for Derby County with a penchant for cigars whose naturally stern expression belied a playful nature.

The FA team's tour took in the breadth of the vast country, with eleven fixtures in all. Having never been out of the country – 'I used to say I took a foreign holiday when I went to the Isle of Man!' – the great North American nation opened Nat's eyes to a world of possibilities, and from then on he would rarely miss an opportunity to see the world beyond

---

*   Matthews flew to join up with the World Cup team in Brazil once the Canadian tour concluded.

Lancashire. Canada wasn't without some reminders of home, however. Nat and teammate Stan Hanson were amazed by the number of people they met who seemed to share a link with Bolton. Mozley was even moved to remark that the town 'must be a poor place for them to come all the way out here', but there was no denying the kinship that the expats clearly felt with the club's two stars. One man, who used to ride the same bus to Burnden as Nat, drove over 1,000 miles just to take in one game. On another stop, Hanson was let off a jaywalking charge when it transpired that the police officer originally hailed from nearby Bootle.

After the opening two matches against Montreal and Ontario – which England won 7-0 (with Nat netting a hat-trick) and 4-1, respectively – the party embarked upon a long train ride across the boundless plains, arriving in Saskatoon to play a hastily assembled team of amateurs. Just before kick-off, it became apparent that England's opponents had been so ill prepared for their distinguished guests that they'd only been able to muster nine players. With the game's result already paling into insignificance, Nat and Derby's Tim Ward drew the short straws and volunteered to swap their allegiances. The final score was an eye-catching 19-1 to the Lofthouse-less England, with Nat seeing the funny side, pointing out that he 'didn't even get the one!'

The only game the England side failed to win came on their next stop, as they played out an entertaining 4-4 draw with Vancouver in front of an enthusiastic crowd. Once again, Matthews was the main draw, off the field as well as on, but despite his considerably higher profile than the other players, he went to great lengths to ensure he wasn't put on a pedestal, insisting the rest of the team be invited to the functions between games that he was. Nat was becoming nicely accustomed to the lifestyle of an England player abroad, and his regular scoring, despite the weak nature of the opposition, was doing his chances of enjoying the role on a more regular basis no harm at all. After their final two Canadian fixtures – one against more familiar opposition in the form of the touring Manchester United that England won 4-2 – the team boarded an overnight train to New York City. Even after the long season and busy tour, Lofty still had the energy to impersonate a conductor and scold passengers who were slow in presenting their passports, until someone recognised his voice. It would become one of his go-to on-tour pranks, particularly after a beer or two!

Nat and the rest of the players were clamouring for a look at Manhattan's famous steel and glass skyline, but no sooner had they arrived than they were whisked to the Triborough Stadium. The attendance of just over 8,000 was something of a disappointment for the final fixture, and was in part influenced by a knee injury sustained by Matthews that prevented him from playing. The game was settled by a single goal in England's favour, a direct free kick from John Hancocks. Nat received what was to be one of his first significant pieces of international press, with the *New York Times*' write up of the game featuring a large photo of Lofty in a typically combative aerial contest. The game would take on considerably more historical intrigue when, nine days later, virtually the same group of US players, many of whom were amateurs who had been rounded up at the last moment, defeated the full England team in Brazil in one of the all-time great World Cup upsets. 'We were staggered,' remembered Nat upon being told the full team's score on the return trip aboard the *Empress of Canada*, the twin liner of the *Scotland*. 'The mere thought that the American team we had narrowly beaten should have defeated our World Cup team left us stunned.' England's blushes were largely spared in the press, thanks to the limited number of reporters who'd travelled to Brazil and the national cricket team suffering an equally surprising defeat to the West Indies. However, the loss and subsequent limp exit from the competition wasn't missed by the FA, who began to look beyond the tried-and-tested stars of the side. Naturally, one of the first ports of call was the second squad.

For Lofty, the representative honours kept coming. Before the 1950/51 season began, he played in an unusual variation of the annual FA Charity Shield. Typically contested between the FA Cup winners and the league champions, the 1950 edition instead pitted England's under-scrutiny World Cup squad against the Canadian tour team. Matthews, who had played for both, was enlisted as part of the Canadian tour side as they went down 4-2. A textbook Lofthouse header late in the game proved little more than a consolation, but did ensure his name was firmly lodged in the minds of the selectors. By the end of October, and despite the turmoil of Rowley's departure, the Lofthouse name had appeared on First Division score sheets no fewer than nine times. As far as Nat was concerned, nothing was out of the ordinary. He was catching the bus to and from Burnden Park each day, training as hard as he could, and doing whatever he could to keep Bolton Wanderers moving up the table. He summed up his playing philosophy at the time very simply: 'If you're playing number nine you've got to go for everything in the box.' Unbeknownst to him, the wheels were in motion at the FA headquarters at Lancaster Gate to reward Nat's no-nonsense, determined and highly effective approach to the centre forward role with the greatest honour of his young career.

Nat recalled different versions of finding out that he had been picked for the England national team. In 1954's *Goals Galore*, he remembered that it was Ridding who first gave him the news in the dressing room before training. In both 1989's *The Lion of Vienna* and a later interview for *Dickie Davies's Sporting Heroes*, Nat recalled hearing about the call on the radio. As England did declare a squad prior to games, it's possible that Nat first became aware of his inclusion via the wireless and then had his starting berth confirmed by Ridding afterwards. However he heard, he was certain of his reaction: 'I felt almost as if Rocky Marciano had hit me on the chin. I had lived for this moment. Now it was here I could hardly believe it.' Lofthouse told the *Bolton Evening News* that he was 'thrilled to bits' to be realising his childhood dream 'to lead England in a full international'.[*] On Davies' programme, Nat remembered being 'scared stiff' and praying on his living room carpet that he'd make the most of his big opportunity. His Bolton teammates and coaches were universal in their congratulations. Ridding had never been called up; George Taylor had been a reserve on one occasion but had never got on to the pitch. George Hunt had received three caps during his Spurs heyday and, having been instrumental in Nat's development through additional training sessions, was quick to offer his young star some sage advice: 'Don't let anything interfere with

[*]   *Bolton Evening News*, 16 November 1950.

your normal game.You've been picked to play for England solely on your form for Bolton Wanderers.' Lofthouse was also congratulated by Tommy Lawton, who took the time to telegram his successor in the role with a message that read, 'Go out and give them all you've got, Nat.' In the press, his call-up was generally applauded, although there was some surprise that he and not Jackie Milburn would be pulling on the number nine shirt.

Even those in his life with less knowledge of the game understood what becoming a fully fledged England international meant. Alma was over-joyed. Nat's mother, Sarah, so often a figure of prototypical Lancastrian down-to-earth stoicism, was so overwhelmed that she broke down in tears, and her son, who had inherited her stiff upper lip mentality wasn't far off doing the same: 'I could almost have cried with her, I felt so happy.' Their joy wasn't solely because of Nat attaining the goal he had strived for ever since he was old enough to kick a ball around on Bolton's cob-bled streets.The long list of promising players who had never truly made the grade and had faded away was testament to the harsh nature of trying to make a living in the game. Being called up for England, however, was special. Barring a disastrous injury, it was very rare for a player of his age to receive the hallowed call and then sink into obscurity.The direct financial incentives of being involved in manager Walter Winterbottom's team were not to be sniffed at either, and made the maximum wage of £12 a week in club football look a pittance. For Nat's ninety minutes of service, he'd receive £30 – a mind-boggling sum that was enough to cover his mortgage repayments for a couple of months. 'I never had a lot of brain,' Nat quipped, 'but it didn't take me long to work out that if I stayed in the England team I'd be alright.'

Nat's debut was to be a friendly against the fearsome Yugoslavia team that had taken silver at the 1948 Olympic Games and would do so again in 1952, to be played on Wednesday, 22 November. Two days before, the players gathered at the Great Western Hotel in Paddington. There were plenty of faces that were familiar to Nat, although most he only knew from the blood and thunder battles he had fought against them. For the first time in thirty-four internationals – a run that covered every game since the war – neither Stan Matthews nor Tom Finney was involved. Ordinarily, the loss of such prolific supply lines would have worried the centre forward, but Nat took solace in the fact that Leslie Medley and Johnny Hancocks, filling in wide left and right respectively, had played alongside him in the Canadian touring team. Wolverhampton Wanderers' Billy Wright, who had come to regard Nat as one of England's best attacking forces based on their bouts at club level, missed out due to injury and relinquished the captaincy to Spurs' Alf Ramsey, who made 'a profound impression' on Nat thanks to his meticulous understanding and analysis of the game. Even with the unsettled nature of the side, expectations were undimmed. Despite their poor World Cup showing just months earlier, pundits and fans alike continued to pride themselves on the fact that England was the home of football and, pound for pound, boasted better players than any other nation. The year before, when England had finally lost at home to a non-British team in the form of Ireland, was acknowledged as nothing more than a fluke; the Three Lions had never succumbed on home soil to a continental European team.

With all the players assembled, Winterbottom led the party to the serene Oatlands Park Hotel in Weybridge. Nat remembered the Victorian country estate, which featured expansive grounds ideal for training, as 'one of the most delightful spots I have visited', although his opinion was no doubt coloured somewhat by his reasons for being there. Nat roomed with Wilf Mannion, Middlesbrough's prolific inside forward known as the 'Golden Boy' thanks to his blond locks and his prodigious record in front of goal: 'It was a tonic to be in his company, for Wilf was astute enough to steer me away from all mention of football and the big ordeal which awaited me.' Despite his alien surroundings and new companions, Nat quickly found himself at home, noting that Winterbottom 'couldn't have been more kind or considerate had he been my own father' and that the England squad were 'a club side in spirit although an international team by selection'. Nat pinpointed Winterbottom's key managerial attribute as his ability to instil pride and a willingness to give everything to the cause in his players. Evenings after training were reserved for rest and relaxation, with the team taking in a film at the local picture house* and enjoying meals in the hotel. Even with these efforts to keep the players relaxed, however, the pressure did begin to weigh on their newest recruit. As the only player in the team who would be earning his first cap in the game, the night before saw Nat overcome by nerves:

> What should have been a period of tranquil sleep developed into a nightmare for me. All night long I tossed about, hardly sleeping a wink. Try as I might I could not get the match out of my mind. All the confidence which had been built up by the kindness of Walter Winterbottom, and understanding of my colleagues, had deserted me.

A team breakfast saw Lofthouse's nerves abate, but they quickly returned as the squad travelled to Highbury and entered the dressing room before the game:

> I hadn't yet overcome my innermost fears … I felt as if I had a million butterflies fluttering inside my tummy and I simply could not keep still. On reflection I suppose it was as well I kept on the move, otherwise my team-mates would have seen me shaking! Seriously, though, it was the most worrying period of my whole career, yet one thing gave me fresh heart. I noticed that even some of the most experienced players were perspiring a little as they changed. I wasn't the only one suffering from a few pre-match nerves.**

As if the pressure wasn't high enough in a game of novelties and firsts for Nat, this was to be the first time that his on-pitch exploits would be

---

*   They likely took in one of two new releases: *Over the Garden Wall*, a low-budget comedy set in Lancashire, or *Wyoming Mail*, a Western about a man tracking down a gang of train robbers.

**   This quote is from 1954.

broadcast live on television; the BBC would be covering the final hour of the match.

Although being denied his first trip to the Empire Stadium was a disappointment, the chance to play at Arsenal's ground was a prize in itself. Highbury was a favourite of many players, with its striking art deco-inspired terracing almost always filled to capacity with vociferous supporters who were known for their appreciation of fine football regardless of which side was playing it. Floodlights weren't installed at the ground until the next year, meaning the game had to kick off at 2.15 p.m. in order to finish before the autumnal gloom set in. Despite falling within working hours, around 61,000 packed the terraces as Alf Ramsey led the England players out of the dressing room, down the tunnel and into a cacophonous atmosphere.

Unlike some continental sides that were beginning to experiment with revolutionary formations that wouldn't be welcomed into English football for at least another decade, Yugoslavia would go toe-to-toe with England in the classic WM formation. Their two stars were inside left Stjepan Bobek and goalkeeper Vladimir Beara, a former ballet dancer who had swapped his pumps for thick leather boots yet retained all the grace and athleticism that his former discipline demanded. Later remembered by the great Lev Yashin as the 'best goalkeeper in the world',[*] Beara was, like the rest of the Yugoslav squad, an unknown as he walked onto the Highbury pitch. By the time he left it, his was a name that few would forget in a hurry, least of all the England players.[**] 'Beara performed feats that afternoon that no goalkeeper could reasonably be expected to perform,' Nat remembered four years later. 'He stopped shots from all our forwards I wager no ordinary keeper would have seen.'

Almost as soon as the Dutch referee Karel van der Meer blew his whistle, Nat's nerves evaporated and he recovered his mettle. Yugoslavia's players were 'first-class footballers' and Lofty was well shepherded by the towering

[*]   *The Guardian*, 5 August 2008.

[**]   Writing in *The Guardian*, Jonathan Wilson later described the 'cult status' afforded Beara as a result of his performance.

Ivica Horvat, a 'first-rate tackler' who 'stuck so close to me I began to think I owed him money'. For all their virtues, the Eastern Europeans quickly found themselves being overrun by England, with the understanding between Lofthouse, Medley and Hancocks as a result of their time in Canada increasingly evident. Winterbottom's men began to exploit their advantage in possession by switching the ball from one wing to the other, stretching the Yugoslav defence out of position. Several good chances came and went, including one in which Nat bettered both Horvat and Beara in an aerial battle before sending his header just over the bar. Then came the moment that Nat had dreamed about for his entire life. Eddie Baily swung the ball across to Medley, who fired it back across goal. At the far post was Lofty, who had to wait what seemed like an age for the ball to reach him before tapping it home. Despite colliding with the upright, Nat wheeled away in delight, arms aloft as he jogged back towards the halfway line, 'so excited I felt like jumping over the famous Arsenal clock'. With the wind in his sails and the pressure of leading England's line somewhat diffused, Nat took just four minutes to get his second. 'Medley was the architect,' Nat recounted, 'placing the ball so accurately in the goalmouth that all I had to do was nod my head and the ball was nestling snugly in the back of the net.' Typical of Nat's humility, footage of the goal tells a rather different story, as Nat powers past Branko Stanković and then executes a trademark diving header with unerring accuracy and devastating power past Beara into the far corner.

Having been beaten twice, Beara began to redeem himself with a string of exceptional saves. Such was the debt owed by Yugoslavia to the keeper that it came as a complete shock when they managed to get one back just before half-time, Bernard Vukas' shot deflecting wickedly past the helpless Bert Williams in the England goal. The second half would follow a similar pattern, with Beara again frustrating England's rampant forward line. It appeared that it was only a matter of time before England scored a third, but again their opponents proved in receipt of the luck of which Winterbottom's side were sorely lacking. Ramsey sliced a clearance straight into the path of the onrushing Toša Živanović, who slotted home easily. To find themselves drawing despite so utterly dominating the game had England's players worrying that their unbeaten home record against continental sides was about to fall, but they pushed on for a winner regardless, only to again find themselves thwarted by Beara. The newsreel summariser put it best, simply exclaiming 'oh, bother' as van der Beer blew for full-time.

Despite the disappointing result, Nat's first England game had been a triumph, with two goals against a sturdy defence and exceptional goal-keeper giving the selection committee plenty to think about. He and Beara shared the plaudits at the FA banquet held after the game and in the coming days – newspapers across the country lauded his performance as a 'striking debut' and described the Bolton star as being in 'grand form'. Nat's natural pragmatism refused to allow him to get carried away: 'In my heart I knew that I had much to learn. I still refused to believe I was international class.' There were plenty of players waiting to take his place, and in the days before uninhibited access to hours of highlight footage, a player's selection could come down to something as trivial as whether or not an FA representative had managed to make it to one of their club fixtures – or worse, if the player had an off day on the one occasion he had been watched. Nat only needed to look at the omissions of Jackie Milburn, now his main competition at centre forward, to see the unfair, undemocratic machinations of the England selection committee in full effect. He was acutely aware that no matter how well he had just played, there were no guarantees of him retaining his place.

As it transpired, Nat was right to be apprehensive. After the Yugoslavia game, it would be eleven months and four fixtures before Nat was recalled: 'I didn't beef about it. I didn't grumble … I'll tell you why I was dropped … because they had someone better to put in. Stan Mortensen.' In Nat's absence, England turned first to Stan Mortensen and then Milburn. Looking back on the aftermath of his debut, Lofty was philosophical and upbeat:

The important thing was that I had played for England. I'd been blooded. They knew about me. I'd gone to London, pulled on the white shirt and scored two goals. That was a gift to me, not a right. Now, if someone was playing better than me he deserved to be in the side ahead of me. It was up to me to prove I was worth another chance.

Despite the unexplained omission, Nat remained sanguine about the situation, much in thanks to George Taylor's steadying influence on his star striker. One of the first things Taylor told Lofthouse 'with some force' upon his return was, 'It wasn't just me out there at Highbury; there were 10 other players who had all played their part.' Taylor was moved to have another word with Nat after his second game for Bolton following the Yugoslavia match – an away fixture at Turf Moor against Burnley.* The 1-0 defeat to their Lancashire neighbours saw Nat put in a performance that he freely described as 'a stinker; a real shocker, I could do nothing right'. Even the *Bolton Evening News*, which typically strived to take a glass-half-full approach to its Wanderers appraisals, commented that the 'attack was held and made its efforts look worse by some wretchedly directed passing'. Taylor asked Lofty to meet in his office the following Monday morning, despite Nat's grumbled protestations that Monday was the players' day off.

Nat believed the meeting would be one of a congratulatory nature, a chance for Taylor to:

> tell me what a good game I'd had at Highbury. Instead, he gave me the biggest rollicking I've ever had – before or since. 'On Saturday afternoon, you were trying to do something you are just not capable of,' he told me when I arrived. 'And what's that, George?' 'Play football.' I thought … he's got to be winding me up here. 'You were coming back deep for the ball, trying to trap it. You couldn't trap a bag of wet cement. There are only three things you CAN do at this game. Run, shoot and head. That's what you did for England against Yugoslavia … why didn't you do it for us on Saturday? We've got plenty of people at this club who can turn on the fancy stuff. Leave that to them and concentrate on what you're good at.'

---

*   In *The Lion of Vienna*, this game is erroneously identified as a home fixture against Chelsea, which took place over two months before Nat appeared for England. The account in *The Lion of Vienna* also states the incident took place after the first game Nat played following the England game; it was unlikely that Taylor spoke to Nat after this game, as he scored twice in a 4–3 victory.

Lofthouse, fully aware of the debt he owed to Taylor for the role he'd played in his development, heeded the coach's instruction rather than rejecting it, later calling it 'the best piece of advice I ever received'. Nat would never shy away from discussing the limitations of his ability and his unflashy, sometimes industrial style. What would set him apart from similar players was the amount of time he spent honing those three key attributes identified by Taylor and the unbridled fearlessness with which he applied them.

Taylor's 'chat' certainly had the desired effect on Lofty, as he netted twenty-one league goals that season. He wasn't the only one to find his footing under the new coaching team. Bobby Langton turned in consistently impressive performances from the outside left position. Harry Webster produced the best football of his career in the number ten shirt, while Willie Moir continued to prove himself one of the league's best inside forwards. Malcolm Barrass, Don Howe and new recruit John Ball all provided defensive versatility and stoicism. The end result was a highly respectable seventh place finish in the league: Wanderers' best showing since 1938.

The strong performance of the 1950/51 campaign imbued Bill Ridding's young charges with a new belief and purpose. No longer was it Cup or bust. There was a palpable sense that, despite the bigger spending of other clubs, Wanderers had a core that was as good as any other side. Ridding's men flew out of the gates in the 1951/52 season, winning seven, drawing two and losing just one – a run that put them top of the table. With George Taylor's rebuke still ringing in his ears – Taylor had taken the time to again remind his young forward of his stern advice on at least one occasion since – Nat had spent the summer working relentlessly on fine tuning his three God-given attributes: running, shooting and heading. His sacrifices didn't immediately manifest themselves in his personal goal tally, but the threat he posed allowed Moir and Webster to fill their boots. Nat took his tally to four for the season with goals in consecutive games at the start of October, and his all-round play was enough to convince the suits in London that the time had come to give the lad from up north another chance in an England shirt. His second cap would be against Wales at Ninian Park for England's first game of the annual British Home Championship tournament.*

In the four games since Nat's debut, England had fallen to an embarrassing defeat at Wembley to Scotland before beating Argentina 2-1, thumping Portugal 5-2 and drawing with France. Jackie Milburn took over at centre forward from Stan Mortensen for the latter two games, but despite netting twice against the Portuguese, his failure to score against *Les Bleus* had the selectors once again doubting Newcastle's talisman. The FA had clearly taken note of Bolton's excellent form, as Nat's teammate and fellow Lancastrian Mal Barrass was also rewarded for his fine club performances with his first cap. It was neither a dream debut for Barrass, who would be cruelly dubbed 'Malcolm *Em*Barrass' by the *Daily Mirror*, or a triumphant return for Lofthouse, despite the presence of the explosive Tom Finney on the wing. Wales had the better of a 1-1 draw as they hunted for their first victory over the English since football had resumed following the war.

Despite his nondescript performance in Cardiff and failure to score in his next three games back at Bolton, Nat retained his place for the next Home Championship international, against Ireland at Villa Park. Nat's somewhat surprising selection was perhaps a result of sheer stubbornness on the FA's part, refusing to bow to pressure to reinstate Milburn, and was no doubt helped by Nat's strong record (five goals in three games) against the League of Ireland for the Football League representative side. Whatever the reason for his selection, the Ireland match would prove a watershed moment in Nat's career and life – the game that truly signalled the beginning of an international career that, by the time it came to an end, had enshrined his legend forever.

The game began in frenetic fashion, with first England and then their opponents going close. After another near miss, Nat went one better,

---

* The Home International Championships were an annually held set of fixtures between England, Scotland, Wales and Northern Ireland, with the season's results ending in a league table and a yearly champion. These fixtures formed the bulk of England's international commitments during the 1950s.

breaking the deadlock with a demonstration of both his burgeoning ability to bring his teammates into play and a telling reminder of his prowess in the air. Playing a neat one-two with Sheffield Wednesday's Jackie Sewell, Nat spotted Finney charging down the right wing. He fed the ball into the channel before ghosting into the box at the far post and deftly guiding the ball past Norman Uprichard with a diving header. As they jogged back to the halfway line, Finney and Lofthouse embraced. What appeared then to be a relatively innocuous moment was the first time that two of English football's greatest players would combine. It certainly wouldn't be the last. From then on, England laid siege to the Irish goal. Lofty was denied his second by a good save from Uprichard after wrestling free of the attentions of an Irish defender. The longer England pressed, the more fatigue began to show in Ireland's play. With just seven minutes left on the clock, Finney and Lofthouse were again the architects of the Irish's downfall, albeit in far scruffier fashion than in the first half. Finney worked some space for himself in the corner of the 18-yard box and struck the ball toward the roof of the goal. Uprichard attempted to catch the ball rather than palm it over, and in doing so merely dropped it at the feet of Lofty, who duly poked into the unguarded net from practically on the goal-line.

Nat's triumph over Ireland cemented him in the national team in both the hearts of the fans and the minds of the selectors. It would be almost two years before anyone else donned the number nine shirt. His next game, against the might of Austria, then one of the world's most feared teams, was another in which the proud record of never having lost to continental European opposition at home was put to the test. Such was the anticipation that newsreel footage referred to the fixture as 'the most discussed of the year'. For Nat, the game took on an added significance, as it was now, in his fourth cap, that he would finally sample the hallowed turf of Wembley's Empire Stadium for the first time. Despite cherishing every opportunity to play at Wembley, Nat was less enamoured with the crowds that England's fixtures there attracted, finding them emblematic of the suffocating pressure and often unrealistic expectations that dogged the national team: 'It is a pity that some of the spectators who enjoy [Wembley's] handsome facilities are not among the best-informed or most appreciative of football supporters.' Lofthouse became the first Bolton Wanderers player to wear the shirt of the national team beneath the Twin Towers since David Jack and Billy Butler in 1924.

The eager anticipation that surrounded the fixture was reflected in the capacity 100,000 crowd that crammed into the famous stadium to watch England face off against some of Europe's finest. Nat's performance against Ireland meant that, for once, the choice of centre forward wasn't paramount on the selection committee's minds. Instead, an injury to Finney forced them into unwanted action, with Arthur Milton, a professional cricketer with only twelve league appearances for Arsenal to his name, being the recipient of what was to prove his only cap. With adrenaline coursing through the makeshift England team, they began at a frantic pace, seeking to be out of sight before Austria got a chance to put a stranglehold on the game. Two good chances for Ivor Broadis were passed up, and the half-time interval allowed the Austrians time to take stock of the situation and adapt. They emerged with a greater incisiveness to their play, and took the lead when Ernst Ocwirk's superb raking pass from near the halfway line eluded everyone but teammate Ernst Melchior, who volleyed home. England were forced to continue defending Austrian attacks before a rare foray forward saw Eddie Baily taken down in the area for a penalty, which was unerringly dispatched by Alf Ramsey. Ramsey's dead ball prowess came to the fore again moments later, when he floated a free kick into the area towards Nat. The ball's looping trajectory meant Nat had time to pick his spot before flinging himself at the ball, sending it over the helpless Walter Zeman and into the net. The Bolton forward's arms-aloft celebration was on show for the fifth time in only four internationals, and rarely had it been exhibited so joyously.

The joy was short-lived, however, as Austria set about reminding the home side how they had earned their stellar reputation. England's resolve lasted just two minutes before Bill Eckersley resorted to punching the ball off the line after England custodian Gil Merrick had been beaten, and Ernst Stojaspal opted for power with his penalty rather than the placement of Ramsey to make the final scoreline 2-2.

7

THE LION OF VIENNA

IN THE SECOND half of the 1951/52 season, the pressure was well and truly on for Bolton Wanderers. Unlike previous years, where they had been threatened by relegation, this was a pressure of a different kind. Bill Ridding was acutely aware that many of the talented team under his command were reaching their respective peaks. Nat had turned 26 early in the season, Mal Barrass was almost a year older and Willie Moir would be 30 before the season's end. Tottenham Hotspur's ascension from newly promoted starlets to champions the season before had underlined the lack of a truly dominant team in English football, and with just ten points between first and fifteenth at the start of January 1952 there had been few better chances for Wanderers to claim that elusive first league championship.

For Lofty, the pressure was even greater. Not only was he shouldering the burden of being his club's talisman, but he was now attempting to prove himself worthy of his England berth. Although he had learned to give as good as he got when supporters took umbrage with his performances, the local press in Bolton were rarely moved to criticism. The attention that came with being a national team player was a different beast entirely. The acid tip of a writer's pen was now another thing to weigh on the mind of the young Wanderers forward.

Bolton began the new year poorly, losing three and drawing two, leaving them six points adrift of first placed (and eventual champions) Manchester United. Walter Rowley had been all too ready to chop and change his team when things weren't going his way. His successor, Ridding, was far more stubborn in his choices, more confident that the team he had deemed his best was the correct one, and his instincts served him well. Things began to turn around from late February, where three wins in four propelled the club back up to fifth, although crucially they gained no ground on their Mancunian neighbours. Importantly for Nat, through the highs and lows he was still scoring, with fifteen strikes to his name by the time the next England game rolled around in April. By now, he was well aware that the three goals he'd scored in his last two games for the national team wouldn't necessarily guarantee him a place for the Three Lions' trip across the border to Scotland's Hampden Park. However, he could be quietly confidence that the selection committee's apparent aversion to watching club football, particularly in the more northerly reaches of the country, may have blinded them to Jackie Milburn's goal-scoring exploits that season; he had nine more than Nat.

If appearing in an England shirt at Wembley was a rite of passage for an international, playing against Scotland in Glasgow was a baptism of fire. 'I don't think an Englishman can really call himself an international player,' said Nat, 'until he's played against Scotland at Hampden Park and at Wembley.' Going into the fixture, England had recorded three away wins over Scotland on the bounce, but these were exceptions to the rule. Since 1900, England had played their northerly rivals nineteen times in Scotland, losing eleven and winning just two before the recent run. Home advantage had done little to improve England's record against the Scots; in the last five games at Wembley, England had drawn two and lost three – a run that stretched back nearly twenty years.

The ear-splitting atmosphere of Hampden – so famous it was dubbed the 'Hampden Roar' – was not for the faint hearted. 'As you trot on to the field,' said Nat, 'you are conscious of being literally fenced in by thousands of people. Glancing round the massive bowl first impressions are of thousands of people standing on each other's shoulders. When they start to roar, the deep-throated Scots really let themselves go. The ground beneath your studs seems to shake.'* The occasion needed no extra spice, but was given some anyway by virtue of it being the final game of the season's Championships. A win for Scotland wouldn't be enough for them to win the tournament, but crucially it would stop England from doing so.

England survived an early scare when goalkeeper Gil Merrick was fortunate not to concede a penalty for hauling down Lawrie Reilly after fumbling a routine catch. Scottish bemusement at the referee's failure to award a foul turned to anger when England immediately proceeded to open the scoring – a superb close-range strike on the half volley by Stan Pearson arrowing into the top corner. It was to be a rare moment of attacking threat from England, who spent most of the remainder of the first half defending doggedly against the increasingly frustrated Scottish forwards. Lofty cut an isolated figure up front, while the mercurial talents of Tom Finney and Ivor Broadis were kept largely under wraps. Moments before the half-time whistle blew, Pearson struck again after a mix-up allowed him to sweep the ball home. The second period saw Walter Winterbottom's men, their white shirts by now caked in Hampden mud, become more comfortable, with the pitch becoming a quagmire and forcing the game into a pattern of miscontrol and robust challenges. A mistake from Alf Ramsey allowed Scotland to halve the deficit, but despite some late pressure the level heads and no-nonsense approach of the likes of Jimmy Dickinson and Billy Wright saw England emerge victorious.

England's victory was cause for much celebration for the few brave souls who had ventured on to Hampden's terraces to support the away side. However, Nat's subdued performance – more a result of Scotland's superiority than his own form – had not gone unnoticed. Although an

---

*   In typically mischievous fashion and fully aware that the Scottish fans considered England their key adversaries, Nat continued, 'But Hampden Park has nothing on Ninian Park, Cardiff, when it comes to giving you knocking knees. Man for man the fans at Cardiff are twice as powerful in their vocal efforts as the Scots of Glasgow.'

England victory was often enough for the selectors to continue with the same squad, there was always a nagging doubt in Nat's naturally worrisome psyche that each England cap could be his last, particularly when he hadn't scored. While awaiting the train to take him and Alma, who had come up with the England party to watch the game, back to Bolton, Nat experienced a déjà vu moment of the incident when a Wanderers fan on the bus had critiqued his performances, while, unbeknownst to him, Nat sat behind him:

> A rather big man, accompanied by a very small companion, came into the tea-room … 'If Milburn had been out there he'd have had three or four,' said the big man. 'If Nat Lofthouse was here I'd tell him so.' Suddenly the little man turned, looked me full in the eyes. He gulped, turned pale, glanced around and carefully placing his cup on the counter, turned to his friend and said, 'I'll be seeing you on the train, Charlie.' And like a man walking to his execution he left the tea-room. My wife and I doubled up in mirth.

Nat's England duties saw him miss two games of Bolton's run-in, where his importance to the team was underlined by the use of wing half Johnny Wheeler as centre forward. Lofty scored in the next three games as Wanderers finished the season with a flourish. Had it not been for their barren winter run, their eventual finish of fifth, nine points behind champions Manchester United, would have been even better.

Despite Milburn's brilliant form, Nat held on to his England spot into the summer, when the team would embark on a prestigious post-season tour. With no European Championships and England's involvement in the World Cup still in its infancy, the matches against some of Europe's finest nations were held in high esteem. 'They might have called the games friendlies but that didn't mean they weren't important,' said Nat. 'They were a yardstick; our chance to see how we measured up against the continentals.' The nerves Lofty felt were exacerbated by the fact that the tour was to be his first time flying, something his more experienced teammates cottoned on to, wasting little time in giving him some stick. Alma's gift of anti-sickness tablets may have only served to heighten his anxiety – and the banter at his expense.

England would play Italy, Austria and Switzerland, all in their home countries. Italy had won two of the first four World Cups, and although the Superga air disaster* had robbed the country of many of its most promising players, they were still formidable. Switzerland, despite their country's size, were another tricky opponent, having reached the quarter-finals in two of their three World Cup campaigns – a feat they would repeat in 1954. It was Austria, however, who posed the biggest test. Blessed with brilliant players and innovative thinkers, *Das Team* made use of formations completely alien to the English, and were considered on a par with Hungary as the world's best. The 2-2 stalemate the sides had played out at Wembley the year before had failed to fully showcase their power. Nat would note how impressed he was by the knowledge of the average continental fan, musing, 'It made one appreciate just how little we know soccer as a worldwide game.'

England's first game was in Florence. Nestled among rolling Tuscan hills and the city's Renaissance-era architectural splendour was the Stadio Comunale di Firenze, with its striking modern facade that played host to over 40,000 passionate, 'typically partisan' Italians. The England touring party were treated 'like royalty' thanks to the fanatical interest in football and the deep impression left by British servicemen, including the Bolton players, who had served there. 'Nevertheless,' wrote Nat, 'the Italians made no secret of the fact that they were going to make amends for the 4-0 defeat by England at Turin in 1948.' Billy Wright and Tom Finney, the only remaining England players from that day, were 'specially singled out' and assured of an Italian victory.

---

* On 4 May 1949, the majority of the all-conquering 'Il Grande' Torino team were killed when, on their return from a friendly in Portugal, their plane collided with the Basilica of Superga in Turin. The Torino team had boasted so many fantastic players that, in one game in 1947 against Hungary, every player fielded by Italy but the goalkeeper belonged to the club. Not a single representative of the club appeared in the game against England in 1952.

The day of the game was stiflingly hot and humid – alien climes to the English players more accustomed to a light drizzle and a brisk wind to keep them cool. Nat would later claim that his imperious heading ability – one of the chief weapons in his arsenal – was impaired due to having a constant headache from the heat: 'Whenever I headed the ball really hard I literally saw stars.' Aware that the temperature would drain their reserves quicker than their opponents', Winterbottom encouraged his men to take the game to the Italians while still fresh. They were rewarded just four minutes in when a marauding run by Stan Pearson was touched home by Ivor Broadis, who wheeled away while a tiny pocket of England fans with a comically large Union Jack celebrated wildly. 'Even now I can picture that goal,' remembered Nat. 'The astonished look upon [goalkeeper Giuseppe] Moro's face, the silence of the crowd, the smile which creased the usually serious face of Ivor Broadis. All these things happened in a matter of seconds, yet I shall never forget them. The Italians seemed stunned.'

Even with the early lead, Lofty quickly got the feeling that this was not to be his game. He knew of the Italians' reputation as particularly tough customers, but he hadn't considered to what degree they'd live up to their billing. Finney recalled Nat in particular being 'kicked from pillar to post'.[*] Writing in 1954, Nat remembered, 'Several times I was given the worst physical shaking I have experienced.'

> On one occasion, in going up for a high cross well placed by Tom Finney, I suddenly found an Italian defender's legs wrapped round me in what would have been a splendid wrestling hold. With a thump which knocked most of the wind out of my body I went full-length. Without hesitation the referee sounded his whistle for a foul, and as I rose groggily to my feet and moved forward towards the Italian goal I got the biggest shock of the game. The referee was pointing towards Gilbert Merrick. He had awarded a foul against *me*!

---

[*]   Tom Finney, *My Autobiography*, p. 7.

Despite the Italians' decidedly robust approach to the game, England remained on top. Italian goalie Moro was forced into a string of tremendous saves, denying Lofty when he was able to free himself from the vigorous attentions of his markers. Just after the hour mark, Italy finally punished England's profligacy when their inside left Amedeo Amadei sent a shot swerving past Merrick at his near post. The crowd behind the goal burst from their seats and on to the track behind the goal. The two sides, both exhausted by the sapping heat, were content with a draw, and the main drama of the final minutes was a small number of the spectators pelting the playing surface with pieces of broken glass bottles, one of which narrowly missed Nat's eye. The Italian players, 'black with anger', were forced to remonstrate with the troublemakers.

Nat had little time to soak in the appreciative ovation that greeted the two sets of players at the final whistle. No matter the circumstances, the quality of the opposition or the ultimate result, two games in the England team at centre forward without a goal was tantamount to complete and absolute failure, the sort that had spelt the unceremonious end of many a promising international career. Bolton's all-time leading scorer, Joe Smith, had been dropped after failing to net in either of the first two England matches after the cessation of the First World War and was never recalled, despite equalling the record for league goals in a season in 1921 with thirty-eight. Even with the comforting reassurances of his teammates in the Stadio Comunale dressing room that he was safe and the gregarious, light-hearted persona he projected, Nat knew that his place was now under serious threat. His response to this challenge would prove to be one of the defining moments of his career.

Back at the hotel, Nat called Alma to let her know how he was getting on and check in on things at home. Alma informed him of the response he knew was inevitable: 'You must have had a bad game, Nat, they're all saying Jackie Milburn should be flown out for the game against Austria.' In fact, the clamour for Milburn's reinstatement in the team at Nat's expense had reached fever pitch, with one journalist declaring England ought to 'Fly Milburn out by Comet'. At an earlier juncture in his career, Nat may have wilted with self-doubt in the face of such public pressure. Instead, he now displayed his trademark on-pitch bullishness and resolve off it. It was 'the first and only time in my career I was flaming mad', remembered Nat. 'I had given everything I had in Florence and taken some of the hardest knocks of my career and I felt this personal attack completely unjustified. There and then I decided I was going to make that writer eat his words – even if he choked!' Several of the seven days before the game against Austria were spent training in Siena, away from the full glare of the Italian media and, to Nat's great relief, any celestial bodies bearing Geordie footballers.

The match against Austria represented a seismic meeting between the new, expansive, fluid way of playing, pioneered by Austria and Hungary, and the old-fashioned ideals that England had unwittingly come to represent. So relished was the fixture across the continent that newspapers in countless languages billed it as the unofficial 'Championship of Europe'. If Lofthouse and the rest of the England squad had been under any illusions about the importance of the game, they were quickly set straight upon their arrival in Vienna. More than 30,000 British Tommies were stationed in Austria, and many had swarmed the capital in the hopes of catching a glimpse of their heroes, if not the game itself. A good deal had staked vast portions of their military pay on England earning what objectively appeared an unlikely win. Although the England players were relieved to have some support, it undoubtedly brought some additional stress that had been almost entirely absent in Florence. Nat felt 'disturbed' by the betting, noting that England were facing 'what many considered to be the finest team in Europe, not only on their own ground, but in front of a crowd reputed to be one of the most partisan on the Continent'. After being told by a soldier that many of his friends had put everything they had on an England victory, Nat told Bill Eckersley that 'there's nothing for it … we'll simply have to win'.

The Austrian climate proved far kinder to the English sensibilities than the humidity of Italy, with a light drizzle on the day of the match more reminiscent of Burnden or Ewood Park than the European mainland in late May. As England's coach was guided through the thronging crowds flanked by police, Nat noted that 'unlike our fans, who equipped with their rosettes and rattles are usually a cheerful crowd, the Austrians looked most determined'. Billy Wright believed the Austrian fans were taking football more seriously than the Brazilians did.

The trepidation surrounding the fixture was compounded upon arrival at the Praterstadion, an imposing bowl structure worthy of comparison to the gladiatorial arenas of ancient Rome. Awaiting them was a team that lived up to the stadium's combative appearance. Ernst Ocwirk, the team's star, was nicknamed 'Clockwork' for his reliability in the centre of the field. Striker Robert Dienst would finish his career with more than 300 goals to his name. Ernst Happel was a superb defender whose astute reading of the game would later translate into an incredibly successful managerial career. Such was his brilliance that, four decades later, the venue for the game would be renamed in his honour.

As the teams lined up and the national anthems played – 'I always felt ten feet tall when they played the national anthem before a big game overseas,' said Lofthouse – each set of players got their first proper look at the opposition:

> In those days continental teams often used to wear numbers on their shorts as well as their shirts, so while their long, drawn-out anthems were playing, I'd be looking along the line. Looking for the number five.
>
> He was usually a big lad! 'By, Lofty, you're up against a big 'un today,' I'd think. Then I'd see him looking at me. You know how boxers try to stare one another out when they get in the ring before a big fight? Just the same.
>
> When they played our national anthem it would be shoulders back, chest out, try and look a couple of inches taller. Make sure he thinks I look a hard man, too. Still the eyeball to eyeball stuff.

Looking down the line on 25 May 1952, Nat's steely gaze met not one 'big 'un' but several. For all their technical wizardry, the Austrians appreciated the need for steel and raw power, and were capable of out-battling teams as well as out-thinking them. On the vast banked terraces of the Praterstadion, the English servicemen, even those who had an unwise amount riding on the game, were in jovial spirits and good voice.

In contrast, the Austrian fans were nervy and tense. Their country had fared badly in the years following the war, victims of a tug of war between the Soviet Union and United States. Their exceptional football team was one of the few bright spots in an often gloomy, depressing time. 'The Austrians had had precious little to cheer about since the end of the war,' wrote Nat, 'but in their magnificent soccer team they knew they had something extraordinary.'

Before the game Walter Winterbottom had been at pains to tell his players to keep focus during the opening moments, astutely predicting that Austria would attempt to snatch a lead and then switch to a counter-attacking system to exploit England's desire to achieve parity. Expertly shepherded by on-field general Alf Ramsey, England stood firm, content to restrict Austria and frustrate them before trying anything too adventurous themselves. As mistakes began to creep into the Austrian play and England's defence proved particularly stubborn, the Three Lions conjured their first attack of the game, with Nat bundling his way through in characteristically muscular fashion before Austria's keeper Josef Musil smothered the ball at his feet.

The Austrian stars continued to be repelled no matter which way they turned. The frustration this caused, Nat felt, was their opponent's undoing: 'Ocwirk and the rest were just a bit too desperate to prove themselves … Instead of patiently waiting for their chance, they threw caution to the wind. That was their greatest mistake.'

Despite Nat's recent drought for the national team, he was still a marked man. Determined not to be squeezed out of the game by the Austrian defence as he had been in Glasgow and Florence, Lofty began to drop deeper to get the ball, and it was one such move that led to the match's first major incident. As England broke, Lofthouse found Eddie Baily, who then slipped the ball through to Jackie Sewell. The pace of Baily's pass caught Sewell out and he miscontrolled slightly, allowing the ball to bobble into the air just behind him. With lightning-fast reflexes, he pirouetted and with almost preternatural accuracy found the left boot of Lofthouse, who took a split second in the box to adjust his body shape before firing calmly past Musil. The man who had once described his left foot as 'little more than a swinger' had just scored the most important goal of his career with it. 'But for the cheers of the British Tommies,' Nat recalled, 'I don't think we would have heard a whisper.' The England players were jubilant, but their joy at their calculated game plan coming to fruition allowed them to lose their concentration. In Austria's next attack, England were found lacking in defensive numbers. In his desperation to get across to cover Dienst, Portsmouth's Jack Froggatt sent the Austrian tumbling in the penalty area. Merrick didn't even have a chance to dive before Adolf Huber's penalty was nestling in the right corner of the net.

The Praterstadion was still shaking from the celebrations of the crowd when England retook the lead, as Sewell surged down the centre of the pitch and buried a superb effort past the despairing dive of Musil. Austria again set about laying siege to Merrick's goal but having been stung once immediately after scoring, England's defensive unit this time stood firm. Frustration again crept into the Austrian play, with rough challenges in equal evidence to the fleet-footed flair the team were famous for. England nearly went further ahead when a typically pinpoint Alf Ramsey free kick looped on to the bar off an England head, before parity was restored at 2-2 on the stroke of half-time when Dienst fired low past Merrick.

As the second half wore on, England's raids into enemy territory became fewer and fewer, with Lofty rarely seeing the ball and being forced to perform more defensive work. Winterbottom had warned them that this sort of sustained pressure was to be expected, but such was the Austrian pressing that England rarely had a chance to execute any sort of counter. Entering the final ten minutes of the game, however, Austria had still failed to breach England's defence. A shot deflected over the bar gave *Das Team* a corner and, sensing blood, they poured forward in anticipation. Nat remained on the halfway line with just one Austrian defender for company and the distant figure of goalkeeper Musil ahead of him, camouflaged by the sea of bodies crowded behind the goal.

What ensued would live long in the memory of all who witnessed it. The corner was floated in from the left and, despite pressure from Dienst, Merrick confidently plucked the ball from the air. Landing heavily, the custodian kept his footing and spotted Tom Finney racing forward into space down the right. Instinctively, he hurled the ball to the feet of the Preston winger. Nat, reacting quicker than his marker and trading on the innate understanding he'd developed with Finney, turned and accelerated toward the Austrian goal. Finney took one touch before lacing a perfectly weighted through ball to Nat, leaving the stranded Austrian defender completely flatfooted. Finney and several others shouted 'on your own, Nat!' and he set off 'as if my life depended on breaking the 100 metres record'.

Austria's defenders gave chase 'like a pack of hounds after a fox' but, despite being aware of the thudding of Austrian boots growing louder, Nat remained fixed on his target. 'Musil wasn't a good goalkeeper. I don't really think he knew what to do. He started to come … then he stopped … then he went back … hesitated … and finally came dashing out.' Perhaps employing some poetic licence, Nat said that at that precise moment, his mind flashed back to a similar chance he'd had a week earlier in Florence when he'd rushed into shooting from range. This time, he continued to advance until Musil finally made up his mind and raced from his goal. With the goalkeeper bearing down on him and Austrian defenders swarming behind, Nat composed himself and slipped the ball past the goalkeeper into the right corner of the net. The timing of the shot couldn't have been more perfect, evidenced by the spectacular clattering Nat took milliseconds after striking for goal, as he and Musil met each other with a crunch.

It was, in the words of the usually diplomatic and reticent Winterbottom, a 'wonderful solo goal'.* The muted cheers of the vastly outnumbered Tommies were only momentarily evident to Nat before the toll of the collision and the resulting crashing fall caught up with him and he blacked out. His next memory was waking to see a mixture of concern and jubilation upon his teammates' faces as they told him he'd scored – ironically – the most memorable goal of his career thus far. Though still dazed – he always remembered being stretchered off the pitch, while he was actually heaved off by Finney and others – and aware

---

★   John Gradwell, *Legend: The Life of Roy 'Chopper' Hartle*, p. 37.

of a throbbing pain in his shin, Nat was able to limp back onto the pitch to complete the game.* Austria were punch-drunk after the late blow: 'From a streamlined team which all afternoon had revealed poise and great constructive ability, they quickly became a number of individuals anxious to make amends but never again clicking as a great combination.' As the Austrian efforts to find another equaliser foundered, the hobbling Nat almost extended England's lead further with a fierce strike that hit the base of the post.

At the sound of Giuseppe Carpani's whistle to signal full-time, the England players celebrated to the sound of an eerie silence within the Praterstadion, punctuated only by cheers from the small number of English supporters, some of whom burst on to the pitch to celebrate with their heroes. Although still feeling the after-effects of Musil's challenge, Nat was left in little doubt by the exaltations of his teammates of the magnitude of what he had just done.

Vanquishing Austria was a remarkable feat. Doing so under the circumstances that Lofty was playing under was little short of miraculous. Nat's place in the England team had been under grave threat before the game. He knew another match without a goal could have easily ended his chances of ever playing for England again. Instead, his performance was a definitive moment, one that he proudly claimed had altered 'my career and my life completely'. Despite his niggling doubts about his own ability, the Vienna game gave Nat a brief respite from his insecurities: 'I felt I had "arrived" at last. For the first time I felt that at last I had really qualified to play for England.'

The British journalists in attendance struggled to keep their occupational objectivity in check as they wired their match reports back to Fleet Street that evening. The writer who had fired Nat's desire to perform in the game more than anyone with his insistence that Nat should be dropped for Milburn sent him a bottle of wine as way of an apology, and the England players spent their evening making the most of

---

* Substitutes were first permitted in international football during the qualifying rounds for the 1954 World Cup.

the Tommies' hospitality. The most lasting impact belonged to the *Daily Express'* Desmond Hackett, who bequeathed upon England's goal scorer one of the most memorable monikers in all of English football. From now until the end of his life, Lofthouse and the sobriquet 'The Lion of Vienna' would be synonymous with one another, long after the exact circumstances of its awarding had been lost to most.

Three days of recuperation before the final game of the tour in Zurich gave Nat time to allow the daze from his injury to dissipate and the enormity of his winning goal in the 'Championship of Europe' to sink in. The squad was brimming with confidence and it was little surprise when they made light work of Switzerland. Nat scored twice in a comfortable 3-0 win that took his tally to nine goals for his country in just eight appearances, giving him further confidence that he would retain the centre forward berth for at least the next round of internationals.

Arriving home at the beginning of June after a considerably less turbulent flight, Nat was afforded two and a half months of well-deserved rest and relaxation. While his time on the England tour had been a near-unmitigated success, his nightly calls to Alma to update her on his progress and to check in on her and Jeff had served as a constant reminder of missed home comforts. He quickly set about what were now his familiar retreats from the pressures of football and growing fame. Nat took great pleasure in responding to the regular pieces of fan mail he received, typically written from schoolboys who harboured an ambition to follow in his footsteps as England's centre forward. What had begun as a trickle of letters as he broke into the Bolton team had developed into a steady stream, and in the wake of his performances for his country that summer he was receiving more than fifty letters a week. In typical Lofty fashion, he always endeavoured to return the favour to everyone who took the time to write him. While the maximum wage for professional footballers was to be raised by £1 to £15 in 1953, Nat followed the example set by many of his contemporaries – close friend Tom Finney bore the moniker of the 'Preston Plumber' – by taking a part-time job as a paint salesman. The face-to-face nature of the role suited the naturally charming and personable Lofthouse to a tee, and he no doubt found the job less challenging than it would have been had his customers not been able to boast that they'd just bought their paint from *the* Nat Lofthouse. To enable him to make his rounds and make family trips to the countryside easier, Nat purchased an Austin Somerset saloon car, although he still often opted to take the bus to games, perhaps due to the value he placed on understanding the mood and the gripes of the Bolton fans. He also began to put great stock in brisk walks each night before bed, finding they helped him get to sleep easily, even on the eve of a big game.

Once his sales rounds were complete for the day, he was free to play with Jeff, go on drives out or indulge in one of his new-found passions, rock gardening. The absolute control and clear organisation of the hobby provided a pleasing counterbalance to life within the vast, constantly shifting mechanism of professional football. When Nat's parents were available to babysit (Alma's mother and father passed away before she and Nat had married), he and Alma would go out for supper in town, and they would still sometimes treat themselves to a night on the Palais dance floor at weekends. Nat and teammates Willie Moir, Stan Hanson and Malcolm Barrass,* all now fathers themselves, began a tradition of taking their children for ice creams at Tognarelli's – an activity they'd continue into the season on Saturdays before home games, as well as giving the children the run of Burnden Park. This outside work socialising was typical of the tight-knit Wanderers team, and the players would usually enjoy a few pints together after the game, often in the tiny wooden hut that passed for a tea room at Burnden Park. So cramped was the room that it would take mere minutes for the air to be thick with pipe and cigarette smoke. It wasn't unusual for Nat and the others to lose track of time, particularly if the beer ('We only supped ale,' Tommy Banks told me. 'We weren't bloomin' drunkards!') was flowing after a victory. On more than one occasion Alma was roused in the wee small hours by her husband returning home with several cohorts and requesting a round of bacon

---

* Such was the bond between this generation of Wanderers players that Nat became godfather to Barrass' daughter Lynne.

butties. It was around this time that Alma and Nat learned that they were to be parents again; daughter Vivien was born in 1953 and, just like Jeff, was doted upon by her mother and father. Even with his confidence in his own abilities and staying power growing with each passing season, Nat nonetheless remained eternally thankful for Alma's calming presence on his occasionally jangling nerves.

8

MATTHEWS' FINAL HEARTBREAK

FOLLOWING THE SEISMIC upheaval in his status, Nat took stock of his situation. He'd turn 27 four days into the 1952/53 season, traditionally the point in a centre forward's career where his experience and physical fitness would be at the optimum balancing point. Aside from the ankle injury that had sidelined him for two months in 1948, Nat had been blessed with a remarkable freedom from injury, despite his no-holds-barred style of play. He was no longer simply the main man on a successful but relatively low-key team. Now he was a national star, as secure a fixture in the national team as it was possible to be. Wanderers' finish of fifth the year before had been their best showing in well over fifteen years.* Now, all eyes were on him to help the team better it.

The new season represented the crystallisation of Nat's playing style and saw him at his imperious, irresistible best. Unlike many contemporary accounts that have him as a lumbering bruiser of a centre forward, Lofty's build was relatively slight given his reputation for physicality and

---

★   This increase in expectations led Nat to initially turn down the club's next contract offer, before eventually re-signing on slightly better terms.

lent him a good turn of speed. Many match reports at the time offer his agility and nimbleness as a given, while it was his prowess in the air and strength that were considered his deceptive qualities. 'He weren't a giant of a fella,' recalls Tommy Banks, 'but he could get up and he was strong as ox.' His passing ability was rarely more than adequate, but he helped his side in other, less appreciable ways. His reputation was now such that his runs off the ball were almost as destructive as his work with it, dragging defenders, who were duty bound to shadow him as closely as they could, away from his fellow forwards. A story in the *Sports Argus* that year referred to him as 'the complete master' of making a nuisance of himself without possession. Nat made no secret, then or later, of his recurrent use of the shoulder charge, then a perfectly legal manoeuvre. Years later, Franny Lee would recall how Lofty liked crosses to be aimed between him and the keeper, because Nat knew the goalie would think twice before coming out to challenge. However, it was utilised solely for practical purposes rather than any sort of score-settling or malice. Even on sodden pitches, playing with a ball leaden with water, he seemed to have inexhaustible reserves of stamina, and would help himself to plenty of late goals by playing as if the match had just started while all around him were running on empty. His unerring ability to find the net was, by now, second to none, and would never again desert him in the manner it had in the fledgling years of his career.

These qualities made him a fine First Division player. What took Lofty beyond and made him an overpowering force of nature was his relentlessness and desire, a superhuman will to force his body through fatigue, through pain (one newspaper quipped he should have carried his own stretcher given the physical punishment he took) to produce the extraordinary. When, as the *Daily Dispatch* put it, he was in the 'Vienna mood', there was simply no other forward in the country, possibly the world, who could produce such irrepressible performances. Doug Holden recounts the psychological impact Nat had on the rest of his team, saying, 'We always felt that while he was still on the field, there was always a chance.' Banks, of those forced to defend against Lofthouse, says simply, 'they knew they were playing against somebody when they played against Lofty.' The feeling among Ridding and his coaches was similarly adulatory: Holden, who broke into the side the year before, remembers one of his few instructions being, 'If you get in any kind of trouble with the ball, knock it down the line and Nat will get it.'

Within the club, belief in the team's potential was at a similarly high watermark. The Trotters were in possession of a core group of players who were arriving at the pinnacles of their careers together and had developed intrinsic understandings between one another. The names in that team became part of Wanderers folklore. The defensive contingent of Stan Hanson, John Ball, Roy Hartle, George Higgins, Johnny Wheeler and Mal Barrass were dependable and as tough as any side. In the attacking department, it was a mixture of silk and steel, with Nat assisted by Moir and Howard Hassall, with Holden and Bobby Langton on the wings.

Though Bolton's league form failed to match expectations, hope abounded that if the draw was kind to them, the team had all the ingredients to make a run in the FA Cup. Nat had begun the season slowly, partially as a result of his long summer with England. In October, however, he exploded into life, scoring nine in eleven for Wanderers. He was even more prolific in representative games. He added to the hat-trick he'd scored against the Irish league at the end of the previous season with an incredible six-goal performance as the Football League romped to a 7-1 rout. With his England spot as secure as it could be following his heroics in Vienna, he now began to show what he was capable of without the sword of Damocles dangling precariously above his head. England's first engagement of the season was in front of a 60,000-strong sea of faces at Belfast's Windsor Park against Northern Ireland. Nat continued his incredible year against Irish sides when he scored in remarkably similar fashion to his winner in Vienna within ninety seconds, though the Three Lions were eventually held 2-2. The final two England games of the year were Wales and then Belgium, both at Wembley. It was to no one's surprise when Nat, newly crowned the nation's footballing golden boy after his remarkable year, netted braces in both games. His performance in the Wales game, in which he scored an opportunistic lob from well outside the box, drew particular praise; upon his retirement, the *Bolton Evening*

News highlighted the game as one of Nat's greatest ever showings. The *Birmingham Daily Gazette* declared that Lofty was displaying such incredible form that he 'will yet rank with the great'.

At Burnden, the situation was looking less rosy. Not only had Christmas brought the team back down to earth after a small revival in fortunes, but a number of players were beginning to feel that they deserved better than to be playing in a team looking over their shoulders rather than up the table. Two big-money signings, Langton and Hassall, took their discontent with life at Bolton a stage further than changing room grumblings, submitting formal transfer requests. Neither was permitted to leave the club, but the fact that the pair had taken the step of publicly declaring their desire to leave left Bill Ridding and George Taylor with plenty to mull over.

Against the backdrop of player unhappiness and shaky league form, Bolton's hosting of Second Division Fulham for the Cup's third round in mid-January was little more than an unwanted distraction for the club's upper echelons. However, the fans continued to take an altogether more positive view of the competition, with more than 32,000 filing into the ground on a wintry Saturday afternoon. Those that braved the freezing temperatures were rewarded with a confident display that belied Bolton's league form, with Doug Holden, Willie Moir and Nat all finding the net in a 3-1 win. The reward for the players' endeavour and the crowd's hearty resolve was another home tie, this time against even lowlier opposition than the Cottagers. Notts County had boasted Nat's personal hero and Bolton lad Tommy Lawton on their books less than a year before, but were enduring a tough first season without the talismanic striker, and travelled to Burnden Park with their spectre of relegation to the third tier looming. Despite that, they were able to restrict Lofty to a single goal and earn a replay back at Meadow Lane following a 1-1 draw.

There, even a period of extra time was unable to separate the two sides, with Willie Moir's brace taking the tie to a third game at a neutral location. Despite many Bolton fans now firmly believing in the team's fourth round hoodoo — they'd not reached the next stage of the competition since the Burnden Disaster campaign, seven seasons before — 23,000 were in attendance at Sheffield Wednesday's Hillsborough ground to see the Whites finally overcome their lower league opposition 1-0 courtesy of another Lofthouse goal. The same scoreline and goal scorer would be repeated in both the fifth and sixth rounds. After beating Luton Town away, Bolton moved on to the quarter-finals and what was, on paper, their easiest game in the competition so far, against Third Division Gateshead FC. Mere weeks before Edmund Hillary and Tenzing Norgay mounted their successful assault on Everest, the minnows from the north-east had staged a similarly stirring challenge, capturing the nation's imagination by collecting the scalps of Liverpool, Hull City and Plymouth Argyle. Having never moved beyond the fourth round of the competition before, Gateshead and their fans were torn between the desire to keep progressing and wanting a true glamour tie against major opposition. As it was, they got the latter in the form of four-time winners Bolton. Over 17,000 crammed into the club's tiny Redheugh Park, only to be left disappointed as Lofty once again punctured a plucky display with a close-range header.

Bolton had garnered a reputation for professional, workmanlike displays that, while effective, were winning them few admirers, particularly among the bookmakers, where few punters fancied the Wanderers' chances for progressing once they met opposition of serious quality. Their semi-final opponents, Everton, were another Second Division side but their pedigree was of an entirely different class than the likes of Notts County and Fulham. As well as their two successes in the competition, their status as a Second Division club was a rarity; this was only their second (and, to date, last) stint outside the top flight. Despite their league standing, their form in the Cup had recalled the halcyon days of Dixie Dean, as they overcame first Manchester United and then Aston Villa, both First Division teams.

The atmosphere in Bolton in the lead-up to the game was in stark contrast to the malaise that had accompanied the last time Bolton had reached the final four of the competition. Seven years earlier, Bolton's semi-final had been played under a cloud as the magnitude of the Burnden Disaster had become apparent. This time, the Bolton fans had little to worry about other than the game at hand as they travelled the short distance to Manchester City's Maine Road ground. Under leaden Lancastrian skies, those that made the trip were treated to a game for the ages.

On paper, Wanderers had by far the better team. Bobby Langton and Doug Holden had the pace and trickery to worry Everton's fullbacks, while the Trotters' central attacking trio of Lofthouse (who had scored in every round), Hassall and Moir was now established as a potent force in the top flight. The Trotters made this advantage tell almost immediately. After an early attempt from a corner had been cleared off the line, Bolton took the lead within ten minutes when Lofthouse found Holden, whose attempted cross looped off an Everton defender and lobbed the stranded Jimmy O'Neill in the Toffees' goal. Moments later, Wanderers doubled their lead when Moir beat O'Neill at his near post. Things continued from bad to worse for the Merseysiders when Nat was played in and calmly slid the ball into the far corner, before Everton were presented with a lifeline in the form of a penalty. However, in keeping with the day they'd had so far, Tommy Clinton conspired to thump the ball hopelessly wide of Stan Hanson's left post. A fourth goal from Nat wrapped up one of the most one-sided halves of football that anyone in attendance could remember. 'It looked as if we were going to be on for a very big win,' recalled Nat, 'but … Bill Ridding wasn't so sure. "For goodness' sake don't ease up," he said. "Remember if you got four in the first half, there's time for them to get four as well."' As wise as Ridding's cautionary words were, they had little effect in stemming the tide of the second half.

John Willie Parker's header early in the second period appeared little more than a consolation, but when Nat again surged through before seeing a sweetly struck half volley hit the upright, there was a sense that the tide was turning. A free kick, then another header for the Toffees reduced Bolton's lead to one. Everton were dealt a blow when their centre forward Dave Hickson was forced off with an injury – a moment that the *Daily Mail* felt showed Nat as 'not only … England's best centre forward … [but] the perfect sportsman', as he checked on Hickson as he departed. With Wanderers' lack of experience in high-stakes Cup games showing, Hanson and Moir appealed for calm, reminding their teammates of their dominance in the first period. With a renewed resolve, the Trotters' defence held firm and halted the Toffees' charge until the final whistle. For the first time in a generation, Bolton Wanderers fans were plotting the long journey down to the Empire Stadium.

The excitement of Bolton reaching the most prestigious game in club football was magnified by the time since their last final, in 1929, and by the sense of occasion that surrounded the match. The game would take place exactly one month before the coronation of Queen Elizabeth II, the first televised coronation in history. The opportunity to witness such a momentous occasion was too good to pass up for vast swathes of the British public, who bought sets by the thousands. Many that couldn't afford a set outright rented them, and the close proximity of the final to the coronation meant that a month's lease was a worthwhile investment. Ten million would watch the final on TV, with the same amount again tuning in on the wireless.

Even accounting for the uptake of new technology, interest in the game needed little bolstering. Bolton's participation, a slumbering giant threatening to reawaken after several years, was one thing; their opponents Blackpool's involvement was another entirely. Formed ten years after Wanderers, Blackpool had spent the majority of their early existence in the shadow of their more illustrious Lancashire neighbours, watching the likes of Bolton, Blackburn Rovers and Preston North End enviously from the Second Division, before a pre-Second World War promotion finally led to a sustained spell in the top flight, the first sign of the club's increasing stature. The second such indication, one that made the footballing world sit up and take note of the town more synonymous with summer holidays than sporting prowess, came on 10 May 1947. Stanley Matthews had fallen in love with Blackpool while serving in the RAF, and when told by Blackpool's manager, Joe Smith, that the 'shackles' placed upon his natural creativity and flair at Stoke City would not be applied at the Seasiders, there was only one club for him. 'Play your own game,' Smith told Matthews, 'and whatever you do on the pitch, do it in the knowledge that you have my full support.'* While some at Stoke scoffed at the idea of giving Matthews such an unencumbered role, he repaid Smith's faith in spades, leading the club as it embarked upon the most fruitful spell in their history. Blackpool finishing third in the 1950/51 season and lost in the FA Cup Final that same year, having also fallen at the final hurdle in 1948. Matthews had turned 38 two months before the 1953 final, and in a year in which attentions were drawn to the beginning of a new era in one British institution as a new monarch was crowned, there was an inescapable sense of national sentimentality about the idea of Matthews finally capturing the medal that had somehow eluded him throughout his illustrious career.

Despite the cost of travelling hundreds of miles down to London, the clamour for tickets was huge. Even Bill Ridding was drafted in to help the club's beleaguered staff sort through the tens of thousands of ticket application envelopes. Given the support that the neutral spectators would be giving to Matthews, it was even more vital that the Bolton Wanderers faithful travelled to Wembley Stadium in numbers enough to make their voices heard over the din of the Tangerine fans and the appreciation of the rest of the crowd for the wizardry of the winger.

In stark contrast to Wanderers' first FA Cup victory – the 'White Horse Final', where the crowd was reputed to have reached north of 300,000 – Blackpool and Bolton were officially allocated just 12,500 tickets each, barely half of what the Trotters had been given for the semi-final at Maine Road. That game had been so oversubscribed that tickets were said to be going for four times their face value on the black market, and the meagre allocation for the final led to thousands of regular Burnden patrons missing out on a trip of a lifetime.

Some of the only people in Bolton guaranteed tickets, which quickly became the most sought-after commodity in town, were the players themselves. Lofty reckoned he had received almost 500 individual requests, most from strangers, asking if he'd be able to help them

---

★   Stanley Matthews, *The Way it Was: My Autobiography*, p. 270.

procure a ticket. 'Until Bolton reached the Cup Final I did not realise I had so many friends,' Nat quipped. 'By the time I has paid postage and had small slips printed regretting the fact that I could not oblige, the Cup Final cost me a great deal in out-of-pocket expenses.' Even with tickets so scarce, some had no intention of trying to butter the players up. 'There was no shortage of Red Rose rivalry. I lost count of the number of times I was hailed in the streets with: "Don't bother coming home if you don't bring the Cup with you, Lofty!"' Others were more genial. One Bolton fan had found a nail in the centre circle of the Wembley pitch before the final in 1923 and, believing that the club's success that day and their two subsequent triumphs had been related, posted it to Nat. Another sent him a lucky rabbit's foot. Despite an upbringing in which hard work was heralded above all else and an ensuing scepticism of superstition, Nat couldn't resist pocketing the foot before he ran out on to the pitch on 2 May.

As Bolton was overcome by feverish anticipation, the players quietly slipped away to a somewhat unlikely location for their preparations – Blackpool. Ostensibly, it was to give the Bolton team a chance to train with fresh sea air in their lungs and to exchange the joint-jangling crunch of the Burnden running track for the soft sands of Blackpool's beaches. Underpinning the decision was Bill Ridding's desire to extract his charges from the nervous excitement that was building among the fans. The players did, however, elect to return to Bolton at the start of the week of the game, getting suited up by Jackson's the Tailors and trying to enjoy some last-minute home comforts before the biggest game of their lives. The team then travelled down to Hendon, their headquarters for the final. Ridding and Taylor intentionally kept training light and as similar to the club's usual routine as possible in order to avoid building the final up as anything other than another routine fixture. The desired effect appeared to have been achieved. Nat stated that:

Contrary to expectation I found myself viewing the prospects of the match with complete calm, and the last few days before the match were no.able for the fact that none of the players showed the slightest signs.

of nerves. I slept like a log on Friday night and at breakfast next morning the players looked as poised and cool as they do on the morning of an ordinary League match.

In fact, the only notable abnormality of Wanderers' preparation was the evening before the game. Nat would have preferred a simple, unfettered night in which to steel himself mentally for the challenges ahead, including consuming the 'cup drink' – a stomach-churning concoction of two dozen eggs combined with two bottles of sherry that the team shared the night before each round.* However, a quiet night in before the game wasn't possible. Nat had been summoned to the London Press Club, where he was to become the sixth annual recipient of the Football Writers' Association Footballer of the Year award, having beaten out competition from Tom Finney and Ron Burgess. At a time when it was immensely difficult to follow any players beyond those that played for your local team, the FWA award had quickly taken on a respect and significance. The journalists voting for the winner were some of the few people in the country capable of a fair comparison between players from the likes of Portsmouth and Preston. Two of the fledgling award's previous winners would be playing against Nat the following day. Matthews had won the first edition in 1948, as much a recognition of his already sixteen-year-long career as his performances that particular year. Blackpool's captain and elegant defensive bulwark Harry Johnston was the recipient three years later. As fate would have it, both Matthews' and Johnston's victories came on the eve of Blackpool appearing in the FA Cup Final; both had ended in defeat.

Nat's receipt of the award came as no real surprise to even the most partisan of football supporters. Although he had finished two shy of Preston's Charlie Wayman's total of twenty-four league goals, his form for the national team had pushed him to the front of the pack. Seven goals in his last four internationals, including his heroic showing in Vienna,

---

* The answer to Nat's wry quip, 'If it was such good stuff, why didn't we have it every week? We'd have been world beaters!' lies in the fortitude of the human stomach.

had left nobody in any doubt as to who now owned the previously hotly contested centre forward role. It certainly didn't hurt Nat's chances that he enjoyed a friendly, genial relationship with several journalists, appreciating their knowledge of the game. In his speech, he credited his teammates for giving him a platform on which he had achieved this personal victory and the Bolton fans who had vocally championed his cause. He would later state that, along with the Cup victory of 1958 and playing for England, it was his greatest playing honour.

As the sun rose on a magnificent late spring day in England's capital city and his players stirred in adjacent rooms, Bill Ridding began mentally scripting what he would say to his team before he handed Bolton Wanderers' destiny over to them. Their Cup run had handed them plenty of tests, all of which they had overcome. They had shown tremendous resolve to hold off Everton in the semi-final. Now it had all come down to one game.

Wanderers' league form had stabilised in the lead-up to the final, with the players given added confidence by their progress and incentivised by the hope of maintaining their spots in the team. Between January and the start of April, the team won more times than they lost and briefly threatened the top ten, before a slump saw Ridding's charges fall to five defeats in their last seven games. Without doubt, the highlight of the second half of the league season, other than securing the club's top-flight status for another year and some morale-boosting derby victories, was the form of Lofty. Nat continued his goal-scoring exploits with hat-tricks against Middlesbrough, now under the stewardship of Walter Rowley, Sunderland and Newcastle United. Bolton's two games against Blackpool had resulted in suitably contrasting scorelines given Wanderers' inconsistencies. A 3-0 loss at Bloomfield Road had formed part of the club's barren early campaign form, but it had been offset by a thumping 4-0 victory at home in January. Although the disparate nature of the results suggested that there was little between the sides, the game in which Bolton had won was still fresh in the memories of the players and fans. With Lofty injured, Bill Ridding had turned to wing half Johnny Wheeler to lead the line. Ridding could have scarcely believed his luck when his makeshift centre forward netted three times; who knew what joy Nat could have against the Tangerines?

Any psychological edge this result gave Bolton was eroded by Matthews' presence in the Blackpool team. While a Cup final frenzy gripped Bolton and Blackpool, so did 'Wizard of Dribble' fever take hold of the rest of the country. By the day of the game, the clamour was such that tickets were now trading hands for sums of money that made a mockery of the notion that football was the working man's game. For Bolton, the 38-year-old Matthews undoubtedly still represented a threat, but Ridding and George Taylor were at pains to impress on Nat and his teammates that their work would not be done just by shutting down the stalwart winger. Joe Smith, himself a legendary Bolton hero, at the time the all-time top goal scorer at Burnden Park and captain of the FA Cup-winning sides of 1923 and 1926, had built a team brimming with talent and experience.

What the Blackpool defence lacked in solidity they made up for in helping out the forward line. Captain Harry Johnston quietly and efficiently made the Blackpool team tick from centre half. A bastion of solidity in the middle of the pitch, Johnston was the central pivot of the team, lauded for his ability to dictate the flow of a game with his passing. Going forward, they had flair and power in abundance. Ernie Taylor, Jackie Mudie, Billy Perry and Nat's old rival for the England team Stan Mortensen were all top-quality attackers, capable of punishing the slightest mistake, and veterans of previous finals. Matthews' reputation as a showboater was entirely justified, sometimes to the frustration of teammates, who found his desire to embarrass defenders sometimes proved detrimental to the pace and effectiveness of an attack. Nat would not shy away from stating his preference for playing with Tom Finney on England duty rather than Matthews: 'He wasn't as easy to play with as Tom ... but I'm not complaining. Tom knew exactly where I wanted the ball; Stanley knew exactly where he was going to put it. It was up to me to be there when it arrived.' However, even with his ageing legs, Matthews could be utterly unstoppable when the mood took him.

Ridding wasn't nearly as fortunate in terms of the experience he had to call upon; none of his chosen starting eleven had ever faced English football's showpiece occasion before. While the Blackpool players were anxious not to fall at the final hurdle again, even a group as battle hardened as the Bolton lads were hard pressed not to feel slightly overawed as they walked out onto the Wembley turf in front of 100,000 roaring spectators.

As with all Cup finals, Ridding and Taylor faced some invidious selection decisions. The most notable of these was the dropping of Roy 'Chopper' Hartle, who'd appeared in every previous round, for John Ball. Although there was considerable disappointment felt for Hartle by his teammates when he learned of his omission, it did lend credibility to Ridding's stance that the final was best treated unemotionally as just another match. The same was true of how Taylor planned to deal with the threat that Matthews posed. While undeniably one of the greatest players of his generation, Taylor was well aware that 'the Maestro' was just one of several attacking threats Blackpool posed, and so made no tactical arrangements for the winger specifically. As Lofthouse remembered, 'You'd probably find it hard to believe but we had made no special plans to deal with the threat from Matthews. Yes, he was a great player and a match winner but we were happy with our own ability to deal with him.'

Although Matthews' eventual impact upon the game came to make this decision appear foolhardy, the faith placed by the Bolton Wanderers manager and coaches in the team was warranted. Stan Hanson had been a cornerstone of the team since 1936, save for his heroic stint in the forces alongside his teammates during the Second World War. Ahead of him was Ball alongside Mal Barrass and Ralph Banks, a defensive unit who were, on their day, capable of mixing it with the strongest of opposition. Bolton's wing half pairing, Eric Bell and Johnny Wheeler, performed the invaluable task of holding the team's shape and setting the attackers on their way. The forward line's undoubted star was Lofthouse, the only fully fledged international on either side at the time of the final. His success over the previous seasons, however, owed almost as much to the players either side of him as it did his bull-like strength, unfaltering courage and the honing of his instinctive, incisive finishing. On his left was Harold

Hassall, another Bolton-born star whose robust, industrious playing style was cut from the same cloth as Nat's. Although he lacked the goal-getting acumen to make him one of the league's most prolific inside forwards, he and Nat operated an effective one-two punch. Opposing players knew that if they were fortunate enough to evade the rampaging charge of one of Bolton's powerful forwards, the other would be right behind. On Nat's right was the club captain Willie Moir, the skilful Scottish forward capable of slotting in anywhere within the attacking 'W' of the WM. Moir and Lofthouse's relationship on the pitch had been, for several years, one of mutual assistance. In Nat's early days, before his skill as a goal scorer had fully developed, it was Moir's goals that helped gloss over this shortcoming in his game. For Moir, his scoring rate benefited enormously by the emergence of Lofthouse and his reputation as a physical threat that simply couldn't be ignored, which created more time and space for the Scot to work with. Outside left Bobby Langton had been in and out of the team during the league campaign despite his billing as the club's one-time record signing but he had featured in every Cup game, apparently thriving on the increased pressure of playing knockout football. On the other flank was Doug Holden, an understated yet direct pillar of reliability whose only time out of the team that season, enforced by injury, had coincided with a noticeable blunting of Bolton's offensive output.

As the pre-game formalities took place, the Bolton team were focused on Taylor's instructions and Ridding's few words of advice: 'dictate the play'. If Ridding's team talk appeared simplistic in comparison to modern tactics, his counterpart Joe Smith offered his Blackpool team even less, taking the view that his influence extended to the team sheet and no further. 'Get two goals up before half-time, lads, so I can enjoy my cigar in the second half' was one of Smith's favourite maxims, and it was often left to Johnston, after a sigh and a wry 'we haven't got a bloody clue what we're doing, do we?', to warn his teammates about particular threats to their game.[*]

[*]   David Tossell, *The Great English Final*, p. 97.

The players lined up together in the tunnel, some paralysed into stony silence by the noise of 100,000 spectators crammed into the stands directly above their heads. Others, including the England international contingent, indulged in a bit of banter before emerging on to the sun-drenched pitch to a deafening roar from the crowd. The teams lined up and shook hands with the Duke of Edinburgh, who stopped for an extended chat with Nat after noticing he was sporting a bandage on his hand, as he had done when the two had previously met before an England game in November. Prince Philip also remarked upon the Wanderers' special kits they'd commissioned for the occasion, made from satin silk rather than cotton, saying that the normally intimidating Bolton team looked 'like a bunch of pansies'.* The pre-game niceties were considerably more regal than what the Blackpool players had become accustomed to; as the team had risen to prominence, so had a small band of eccentric fans known as the Atomic Boys. The group were garbed in eye-catching tangerine regalia and had a ritual of placing a live duck – dyed tangerine – on the pitch before a game.

Finally, there was nothing left to do but to play the game that millions had been waiting for. Blackpool kicked off, but Ridding's desire to see his team dictate proceedings was gratified as they almost immediately won the ball and advanced up the field. Holden played a cross in front of the Blackpool box that was miscontrolled by Moir but recovered by Hassall, who returned the ball to Holden. The winger realised that the usual target for his crossing, Lofthouse, was just to his left rather than in a more advanced position in the box. Nat often took up this position to allow his wingers to outrun their defenders and then feed the ball into them at the touchline, before racing into the box to try to meet their pull-back. Perhaps in the knowledge that this was what Blackpool were expecting, or perhaps simply over-excited by his first sight of goal in the final, Nat surprised everyone with a curving shot from 25 yards out.

Blackpool keeper George Farm won many admirers for his casual, nonchalant style of playing, but the downside to such an approach was

★   According to Ralph Banks, quoted in Tossell's *The Great English Final*, p. 30.

that when he made a mistake, it was all the more glaring. Never would that be truer than just ninety seconds into the game, with millions of Britons glued to TV sets and radios up and down the nation. Lofty's mishit shot ('there was plenty of sting in my effort, but I must admit I didn't quite make contact as I wanted to') bounced toward goal, Farm shifted his weight to the right and went down as if to catch the ball. It continued to bend and Farm, with none of his body behind the ball, only succeeded in shovelling it into the corner of the net. The exclamation of 'Lofthouse … it's a goal!' by BBC commentator (and boyhood Bolton fan) Kenneth Wolstenholme betrayed the sheer surprise of the early strike. Years later, Nat would recall the goal with a grin: 'Oh, that was lucky!' The goal meant that Nat became only the ninth man to score in every round of the Cup in a season.

The next fifteen minutes consisted of Bolton launching successive counter-attacks as they allowed Blackpool time on the ball. Nat's ability to win high balls was enhanced thanks to the fact that Blackpool left fullback Tommy Garrett had broken his nose a week before the final, making aerial battles with Lofthouse – an unenviable task at the best of times – even more problematic. Despite Bolton's ascendency, an injury to Eric Bell threatened to derail them entirely. Bell, who had been struggling with an injury prior to the game but declared himself fit, eventually returned to the fray, but was limited to a hobble by a tear in his hamstring. Ridding was forced to make changes in order to accommodate his left half's lack of mobility. Bell, who Wolstenholme told viewers 'I think we can write off', was moved to outside left, where his injury would be the least burdensome, with Langton moving inside and Hassall dropping back to midfield. Despite this, the shock of conceding in such a manner so early on in the game seemed to still be affecting Blackpool, while Bolton appeared determined to put paid to any chance of Joe Smith enjoying his second-half cigar. A ball was lofted into the Blackpool half, which Nat deftly knocked down. Moir beat his man and slid the ball back through to Nat, who was now steaming towards goal and in a straight foot race with Farm to see who could get there first. Nat won, only to see his poked effort bounce back off the post in agonising fashion. A scrum ensued for the loose ball, with an effort blocked on the line before Blackpool were eventually able to clear.

The game continued in this fashion for the next quarter of an hour, with a shot dragged wide of the far post by Bill Perry and a miscue by Ernie Taylor all Blackpool had to show for their endeavours, before a moment of brilliance turned the game on its head. A long ball from the back bounced through to Mortensen, who controlled, turned, beat Ralph Banks with a marvellous piece of dribbling and then charged around the side of John Ball and shot. His effort looked to be destined for the far corner, but Hassall inadvertently made sure of the outcome by diverting the ball past Hanson in a desperate attempt to block. Having settled into a rhythm of allowing Blackpool time on the ball and then hitting them on the break, Ridding's men now needed to seize the initiative again to avoid the Tangerines gaining the momentum. Holden drifted down the right-hand side of the pitch before finding Langton, who swung in an inviting cross just in front of Farm. The ball was perfectly placed for the onrushing Moir, who nipped the ball from the goalkeeper's fingertips and into the goal to give Wanderers a 2-1 half-time lead.

As the players returned to their dressing rooms to process the events of the first half and to strategise their plans of attack, Mortensen tugged Lofthouse's shirt and congratulated him on matching his achievement of scoring in every round. In the Blackpool changing room, Smith delivered a typically rousing, if tactically bereft, speech, telling his players to keep playing their own game. Johnston then took the stage, telling his attackers to focus on what they were there for while he and the defence did the rest. In the Bolton camp, Ridding implored his players not to get carried away and lose focus while trainer Bert Sproston tended frantically to Bell, who was at this stage unable to break out of a slow limp. Ridding put emphasis on remaining tight and compact defensively for the first exchanges of the second half, believing that Blackpool would attempt to overwhelm the Trotters early on.

Remarkably, Bell had a good chance to put his side further ahead almost immediately after the restart, screwing the ball wide when his ailing leg wouldn't allow him to take another step, drawing sympathetic and appreciative applause from the crowd. Blackpool attempted to force the issue but Ridding's instructions to remain solid and not try anything too adventurous kept Matthews and Co. at bay with ease. Then, ten minutes into the half, the seemingly impossible happened. Holden, who had assisted the first goal and played a large part in the second, worked a yard of space on the right and looped a cross over into familiar Lofthouse territory. Nat, however, was further back on the edge of the box. Instead, it was the badly injured Bell who compelled his weakened legs to propel him skyward. Farm came for the ball, as he had for Bolton's second goal, and once again he was beaten. As Bell's header nestled in the net he wheeled away into the arms of his jubilant teammates and even dared to break into a celebratory jog before the pain in his leg quickly reminded him of why he was in the unfamiliar forward position in the first place.

Even with thirty-five minutes still to play, Bell's goal could well have sealed the game. Nat recalled 'it seemed the Cup was as good as in the boardroom of Burnden Park', while Cyril Robinson, Blackpool's left half, remembered thinking, 'At least I've been to Wembley.'* Blackpool's heads were down, and they sunk further when they somehow contrived to miss a glorious opportunity following a pinpoint cut back from Matthews. With Bolton becoming more assured of their position, they began to allow Matthews more time on the ball, incorrectly believing that, at 38, he simply wouldn't have the stamina to make an impact late in the game. The missed chance could have been Matthews' last roll of the dice, a final desperate attempt to haul his team back into contention. In fact, it was just a shot across the bows – a warning that Bolton failed to heed. With just over twenty minutes remaining, he swung a cross over in a style not dissimilar to Holden for the third Whites' goal. The flight of the ball deceived Hanson and Mortensen was on hand to bundle it home, taking an almighty whack against the post in the process.

Now, with the score 3-2, Matthews moved into another gear. Having been comprehensively outpaced for the second Blackpool goal, Ralph Banks was opting to keep several yards of space between himself and Matthews, knowing that if he got too close then the winger would pass

★   David Tossell, *The Great English Final*, p. 268.

him with ease. The trade-off was Matthews had more and more time to pick his passes. Ernie Taylor recognised the added space and time Matthews was receiving and began moving the ball to the mercurial star at every chance he got. Another move down the right saw Mortensen's close-range strike brilliantly saved by Hanson, but there was no mistaking which side now had the wind in their sails. 'The tide had turned,' stated Lofthouse. 'We knew it. Blackpool knew it.'

With less than twenty minutes to go, Bolton retreated into their own half, determined to stick with what they had rather than twisting in search of a game-clinching goal. Their special silk kits were nowhere near as breathable as Blackpool's standard cotton ones, and the scorching sun was taking its toll almost as much as carrying the injured Bell. Every player had 'ran himself into the ground', said Moir. Bolton successfully repelled attacks until Blackpool won a free kick left of centre, 5 yards outside the penalty area in the eighty-ninth minute. Wolstenholme informed the viewers of the anticipated four minutes of stoppage time that Blackpool would have to find their equaliser. Mortensen placed the ball, walked back several paces before turning quickly and thundering the ball past Hanson's wall and into the top corner. Johnston and Mortenson celebrated so vigorously they ended up in a heap on the floor, while the Bolton players slumped to the turf, unable to quite believe that they had relinquished their lead at such a late stage. Now the focus was simply on earning a replay, one that they would have reason to feel confident in winning given the way they had performed despite Bell's injury. Matthews, however, had other ideas. Almost immediately from the restart, Blackpool won possession and Matthews tore up the right flank, bamboozled the exhausted Malcolm Barrass and swung in another fiendish cross. Hanson came and failed to make contact, before watching with heart in mouth as the ball fell to Jackie Mudie and somehow bounced wide. But if Bolton were thinking that their luck had finally changed, they were quickly shown otherwise. Once again Blackpool swept forward, once again Matthews left his marker – this time Banks – for dead before sliding in an inch-perfect pull-back to Perry, who made no mistake from mere yards out. An over-eager scoreboard operator momentarily credited both teams with a fourth goal, but that would be as close as Bolton would come to restoring parity.

At the full-time whistle, the attention immediately centred on Blackpool's star winger, as Wolstenholme declared 'a great end to a great career'. His teammates hugged him, the Bolton players shook his hand. Nat, one of the last to reach the man of the hour, congratulated Matthews, who consoled the Wanderers centre forward, as did Joe Smith. Years later, Nat would joke that 'If I'd had a gun at the end of the 1953 final I would have shot him [Matthews]!,' but none of the Bolton players were able to see the funny side at the time. Nat silently vowed that he'd one day return triumphant as he trudged disconsolately from the Wembley pitch.

Back in the Bolton dressing room, the stony silence cut through the Matthews-led narrative being lapped up by the rest of the country. The popular support for their opponents and the manner in which the game had slipped from their grasp at the last possible moment made the defeat sting even more. Bill Ridding, never a manager to let his emotions run wild, was 'too full to say anything'. Willie Moir remembered sitting opposite Lofty in the bath with 'tears rolling down our faces'. Nat freely admitted he was reduced to sobs as the sound of the ceaseless support of the Bolton fans continued from the stands.

9

TAKING ON THE WORLD

DESPITE THE BITTER disappointment of the FA Cup Final loss, Lofty had no time to sit back and reflect on what had gone wrong. He had enjoyed a truly spectacular year, scoring twenty-two goals in the league – his best ever haul – and another eight in the Cup. His international form was responsible for his deserved receipt of the FWA's Footballer of the Year title. With England heading on a gruelling tour of South America as a dress rehearsal for the next summer's World Cup finals in Switzerland, the Three Lions needed the Lion of Vienna to be at his roaring best.

If Nat and his national teammates had found the previous year's jaunt around Europe to be a cultural eye-opener, they were about to be blown away. The England tour of 1953 was to take in three stops in South America, Argentina, Chile and Uruguay, before travelling north for a chance for revenge against the United States after they had stunned the English in the World Cup three years previously. While the USA held the allure of post-war prosperity, modern commodities and a burgeoning pop culture industry that was beginning to make inroads across the Atlantic, it was South America that truly held the attraction – and trepidation – for Nat and his compatriots. With commercial air travel still in its infancy, the South American continent was regarded in the UK with much fascination, with the unknowns outnumbering the knowns of this exotic part of the world. The one certain common strand shared between Britain and South America was football.

Eschewing the physical wars of attrition that so often characterised the English game, the South American style was far more engineered towards flair and panache – an entire continent of Stanley Matthewses. The England players weren't naive enough to believe that was *all* their opponents would offer on the tour. They'd been forced to work hard by an industrious Chilean side in the World Cup, and their experiences in Europe the previous summer, and in Florence in particular, were demonstrative of the fact that foreign sides could give as good as they got. Beyond this, however, England were travelling into the unknown. Decades of FA obstinance, aided and abetted by a blinkered view in the media that the national team need not entertain the thought that any style of play other than the British way was worthy of consideration, meant that Walter Winterbottom's men were approaching the tour ill prepared.

The decades-old WM formation had already begun to show its age, and it had taken Herculean performances such as Nat's against Austria to keep England's recent record respectable. So ingrained was the 3-2-5 formation – with two fullbacks, a centre half, two half backs and a forward line featuring a centre forward, two inside forwards and two wingers – in English football that the idea of trying something different was simply never entertained. In South American football, the roles were similar, but the degree to which they were adhered to was wildly different. Players interchanged freely and took up positions in a much more fluid manner than the English players had ever been coached to do. Nat reflected on the trip with admiration, stating:

They played football, football, football all the time. No hopeful kicks up field. I don't mind admitting that we often used to call on the old long ball up field in times of crisis in defence. It's part of the English game; always has been. But the South Americans would never resort to anything like that. Even the centre halves were comfortable on the ball and quite happy to play their way out of the trouble. Even in their own penalty area. It was something completely new to me.

The first game was against Argentina at the Estadio Monumental, the intimidating home of River Plate. After taking part in the usual ambassadorial duties, including meeting President Perón (who informed them of the Argentina national team's proclivity to fade in the second half of games), Nat watched with other first-choice England stars as a second side were comfortably beaten 3-1 in front of a baying crowd of 120,000. Hoping to gain an advantage in the full international, the England players noted that the heat – and the effect it had had on the pitch – was a key factor in the reserve Argentine side's victory. Before the main fixture, Nat and Billy Wright inspected the pitch and agreed that a spot of rain would work wonders in making the surface more suited to the English style of play. Their words would prove to be prophetic, with the months-long drought the country was experiencing breaking in spectacular fashion hours before kick-off. By the mid-point of the first half, any hope of either side managing to impose any sort of game plan on proceedings was obviously futile. English referee Arthur Ellis eventually abandoned the game ten minutes before half-time while 'ankle-deep' in water, joking with Billy Wright as they left the pitch that if he left calling the game any later they would have needed lifeboats. Back in the dressing room, the England players needed help from trainer Jimmy Trotter to get out of their sodden kits.

Tight scheduling put paid to any hope of a replay and the England party flew on to Santiago for their next game against Chile. In their previous meeting in England's opening fixture of the 1950 World Cup, Wilf Mannion and Mortensen had put *La Roja* to the sword, and of the team's three engagements in Latin America, this game was expected to be the easiest. The flight proved to be one of the more enjoyable of Nat's England career, with the pilots happy to allow the guests of honour into the cockpit for a front-row view of the snow-capped Andes below. The match itself, which England won 2-1, proved a far less inspiring spectacle, with England's opponents opting to 'hit us with their shoulders and elbows, and threw in a bit of shirt-pulling for good measure' rather than meet Winterbottom's men on a footballing level. Nat struck the eventual winner with a cool finish that took his record for his country to fifteen goals in fourteen appearances, and hit one shot so hard that the Chilean player that blocked it attempted to give him a kick in retribution.

Despite the victory, it was Chile – the country itself – that was to have the final say. With the players scheduled to remain for the next few days before the tour's biggest test against Uruguay, illness swept through England's slender eighteen-man squad, putting the likes of Alf Ramsey and Tom Finney out of commission. Nat managed to avoid the colloquially named 'Chile tummy' but spent several days laid up in his room as a result of swollen glands and a sore throat. Another biblical storm threw the squad's training and travel plans into further chaos, and the Uruguay match was postponed a day at the behest of influential FA head Sir Stanley Rous.

After finally arriving in Uruguay, where they would be based in a picturesque Spanish-style hotel on the banks of the River Plate ('Just like Southport,' remarked Bill Eckersley), England were relieved to have at last reached the final leg of their South American adventure. As Nat and the others frequently found during their travels with England, they often knew little of the places they visited and the people who lived there, but the people certainly knew them. Once again, they were treated like foreign royalty, and the Estadio Centenario had its capacity temporarily expanded to 70,000 due to the demand to see the match.

When the game finally kicked off, Uruguay sought to quickly establish a rhythm, with rapid passing and the sort of fluid interchange of positions that was an anathema to English football purists. Nat would note after the match that it was the movement above all else that had put England to the sword. ('They were on the move all the time. I never saw one of their chaps standing about with his hands on hips, one of the crowning follies of so many young players in England.') Even in the initial throes of the match, it was clear that the extra day's rest had done little to replenish some of the England players who had been struck down with illness. Sensing this, the Uruguayans aimed to exhaust their already lethargic opponents before going for the jugular. This calculated approach almost cost the reigning World Cup champions dearly when Ivor Broadis slipped Nat through on goal. Lofty powered his shot past the helpless Roque Maspoli in the Uruguayan net, only for it to hit the post, roll along the line and inspire a desperate clearance from a defender. Stung into life, the South Americans hit the bar before taking the lead with a strike from range. England again struck the woodwork, but the humidity and the team's weariness began to become more and more evident. On the hour mark, Oscar Miguez's header looped over Gil Merrick and into the goal. Refusing to cede despite the deficit, England dug in while their foes, with 'the artistry of ballet dancers, and the body control of acrobats', broke out the party tricks. Nat recalled for the first (and quite possibly only) time seeing Billy Wright left bewildered when Miguez tapped the ball over his head, rounded him and continued up field while still juggling the ball. England continued to work and, with just over a minute remaining, earned a consolation when Tommy Taylor lashed home a rebound to make the score a disappointing yet respectable 2-1.

The Latin American leg of the tour complete, the England party headed north for their final game against the USA. The fixture, billed as a 'Coronation Celebration', was to be played at Yankee Stadium and, it was hoped by the United States FA, would do much to help the profile of the sport in the country. However, the tour's recurring theme of torrid weather continued. A torrential downpour saw the match postponed and meant that the pre-match entertainment, including a performance by the Royal Canadian Naval Band, was sacrificed as well as (more crucially) much of the crowd. Just 7,000 of the previously anticipated 40,000 were in attendance when the game finally kicked off the night after originally scheduled. Those that were there bore witness to a highly entertaining if one-sided match. By the hour mark, England were 4-1 up, with Nat again having done his case for being England's starting centre forward at next summer's World Cup no harm at all with two more goals. The US briefly threatened a highly unlikely comeback with two goals in as many minutes, but England helped themselves to two more to settle the score at 6-3.

Beleaguered, battered and in need of a good long rest after four weeks away, rarely had Bolton looked so good to Nat. Granted, there were no Spanish-style villas, no immense, expansive rolling rivers or dizzying skyscrapers like he had seen on tour, but it was home. Lofty had played in some remarkable, historic stadiums, packed to the rafters with crowds that were both hostile and effusive in their praise of the England players. Such bipartisanship was rare to find on the terraces in England, even back in what is now looked upon as the last great era of footballing sportsmanship. Nat knew all too well that often you could expect worse abuse from the fans that were there to supposedly support you than you could from the opposition. But even the majesty of the Estadio Monumental and the revered Yankee Stadium couldn't quite match the somewhat ramshackle charm of Burnden Park and its oftentimes cantankerous and impetuous crowd. It might never have the opportunity to play host to the Royal Canadian Naval Band, but Nat wouldn't have had it any other way.

Before he had embarked on the tour, another offer had come in for Lofty. This time, it was from abroad. Italian side Fiorentina had apparently been deeply impressed by his robust, relentless performance for England against Italy in the match before he was anointed the Lion of Vienna. As was the case with offers for Nat in the previous years, he had no say in the matter. With their improved league performances and the severity of their financial issues easing, it would have taken an astronomical sum to wrest Bolton Wanderers' prized asset from them, and whatever the eventual sum offered was, it wasn't enough. One paper ended their front-page piece on the speculation by saying, 'There is little likelihood of any transfer materialising,'* while another summarised the negotiations between the two clubs simply as 'Bolton Wanderers said: NO'.** The *Bolton Evening News'* story was equally emphatic, with Bill Ridding quoted as saying, 'the club would not entertain Lofthouse's release in any circumstances.'*** As with the interest from Spurs and Villa, however, Nat did allow his mind to wander when he got wind of the bid, imagining life in the sun-kissed bliss of Tuscany, accompanied by a proposed pay packet of over four times what he earned at Burnden Park as well as a home and a car. In later years, and somewhat contrary to the legend of his undying devotion to his club, Nat would reflect candidly that:

★ *Portsmouth Evening News*, 28 April 1953.

★★ *Daily Herald*, 29 April 1953.

★★★ *Bolton Evening News*, 28 April 1953.

Looking back, if there really had been a serious chance of me joining Fiorentina I would probably have gone. For a start they were offering me £60 a week.* Big money. And then I always enjoyed playing against the Italians. I liked their style of play.** Yes, they can be a bit volatile and they know all the tricks of the trade but basically the Italian First Division is a good place to play football.

Although Nat could have pushed harder to leave, either to White Hart Lane or to the Stadio Comunale di Firenze, it is to his credit that he didn't. His upbringing, his time as a Bevin Boy and his relationship with the people of Bolton never let him forget that he was in an extremely privileged position. Although it is unreasonable to expect him not to have countenanced the idea of moving for better pay, the fact that the move never materialised didn't mean Nat lost sight of the bigger picture. 'It didn't really worry me at the time. I was happy to play for Bolton. I was a regular first teamer in a successful side … My £14 a week*** doesn't sound much now but it was a reasonable amount at the time.' He was also acutely aware that, at Bolton, he had something that he would never have been able to replicate at another club, something to which it was impossible to assign a monetary value. 'I learned very early on that you won't find better fans anywhere,' Lofthouse explained:

Yes, they've given some players a hard time over the years but by and large they're among the fairest in the game. They never criticise a trier. I'll tell you how I picked up that lesson. In one of my early games, someone pushed a pass through the centre half and the left back for me

---

* According to several newspapers, Fiorentina's offer was £2,000 a year basic wage, with £25 for a home win and £35 for an away win.

** In the late 1990s, Nat would state his belief that his style may have been incompatible with the Italian league: 'I'd have been sent off more times than I would have played!'

*** Nat would have actually been earning a princely £15 a week at the time of Fiorentina's bid.

to run on to. Everyone in the ground could see he'd hit it too strong, that it was going out for a dead ball. But I thought I'd give it a go. I set off after that ball. I ran for 25 or 30 yards as if my life depended on it. And in the end I didn't miss it by much. It trickled over the line as I was sliding in. When I turned around to trot back to the centre circle for the goal kick I was given one of the biggest cheers I ever received. Just for trying. I remember thinking; 'Hey, Lofty, you've got something here. These people are cheering you just because you tried. You could have let the goalkeeper come out of his box, take the ball back in and then clear it up field. But no, you gave it a try ... and the fans love you for it.'

It was moments like this that meant that even if a bid had been successful, Nat would have been heartbroken to leave his hometown club. This view is advanced by his son, Jeff, despite Nat asserting that if playing after the abolition of the 'retain and transfer' system 'I don't suppose I would have been a Bolton Wanderers player for all those years'. Though moves elsewhere offered adventure and, in some cases, untold riches, Nat was well aware that the grass wasn't always greener, and that his lot was already nothing to be quibbled at. He was adored by the fans, and after some brief contractual squabbles in years past, Wanderers were now in no mind to offer him any less than the maximum wage when it came time for his annual contract renewal. His England career and his part-time salesman role kept a few extra quid in the family coffers, as did the increasing demand for product endorsements. Sponsorships had been a lucrative earner for sportsmen for decades, and Nat, with his profile as one of England's most prominent players, was never short of offers. Among the products he lent his name and image to were Smiths Empire watches, Lucozade, and a table-top football game for children.

Following a summer dominated by the coronation and the ensuing celebrations, every fan in the country, regardless of which team they followed, could be forgiven for approaching the new campaign with a sense of optimism. Now with a settled core of players and a manager and coaching staff that knew how to get the most from them, Bolton

Wanderers were ready to bounce back from their weak showing in the league and agonising defeat in the Cup the year before. The core of the team – Stan Hanson, John Ball, Mal Barrass, Johnny Wheeler, Eric Bell, Harold Hassall, Doug Holden, Nat Lofthouse and Willie Moir – had emerged from the shock of the Cup Final defeat wiser and ready to learn from their mistakes. Ridding's growing stature and influence at the club was reflected in his selling of Bobby Langton back to Blackburn Rovers. Langton had been the club's record signing when he joined, and it took a bold manager to risk not only selling him, but to a local rival where his every success was certain to reach the ears of the Bolton fans.

Ridding's roll of the dice paid off. In Langton's place came 17-year-old former England Schoolboys captain Ray Parry, whose debut two years before had made him the youngest player in First Division history. His performances on the left wing were such that there was never any danger of Ridding facing recriminations from allowing Langton to leave. With Parry and Holden supplying the crosses, Moir and Hassall wreaking havoc from the inside positions and Nat as the fulcrum, the Trotters netted fifteen more goals than they had the previous campaign, but it was their defence that truly shone, finishing with the fourth-fewest goals conceded in the league. Hanson was at his goalkeeping peak; Ball played every game; Ralph Banks was replaced by his younger brother, Tommy, who quickly earned a fearsome reputation thanks to his tendency to give opponents a nasty case of 'gravel rash' courtesy of the Burnden running track. 'The [opposition] players always knew about it, and to Hartle and me, that was alright,' remembers Banks. 'It was always a feature, they didn't like that. When you were gone off the grass you were gone.' Not dissuaded by his failure to break into the England team during the energy-sapping tour of the Americas, Mal Barrass continued his progression to becoming one of the country's most highly rated centre halfs. It wasn't just that the defence had matured into a sturdy unit. The general make-up of the team was one of physicality and a never-say-die mentality that owed a tremendous debt to George Taylor and George Hunt's training techniques, which had made Bolton one of the fittest and most physically imposing teams in the league.

For Nat, the 1953/54 season began in frustrating fashion, as he was forced to watch the opening weeks from the sidelines after breaking a bone in his wrist during training. The first attempt to reset the bone failed, leading to a further setback, before a piece of bone was taken from his leg in order to peg the split. With a place at what was only England's second World Cup at the end of the season at stake, it was the last thing he needed. As soon as he realised he wouldn't be fit enough for the start of the season, Lofty suffered a relapse into the worrisome state of mind that had often dogged him as a developing player before he had secured his place in both the Bolton and England teams:

At once I began to worry. What about my place in the England team? Not being one of those chaps who thinks he's an automatic choice I began to wonder if I would ever get another chance of appearing for my country. I worried so much that it began to get me down.

Things only got worse when he did return, as he failed to find the net in any of his first four appearances of the season:

Apart from the psychological effect which prevented me from taking normal chances for fear of hurting it, I soon found myself completely off-balance. Chances which by normal standards I would have snapped up became near-misses. All my old confidence was drained away and it dawned on me I had lost my touch.

As always, Nat kept his inner demons away from the eyes of his teammates. When asked if he ever saw any evidence of Nat's confidence faltering, long-time teammate Dougie Holden replied, 'No, no, he wasn't that sort of fella.' Terry Allcock was similarly dismissive, remembering Stan Hanson often being a nervous wreck before matches but Nat never appearing less than a pillar of strength and self-belief.

It wasn't long before Nat began to find his feet again, helped by the added steel in Bolton's play and fantastic performances by the men either side of him. Harold Hassall enjoyed by far his best season in front of goal for Bolton, scoring sixteen in just twenty-eight league appearances in a campaign punctuated by injury. Willie Moir, on the other side of Nat, enjoyed an equally splendid year, denying Lofty the accolade of being Bolton's top goal scorer in a full season for just the second (and, as it turned out, final) time in his career.

Despite his stuttering start to the season, Lofty's short-term future with England was secured when he scored twice in two minutes (taking his record to an incredible nineteen goals in seventeen caps) against Wales in the first international of the season. The next match, at the end of October, was a showpiece fixture against a Rest of the World XI to commemorate the FA's ninetieth birthday. 'It was the ambition of every player in England to be chosen for this great match,' Nat recalled. A hat-trick for the Football League against Ireland in Dublin was enough to convince the FA that Nat deserved to keep his place (the Bolton man had to endure a twenty-minute news bulletin that 'seemed more like twenty years' before learning of his inclusion). He would be facing luminaries such as László Kubala, vanquished foes from Vienna Ernst Ocwirk and Ernst Happel, and goalkeeper Vladimir Beara, who had performed remarkable feats to restrict Nat to just two goals on his England debut three years before. The FA hoped that the motley crew of foreign stars would help lend their birthday celebrations some sparks, and so it proved, with a final scoreline of 4-4 reflecting the relatively relaxed nature of the exhibition. Nat had an unusually quiet day by his standards, particularly in an England shirt, as he found his teammates often opting to take advantage of the occasion and shooting from unlikely angles rather than picking him out.

With the fun over, England were still the undisputed 'Kings of Football', as far as most fans in the country were concerned. If this sparkling collection of Europe's greatest talents couldn't beat them then there was no need to worry about the highly anticipated upcoming match with Hungary. Tellingly, some of the few dissenting voices came from the players themselves. Nat, writing the year after the Hungary game had thrown the perception of the national team's standing in the world into disarray, noted that 'We owe much to the FIFA [Rest of the World] side for spotlighting the fundamental weaknesses in our soccer fabric: lack of ball control, speed of thought and movement, and astute positional play'. He even went so far as to call the game 'the turning point in British soccer' thanks to the fact it had been televised – the moment that the average fan realised 'that England's footballers were not facing a badly equipped rabble when they played abroad'. In one respect, Lofthouse was correct – the Rest team had demonstrated a level of skill and guile of which many casual spectators in England would not have believed foreign players capable. However, the game also inadvertently reinforced the long-held belief of superiority within the English game, with even a team consisting of the very best in the world still unable to beat the English. Nat commented perceptively that for years 'foreign sides invariably took a hammering from British teams while they were in the process of learning the soccer business' but few of his fellow countrymen appreciated the head start the game had enjoyed in Britain and how that advantage was disappearing as time passed.

England's next match, a Home International against Ireland at Everton's Goodison Park, had been given added emphasis by the fact that a victory would ensure England's qualification for next summer's World Cup finals. Despite his failure to score against the FIFA representative team, Nat kept his place after netting twice in a 6-1 demolition of Portsmouth, Wanderers' only win in a difficult November. Alongside him was Harold Hassall, who had continued his prolific form for the Trotters and earned his first call up-since his Huddersfield Town days. Both men scored – Hassall twice and Nat once – as England cruised to victory and World Cup qualification. In the process of scoring, Lofthouse demonstrated his characteristic fearlessness by clashing heads with Irish centre half Bill Dickson, splitting his head just above the eye. Unable to continue, Nat was led groggily from the pitch by a trainer and a policeman with a towel draped over his head to try to stem the bleeding. The blood-soaked shirt he was left with became one of his prized possessions and took pride of place among the sizeable collection of memorabilia he accrued over the course of his career.

Second only to the prospect of playing at the World Cup was England's next fixture. Billed as the 'Match of the Century', England would be facing one of the sternest tests of their unbeaten home record against continental European teams. Hungary's 'Mighty Magyars' side were unbeaten since 1950 and had made a near-mockery of the teams they faced during the 1952 Olympics on their way to winning gold. Their success was owed to a combination of star players, including Ferenc Puskás, and the tactical innovations championed by their manager Gusztáv Sebes. More than a contest between two sets of technically brilliant players, it was a clash of two playing ideologies: one forward thinking, one dogmatic in its adherence to what had come before.

After receiving the call for the Ireland game, Nat 'thought that I was halfway towards playing in the Wembley game' against Hungary. Never one to shirk a challenge for club or country and always looking to prove his mettle against the very best, Nat wrote, 'I confess I nursed a great ambition to play against the superb Hungarian side. They had won the Olympic Games title and to all intents and purposes had proved themselves the best side in the world.' However, it wasn't to be. Nat's slow start to the season had been noted, and his wrist injury had certainly contributed to him lacking some of the decisive edge his forward play usually possessed. Nat had, at one point, been so despondent about his form and his prospects with the national team that Alma had been forced to give him a dressing down, reminding him that he had two adoring children who were going to follow their father's moping example if he carried on. Jeff says he wasn't aware of his father's fears and worries 'at the time, but it fits in with his personality'. Nat admitted that 'inwardly I did not feel like I was playing well enough to lead the England attack', despite his incredible goal record for his country and the fact that the draw against the FIFA side had been only the second Home International in which he'd failed to score.

Whatever could be said of Nat's form, or his self-proclaimed lack of it, it wasn't the sole factor in his eventual omission from the team. His replacement, Blackpool's Stan Mortensen, was still noted for what Stanley Matthews called 'lightning speed'[*] in short bursts – an attractive trait given the fluidity of the Hungarian side. Matthews' place in the team

---

[*]   Stanley Matthews, *The Way it Was: My Autobiography*, p. 275.

may have been another contributing factor. He and Lofthouse had failed to link effectively in the last two games, and Mortensen came with a now innate understanding of his Blackpool teammate's style of play.

Despite losing his place and breaking his run of appearing in eighteen straight games for his country, Nat stated a year later that he 'felt no bitterness' – a claim perhaps influenced by the knowledge of the mauling that the Three Lions received in his absence. Lofty took in the game not from a seat in the dugout but from his living room, sat with his family in front of the TV, guided by the familiar voice of Kenneth Wolstenholme. Of all the remarkable games the legendary commentator was to preside over during his illustrious career, nobody would ever forget the events of that overcast November afternoon.

Any semblance of hope for England in the match was quickly annihilated by the fluid interplay of the Hungarian players, who simply moved into positions that England's players had never had to fathom defending before. The fact that the Mighty Magyars frequently interchanged wrought havoc with England's attempts at man marking, even with a stellar defence marshalled by Billy Wright. The famous 6-3 scoreline in no way flattered the Hungarians. England's 'Kings of Football' crown had slipped, their throne abdicated. For those still clinging to the notion that this was a mere aberration, the ensuing months were to make it clear that this was a full-blown constitutional crisis.

Lofty wasted no time in joking to his fellow England internationals that the result would have been different had he played. His words were in jest, but as the season progressed and his form improved, they became coloured with frustration as he found his England exile continuing indefinitely. Though his season with Bolton was a personally disappointing one – his haul of seventeen league goals was his worst return in five seasons, and after his heroics of scoring in every round of the Cup in 1953, he only managed one in six this year – he still showed what he was capable of in flashes. Seven goals in eight games over the winter propelled Wanderers towards a strong fifth-place finish. One of those wins was a 5-1 hammering of Manchester United at Old Trafford in United's heaviest loss at home in well over two decades, which moved the *Bolton Evening News*'

Haydn Berry to write, 'In many visits to Old Trafford down the years …
I have never known such a runaway victory as Saturday's.' Lofty scored
Wanderers' first two goals, the second of which was a deft chip after waiting for the goalkeeper to advance from his line. Nat enjoyed another
purple patch in March in the run-up to England's next match versus
Scotland but was again overlooked, this time for West Bromwich Albion's
Ronnie Allen, who was enjoying a superb season. Ever the gentleman, Nat
sent his warm congratulations to Allen via telegram as Tommy Lawton
had done to him. Allen's goal in a 4-2 victory that went some way to
lifting the clouds left by the Hungary game was enough for him to retain
his spot for the impending pre-World Cup tour. Unlike the relatively
gentle fixtures major international teams now use to warm up for tourna-
ments, in 1954 the FA ran the risk of destroying their players' confidence
before the World Cup even began, with a daunting trip to Belgrade to
face Yugoslavia before a return match against Hungary in Budapest.

Following the end of the club season Nat busied himself on Bolton's
end-of-season tour and then continued to train by himself in an empty
Burnden Park while anxiously awaiting news of England's progress. The
trip to Belgrade ended in a 1-0 defeat, but despite the narrow margin
of defeat, England could have few complaints, having been decidedly
second best throughout the game, relying on sparse counter-attacks.
Allen's failure to find the net against the well-drilled Yugoslavia team saw
him dropped, and he would fail to make the cut when the preliminary
World Cup squad was cut to the twenty-two.

Although Nat professed his regrets at not appearing in the Wembley
fixture against Hungary, he was grateful he wasn't involved in the match
in Budapest. Winterbottom and the FA had been frantically chopping and
changing the team since the 6-3 loss the previous November, while failing to address the tactical reasons why England's defeat had been assured
even before they stepped on to the Wembley turf. No attempt was made
to update the outmoded WM system that Winterbottom was persever-
ing with and to which the England players had spent their entire careers
adhering. Furthermore, many English press writers who had covered
the previous match had noted that ten of the eleven Hungarian starters

came from two clubs, Budapest Honvéd and Vörös Lobogó. The Eastern Europeans enjoyed, in the words of *The Guardian*'s Pat Ward-Thomas, an 'immense advantage' by virtue of their familiarity with one another. By changing their team so incessantly, England were arguably doing themselves more harm than good.

So it proved in Hungary. Ivor Broadis' hammered finish past Hungarian keeper Gyula Grosics with around twenty minutes remaining came only after England found themselves six goals down, and the eventual 7-1 scoreline remains the country's biggest ever defeat, their previous worst result having come in a 6-1 loss to Scotland in 1881, three years before professionalism in the English game was legalised.

With shockwaves from their two games against Hungary – the first a humbling, the second a humiliation – reverberating around English football, the FA took drastic action when the time came to whittle down their preliminary squad to the seventeen men who would make the trip to Switzerland for the World Cup. English football's governing body were in the unenviable position of trying to prepare for the tournament in the wake of the national team having suffered their heaviest, most embarrassing defeat less than two weeks previously. In classic cronyistic FA style, they chose to simply bury their heads in the sand, with the 7-1 battering in Budapest simply not being mentioned at the organisation's annual meeting.

With the FA in damage limitation mode, they simply wanted to put out a team that would avoid embarrassment. With nineteen caps to his name, Nat was by far the most experienced of the centre forwards in the reckoning. Ronnie Allen's chance had gone when he failed to score against Yugoslavia in the first warm-up game. Tommy Taylor was called up after an excellent season at Old Trafford, but he was generally utilised at inside forward for England. Bedford Jezzard, from Second Division Fulham, was placed on the five-man reserve list. Stan Mortensen had been cruelly made a scapegoat for the 6-3 loss against Hungary and never played for England again. Jackie Milburn, despite his remarkable scoring record for Newcastle United, simply never truly found favour with the selection committee. The FA were left with one clear choice.

Bolton had finished the season well, with an identical record to fourth-placed Manchester United, losing out to their local rivals by virtue of goal average (United 'beat us [in the league table] every year, they always got that bloody point!' remembers Tommy Banks). Nat had played a key role, finishing with seventeen goals in thirty-two league appearances, ten of which came in the second half of the season. Bill Ridding and George Taylor, by now accustomed to their star player's proclivity to bury himself in self-doubt when enduring a dry spell, had spent countless hours on the pitch and in the offices of Burnden Park working to build up Nat's confidence. Lofty's faith that, despite his time in the international wilderness, he would make it to the World Cup was proved well placed when the back page of the late edition of the *Bolton Evening News* on 3 June declared, 'Nat Lofthouse for World Cup!'

In contrast to the excitement in the Lofthouse household when the word arrived, there was a gloom pervading the analysis of England's chances in Switzerland. Many prominent scribes wondered in their columns what fresh insults to English football's reputation the World Cup could bring. The *Daily Herald*'s Clifford Webb described the competition as 'a last chance for the English football system. If we are beaten the bottom will have dropped out of everything.' If the FA were doing their best to pretend that the recent Hungary game simply hadn't happened, they were given a stinging reminder that the public were not of such a forgetful mindset. A storm brewed after the press got hold of some photos of the England players engaged in a game of rounders at Roehampton before their flight to Zurich – apparently too leisurely a training activity given the team's recent results.

While no doubt slightly unnerved by the vociferous reaction to what would probably be dubbed by modern media as 'roundersgate', England players had reasons to be cheerful beyond the usual international tour japes that this time included convincing Albert Quixall to have his trademark golden curls shorn off. Their first stroke of luck was that their group's team from pot one was Switzerland, who were only seeded well due to their status as hosts. While playing the home nation would naturally be a tough test, it was a blessing considering that the other three teams in the pot were Uruguay, Brazil and, most frighteningly, Hungary. England's second piece of good fortune came as a result of the structure of the tournament. Although the World Cup in 1954 utilised four-team groups, each side would only play two games rather than facing off against all of their group. England would play Switzerland and their group's fourth-pot team, Belgium, crucially avoiding the underrated Italians who had left such an impression on the minds – and the bodies – of the England players when the nations had met two years before.[*]

Although Basel's St Jakob ground seated more than 50,000, only around 14,000 were in attendance to see the likes of Billy Wright, Tom Finney, Nat Lofthouse and Stan Matthews in England's opener against Belgium. However, those that had come were treated to a remarkable game, even in the context of the high-scoring tournament. The English team, safe in the knowledge that they should have too much for their opponents, went into the game relatively relaxed, even after one team bonding session ended with some of the team stranded for five hours on Lake Lucerne in an immobilised boat. Despite relatively few changes in personnel from the game in Budapest, England had an indisputably tougher, more experienced look to the team. The goalkeeper Gil Merrick, the defence and the midfield were untouched, while into the forward line came Lofty for Jezzard, Stan Matthews for Peter Harris and Tommy Taylor for Jackie Sewell. Nat lacked the international reputation of Matthews, but the Belgians, who had never faced Lofthouse before, needed only look down the line at his imposing frame as he belted out the national anthem to know they were in for a long day.

The 'football feast' the fans were treated to got off to a flying start. Although played in front of a crowd largely made up of locals, both sides played as if cheered on by thousands of frenzied fans. After Nat had thundered a shot just wide, Belgium went ahead when Leopold

[*]   Before their knock-out match with Uruguay, Nat had a chance meeting with Rino Ferrario, the centre half who had meted out a good portion of Nat's punishment on that day in Florence: 'Automatically I prepared myself for a hefty shoulder charge from the Italian "rock". Instead he ran forward and embraced me like a long-lost brother.'

Anoul capitalised on a loose ball in Merrick's box. England focused their attacks down the channels, with Matthews and Finney trading crosses and gradually getting closer to hitting their mark. The Belgian defence held until the twenty-fifth minute, when a weaving run by Broadis ended with the Newcastle United star slipping the ball under the onrushing Belgian keeper Leopold Gernaey. Twelve minutes later, the Three Lions took the lead when one of Finney's centres finally found Nat. The low cross still required a brilliant diving header from Lofty, who contorted his body in mid-air to get himself in position to direct the ball into the bottom corner. Some months after the tournament, Nat described the goal as 'the best I've ever scored with my head … I cannot explain why I decided to try a header instead of a drive, but I threw myself at the ball, [and] my forehead connected in copybook fashion.' Nat's first goal for his country since his exile was greeted with the same celebration that his previous twenty strikes had been, but this one was unique in that it was record breaking, albeit a record that had only existed for three games. At the tender age of 28, Nat had just become England's youngest World Cup goal scorer.

England now took the game by the scruff of the neck, with the Belgian defenders forced again and again to repel Lofthouse's aerial threat. Good fortune and, on one particularly egregious occasion after a clear trip, the referee came to Belgium's aid time and again. Finally, just after the hour mark, Broadis struck from close range to seemingly put the game beyond all reasonable doubt at 3-1. As England continued to press to extend their advantage, Anoul went on a mazy run that would have brought even the most seasoned of Matthews fans to their feet in admiration, before finishing with aplomb. As the game's frantic pace began to catch up with the players, the two defences, who up to that point had repelled attacks admirably, wilted. With England seeking only their second ever victory in World Cup finals and Belgium desperately trying not to squander the momentum that was now in their favour, the question became not whether there would be another goal, but which team would score it. The crowd, who were by now thoroughly enjoying what had turned into a frenetic, pulsating encounter, weren't made to wait long for the answer, as Belgium forward Rik Coppens launched a 'one-man Commando attack on the England goal'. As his shot cannoned off the inside of the upright and past the stranded Merrick, Nat claimed that 'there wasn't a man in the England side who did not ... feel that justice had been done'.

The game remained at 3-3 until the full-time whistle was blown. Under the tournament rules, if games were drawn at ninety minutes then extra time would be played (however, if drawn at the end of the added thirty minutes, there would be no penalties or lots drawn to decide a winner). Any suggestion of the two nations settling for a stalemate were quashed almost immediately after the restart. What Nat humbly described as having had 'the good fortune to see a shot beat Gernaey' did little justice to a move that saw him played in on the right-hand side of the area. With England having launched numerous aerial bombardments from similar positions, the Belgian defence and Gernaey braced themselves to block the onrushing forwards. Sensing an opening, Nat instead smashed a pinpoint strike directly across the face of the goal, beyond the helpless Gernaey and into the far corner. England once again appeared in control, before a hopeful free kick into the England penalty area glanced off the head of Jimmy Dickinson and looped past Merrick to make the final score an extraordinary 4-4.

The England players left the pitch relieved to have avoided defeat yet also bitterly disappointed. 'Believe me,' said Nat, 'when we boarded the train back to Lucerne we felt far from pleased with ourselves.' The sense of the match being a missed opportunity was reflected in the press back home, with *The Times* running with the headline 'England Throw Victory Away', and was exacerbated by the expectation that the game against the Swiss was likely to be a sterner test. Not only were they the hosts, but they had fared well in past World Cups. To make matters worse, when they got back to their hotel the England party learned that their next opponents had secured a sensational victory over Italy in their game, meaning they would be assured of a place in the next round with only a draw, while England had to win to keep their destiny in their own hands. The task was made harder still when Winterbottom and England trainer

Jimmy Trotter came to the solemn realisation that they would be without not one but two of their star men. Stan Matthews had picked up a knock in the rough and tumble of the Belgium game and wouldn't be fit to put the mortal fear of embarrassment into the Swiss defence. Even worse was the news that Nat, having come through the first game as unscathed as a bruising centre forward could, had picked up a nasty cold and wouldn't be ready to take to the field at the Wankdorf Stadium in Bern.

While Lofty was left cursing the fact that his body was apparently more amenable to the smog-choked sky of his hometown than the crisp lakeside air of Lucerne, his national manager was facing an unhappy quandary. In just ninety minutes, Nat had gone from a player being recalled for the first time in months to an automatic selection again. A team that had looked increasingly rudderless and lacking in a focal point suddenly had one, and Winterbottom must have watched the Belgium match wondering why the FA selection committee had chosen to omit the Lion of Vienna in the first place. Without Alma's reassuring hand to guide him through the murk of uncertainty and self-doubt, Nat found himself recuperating in his hotel room wondering if this enforced absence could result in another long spell in international exile. In another room in the same hotel, Winterbottom was likely reminding himself that no matter how well Nat's replacement Tommy Taylor performed, the Bolton striker was his man.

Even without Lofty and Matthews, Winterbottom's men rose to the challenge, with goals either side of half-time from Matthews' replacement Jimmy Mullen and Dennis Wilshaw (who usurped Nat as England's youngest ever World Cup goal scorer in the process) guaranteeing England's place in the knockout stages of the World Cup for the first time. In contrast to the excitement of the previous game, the tempo of the Switzerland match fell foul of the sweltering conditions it was played in, resulting in what *The Times* bluntly assessed as 'a match of extreme mediocrity'. Even with the Lancashire–Yorkshire and Bolton Wanderers–Manchester United rivalry between them, Nat would have never wished failure on Tommy Taylor. Despite this, and even with his characteristic humility, he must have felt slightly relieved as the game ended goalless for the United starlet.

As Nat recovered, the England camp nervously awaited their fate. Another oddity of the 1954 tournament was that, rather than group winners being drawn against runners-up in the next round, the draw was split down the middle, with the winners on one side and second-placed teams on the other. As England were beating Switzerland, Italy were making short work of Belgium, meaning that they were tied with the hosts on two points with England ahead on three, ensuring the Three Lions' place in the harder half of the draw. The teams they were able to draw in the next round made for grim reading: Brazil, Uruguay and Hungary. All three had superb sides, and, unlike England, all had genuine international silverware to compare to England's frequent boast of being the best by virtue of the country's role in the genesis of the game. *The Times* summed up the bleakness of England's chances in their report of the Switzerland game: 'England, in a world sense, represent a Third Division side that has found its way into the last eight of the FA Cup.'

The draw was ultimately as kind as it could be, as Winterbottom was asked to pit his wits once again against Juan López Fontana and his reigning champions, Uruguay. England had never played Brazil, and that unfamiliarity combined with the South Americans' reputation gave them an added dimension that even the most combative and competitive England players were pleased not to have to explore. The two recent fixtures against Hungary had helped England get somewhat accustomed with the Mighty Magyars, but only to the extent where they knew they would more than likely be on the end of another hiding. In contrast, the Three Lions had been overpowered but not out of the running when they had met Uruguay the previous summer in Montevideo. Still, there was no denying that the South Americans were the favourites. *Los Charrúas* had had none of the group stage difficulties that England had, seeing off a good Czechoslovakia side 2-0 before utterly embarrassing Scotland 7-0.

Having come through their test against Switzerland, Winterbottom once again had the luxury of choosing from a fully fit squad. As well as Nat returning at centre forward in place of Taylor, Matthews returned on the right and Finney moved to the left, replacing Mullen. The spine of the team – Merrick, Wright, Dickinson and Lofthouse – was the same as that which had played the South Americans the previous summer, and with the Uruguayans fielding a similar team to their last meeting, England could afford to feel quietly confident. Unfortunately for them, the weather in Switzerland was proving more reminiscent of Latin America than of central Europe. Temperatures were touching 40 degrees centigrade, and proved so extreme that on the day England played Uruguay, the game between Switzerland and Austria became known as *Hitzeschlacht von Lausanne* – the 'heat battle of Lausanne'. The Swiss were able to score three goals in rapid succession after the Austrian goalkeeper began to suffer from hyperthermia. English journalists who'd seen the Uruguayans in training reported that they possessed remarkable stamina and rarely stopped moving, despite the oppressive heat and the players' penchant for a large steak for breakfast.

Although the prestige of the World Cup was not yet fully established in England, there were a number in the team who were acutely aware that the Uruguay game represented a 'now or never' moment. Stanley Matthews was 39; Gil Merrick and Tom Finney were 32; Billy Wright, Jimmy Mullen and Ivor Broadis were 31. These men knew that in all likelihood this would be their last World Cup. Even the players who would still be close to their prime by the 1958 World Cup (Jimmy Dickinson would be 33, Nat 32) were seasoned enough to know that four years was plenty of time for their international careers to be curtailed by injury or falling out of favour. The hundreds of telegrams from back home wishing the players luck that had been arriving since the draw served simply to fuel the fire already lit in the bellies of the Englishmen. 'We could have been excused for feeling a little depressed,' Nat recalled, 'had we not felt so confident … There was not a man in our side, either, who wasn't prepared to run himself into the ground in a mighty effort to make amends [for the Hungary games]. One could not have asked for a more determined spirit from anyone.'

As the game got under way, England quickly discovered there was little doubt as to who the 28,000 local fans were behind. Nat remarked that the crowd was more vociferous in support of England than any Wembley crowd he'd played in front of, thanks in considerable part to the presence of Matthews. Every time he got the ball, there began an 'expectant hush' which swelled to a crescendo as the Blackpool star jinked his way beyond defenders with his trademark verve. Juan Alberto Schiaffino, the Uruguayan inside forward, was doing his best to match Matthews in the flair stakes, and left the England players 'staggered' by the improvement he'd made since playing them twelve months earlier.* The star was soon dictating the game, linking with his outside left Carlos Borges, who was described by the straight-talking Nat as 'a chunky little fellow' (a description made all the more embarrassing when compared to Lofthouse's gushing illustration of Schiaffino as 'blond, tall, quite well built … [with a] languid, effortless stride'). It was the diminutive Borges who drew first blood, reacting quickest to a mis-hit shot screwed across the area and blasting it into the roof of the net after only five minutes. England, who had started well and restricted Uruguay to that one attack, took encouragement from Billy Wright's commanding performance and soon found their feet. Wright had 'put [Omar Oscar] Miguez, rated Latin America's best centre forward, well and truly in his pocket', and after robbing him of the ball again, quickly found Wilshaw with a long raking pass. Wilshaw cut inside as Nat burst from deep, dragging his marker with him. Wilshaw feigned to go on himself, before playing a cute reverse pass into Lofty's path. With the Uruguayan defence completely flat-footed, Nat repaid Winterbottom's faith in him, placing the ball beyond goalkeeper Roque Maspoli to bring England level.

'At this stage,' Nat recounted, 'the England team was playing better than any other representative side in which I have appeared.' Uruguay grew increasingly dependent on their dominant right half Victor Andrade, who spent the period immediately following England's goal as an auxiliary fullback. Even Andrade was powerless to stop another attempt from Lofthouse, who powered a shot in from fully 25 yards out. Maspoli spilt the ball and was relieved when the rebound, too fast for

* Schiaffino would become the world's most expensive player after the World Cup, costing AC Milan 52 million lire.

Wilshaw to control properly, dropped just wide of his upright. The fact that it seemed a matter of time until England broke through again made what happened next such a hammer blow. With just five minutes to go before half-time, Uruguayan captain Obdulio Varela picked up the ball and began to advance. The England players dutifully stuck to their attackers as they surged towards Merrick's goal. The one eventuality they hadn't planned for was for Varela to simply keep going, eventually unleashing a brilliant strike into the corner past Merrick to give his country a scarcely deserved lead at the break. The rapturous celebrations of the Uruguayan team could be attributed to both the sheer brilliance of the goal and because none of them could quite believe they were winning.

Almost immediately after half-time, England found themselves even further behind as Schiaffino found space in the box and hammered the ball past Merrick; 3-1 down and with their hopes of progressing hanging by a thread, the English players could have been forgiven for letting their heads drop. However, although they were 'shaken', in Nat's words, they weren't yet beaten. The fortuitous goal they scored just after the hour mark gave Winterbottom's team fresh hope that their luck had turned. Dennis Wilshaw's cross caused havoc in the Uruguayan defensive ranks, and Finney rose with Maspoli to challenge. The ball dropped at the feet of Nat, who shimmied and shot through the legs of the recovering Uruguay custodian. Maspoli got enough on the shot to stop it, but Finney was on hand to stick out a leg and poke the ball over the line. The Preston winger ran straight to Nat to celebrate and was likely a bit taken aback when his close friend grabbed him around the waist and hoisted him off the ground in jubilation. It was no less than England deserved, and the wind was in their sails. Ivor Broadis, rarely less than an ebullient figure, was particularly vocal in urging his teammates on, telling his countrymen 'we've really got them this time' as they headed back to their half for the restart. 'In our hearts we all knew, as the crowd roared us on,' said Nat, 'that if we could get an equalizer we'd go on and win.' For the next ten minutes, England laid siege to Maspoli's goal, coming agonisingly close to drawing level on multiple occasions, including when Matthews, the unanimous selection for man of the match, struck the post.

Just as it appeared an England equaliser was inevitable, Uruguay roused themselves to put together the best move of the match, sweeping up the field and finding Javier Ambrois on the left of the area. Whether what he produced was a misplaced cross or a highly speculative shot, few would have given it much of a chance of beating a goalkeeper as experienced as Merrick, but the Birmingham City keeper, suffering in the sweltering heat, was caught off guard and the ball flew past him into the corner of the net. It was a cruel blow to England and Merrick in particular, who had been singled out for criticism in the wake of the two defeats to Hungary. With the score now at 4-2 and just over ten minutes remaining, the task proved beyond England's capabilities. Months later, Nat reflected, 'It was a game … I would never have missed. It has gone down in my memory as one of the best England has played since I was fortunate enough to gain my first cap. It was just one of those things that we didn't win.'

His feelings were echoed in the press, who were generally sympathetic to England following their exit. The unanimous verdict was that although England had put up a good fight and on another day could have advanced, their philosophy and game plan was too rigid and ill-equipped to deal with the pace and fluidity of the elite class of national teams. Despite boasting a talented squad capable of matching any other assembled in Switzerland, the players had been the victims of an outdated view of how the game should and could be played. It was, after the first match against Hungary, another watershed moment for English football, albeit one the FA, the press and the fans would take some years to recognise fully.

As the England players flew home, there was an air of disappointment and worry despite what had been a broadly respectable campaign. Just as had been the case following the previous World Cup and the 6-3 reverse to Hungary, there was a widespread expectation that the cruel and often indiscriminate scythe of the FA's selection committee would cut through the squad, despite the fact that teams like Hungary and Italy had credited a good deal of their success to maintaining a consistent team. With four years before the next tournament, English football was at a crossroads. The entire approach to the game, from selection policy to tactics to players, many of whom were now entering the twilight of their careers, needed overhauling. The Home Championships had begun to pale into insignificance, with the competition's credibility being undermined by England's relentless success while they experienced mounting problems against stronger international competition. The next four years presented the perfect opportunity for the FA to re-evaluate the situation.

All of this left the players, as they flew home from Basel, not knowing where they stood. Nat had emerged from Switzerland with his international reputation, on the wane over the previous season, bolstered. Two goals in two games meant he had maintained his remarkable scoring ratio, which now stood at twenty-three goals in just twenty-one games. He was also able to point to a record of having only lost two games in an England shirt – both to Uruguay – and, after the flux and uncertainty of recent times in the centre forward position, had proven himself never anything less than a reliable, consistent threat. He was also now one of the most important members of the international dressing room, bringing plenty of laughs and banter to proceedings and never shy of extending the same reassurance to new call-ups that he had received when collecting his first cap. It was a remarkable turnaround for a player who mere months before had been contemplating the serious possibility that his international career was finished.

An aerial view of Burnden Park. The left-most side of the ground is the imposing
Railway Embankment end, where the Burnden Disaster occured in 1946. (*Bolton News*)

A quick break from the football. Even during the Second World War, the community role
played by Bolton Wanderers and their players was undimmed. Here, Nat pays a visit to
adoring fans at Sunning Hill Youth Institute. (*Bolton News*)

Despite the spectre of the previous year's Burnden Disaster still looming large, Wanderers fans are out in force to watch the team in Cup action in 1947. (*Bolton News*)

'The best I've ever scored with my head': Nat puts England into the lead against Belgium at the 1954 World Cup with a superb diving header. The goal makes him, at age 28, England's youngest ever scorer at the World Cup. (Haynes Archive/Popperfoto/Getty Images)

oyed by their appearance in the Matthews Final the year before, Wanderers fans of all ages
eue to get their hands on tickets for the FA sixth round replay against Sheffield Wednesday.
olton News)

a for two: Nat and best mate and fellow England legend Sir Tom Finney enjoy some
freshments, the day before a match for the Three Lions against Spain at Wembley. (Sport and
neral/S&G and Barratts/EMPICS Sport/PA Images)

'He was a bit special': Son Jeff and daughter Viv pose with their doting father. (*Bolton News*)

Family time: Nat with wife Alma and daughter Viv enjoy a picnic in Rivington. (*Bolton News*)

Cheers! Nat behind the bar during his ill-fated spell at the Castle pub. (*Bolton News*)

Nat prepares for another titanic on-field clash as he leads out teammate Bryan Edwards as Bolton Wanderers captain. (*Bolton News*)

After an almost-three decade wait, Wanderers are FA Cup winners for a fourth time. There's no argument about who the man of the match is: captain and two-goal hero Nat Lofthouse. (*Bolton News*)

Hometown hero: Nat holds English football's most precious piece of silverware, the FA Cup, aloft from the steps of Bolton town hall. To his left are right half Derek Hennin and centre half John Higgins. (*Bolton News*)

Leeds United's Jackie Charlton (right) can only watch as Lofty hammers a volley in. (Colorsport/REX/Shutterstock)

Quite the sign-off: Nat nets his record-tying thirtieth goal for England in his thirty-second and penultimate appearance for his country, against the USSR at Wembley. (B. Thomas/S&G and Barratts/EMPICS Sport/PA Images)

Following his illustrious playing career, Nat endured a harsh and luckless spell as Bolton manager. (Peter Robinson/EMPICS Sport/PA Images)

The Lion roars: Nat takes to the Burnden Park pitch to lay down the law to hooligans who have besmirched the club's image. (*Bolton News*)

This is Your Life: Nat is surprised by Michael Aspel for an episode of the legendary television programme. (*Bolton News*)

10

A LEGEND IS BORN

AS LOFTY AND his Bolton Wanderers teammates trudged from the pitch on 30 April 1955 following a limp 1-0 reverse to Burnley in front of a meagre crowd of just over 20,000, there was a collective questioning of just where it had all gone wrong. After the heroics of the previous season, when the team had finished just nine points off the champions Wolverhampton Wanderers, Bill Ridding's team had slumped dramatically. They would ultimately finish eighteenth, just four points clear of the drop zone. What could have been the year they finally pushed for the title had nearly ended in disaster.

The team was, if anything, stronger on paper than the previous season. Utility forward Harry Webster and half back Bryan Edwards were both available full-time after completing their national service, and although Ray Parry was still serving, the fact he was stationed locally allowed him to make thirty appearances. The quest to better the previous year's finish had begun well, and the first four games had established a pattern: when Lofthouse scored, Bolton won. Five goals (including a brace against Portsmouth) in the opening six fixtures resulted in four wins and established Ridding's team as one to watch.

By November, however, the momentum had been well and truly lost, with seven of the first seventeen games ending in draws. It got even worse in December, as an injury to Nat in a 2-0 defeat at Sheffield

United kept him out for the next four games, all of which would end in defeat. Without doubt the most 'boom or bust' aspect of the Wanderers team was the attack. While Nat once again delivered a consistent (if somewhat muted) season, netting fifteen times despite injuries restricting him to just thirty-one appearances in the league, he was the exception. An article in *Sporting Life* commented, 'What a wonderful forward line Bolton have. Operating a combination of old and new styles which produce brilliant movements they threaten to sweep opponents out of the game.' However, the truth was often far from that assessment. Willie Moir, who turned 33 towards the end of the season, found the net just eight times in the league and was often forced to play out wide as a number seven in order to accommodate the emergence of Parry as a goal-scoring threat. Harold Hassall, having battled injuries and only recently fully recovered from an operation on the cartilage in his knee, was enjoying a strong campaign until New Year's Day, when he damaged his kneecap against Chelsea. Despite months of rehabilitation and a sustained attempt to make a comeback, his enormously promising career was finished at age 25. Nat's return in the next game, a 1–1 draw at Old Trafford against Manchester United, marked the club's best string of results in the league that season, with four wins (including a remarkable 6–1 thrashing of reigning champions Wolves at Burnden Park, a 'triumph for Wanderers' attacking game' that 'only a fanatic could have anticipated', according to the *Bolton Evening News'* Haydn Berry) and a single loss lifting the Trotters away from the lower reaches of the table. Another barren spell followed, with just two wins from the final ten matches to end a thoroughly wretched season.

While the club hadn't been shy of spending money in the post-war years, Bolton's directors still had no intention of trying to compete with the more heavily bankrolled teams. The £27,000 they had parted with for Hassall's services back in 1951 would remain their record transfer fee until 1967, several years after the abolition of the maximum wage had seen the amount of money being bandied about the game increase exorbitantly. The world transfer record in 1951 had been £34,500, just £7,500 more than Bolton's record; by the time the club paid £50,000 for Gareth

Williams in 1967, fees of more than double that had been exchanged regularly for years. Faced with the prospect of much of the 1953 final team moving past their peaks, Ridding and Taylor had little choice but to look inward at the club's youth system in order to replenish and revitalise the side. Ridding, some of the more senior players felt, preferred it this way; youth players were less likely to talk back or question him.

Tommy Banks, who had taken over at left fullback from his brother Ralph, was maturing into a skilled operator who, even in the age where bone-shuddering tackles were commonplace, stood out as someone who opposing players simply dreaded facing. Banks was probably the only player in the squad who could rival Nat in terms of fanaticism and love for the team, having spurned the advances of Arsenal and Manchester United in order to sign for his hometown club. On the opposite flank, Roy Hartle offered a near mirror image to the hard-tackling Banks. Mal Barrass, from Blackpool, and Bryan Edwards, from Leeds, had developed a strong partnership over the years, capable of launching attacks and aiding the side's defensive efforts in equal measure. Manchester-born Doug Holden had been providing a reliable supply of ammunition to Lofty for several seasons, and on the other wing, Ray Parry had emerged as one of the most exciting talents in English football, lending further weight to Ridding's conviction that he could rely on youth players just as much as the volatile and increasingly skewed transfer market. The Bolton manager needed only look at the club's youth team, who won the Central League championship for the first time that season, to be further vindicated. Worries about Stan Hanson's advancing years – the stopper turned 39 during the campaign – were eased considerably by 19-year-old Eddie Hopkinson, who had been poached from Oldham Athletic as an amateur and was now staking a serious claim for first-team consideration.

For all the upheaval on the international scene following the World Cup and the rebuilding that was taking place at Burnden, Nat's home life was comparatively settled. His relationship with Alma had never shown any signs of wavering, and with their two children growing up before their eyes, he was never short of gratitude towards his wife for the long hours she put in caring for Jeff and Viv during the incessant stream of away games and England tours abroad. She had become close friends with the wives of many of the other Bolton players, as well as Tom Finney's wife, Elsie, and the women kept one another company while their husbands were away. Lofty liked to give Alma a reprieve from looking after the children whenever he could, and they still regularly enjoyed a trip to the pictures and going out for meals. The old adage of there being a great woman behind every great man was undoubtedly true of the Lofthouses. For all the work that George Taylor and George Hunt had put in to develop Nat as a player, it was Alma who had the job twenty-four hours a day, and she had developed a knack of knowing when to lend a sympathetic ear and let her husband talk his worries out and when he simply needed to be told to stop griping or worrying about whatever injury or poor spell of form was affecting him. She was no shrinking violet, and never failed to give as good as she got in the banter stakes (she 'would let me know when I'd had a bad game!'), even though her husband had been seasoned by the naturally bawdy nature of First Division dressing rooms.

With the flurries of excitement that his job brought week in, week out, it was little surprise that Nat had strived to keep his home life and activities as uncomplicated as possible. To say that the cliché of the 1950s footballer being a man of the people, happy to walk down the street and enjoy a kick about with the neighbourhood kids on his way to pick up the paper, has been well worn is to make a considerable understatement. Yet, as with so many common platitudes, it is grounded in truth. Many a Bolton youngster from the time remembers a game of street football being briefly interrupted by the very man they all dreamt of emulating and who they pretended to be when playing. Nat delighted in the simple pleasures of life. Unlike some who found fame (although he would scoff at the notion that he could be considered 'famous') to be burdensome or a source of worry, he considered the fact that people knew his face and would volunteer their thoughts on the game he loved an added bonus of being a player. From his playing heyday through to his later years, one of the recurring themes in the memories of the fans he met was that he made each and every one of them feel special, whether by greeting them as 'cocker' (which he used ubiquitously) or by simply taking the time to stop and chat. Jeff remembers one particular school sports day that was 'completely disrupted' when his schoolmates noticed the illustrious member of the watching group of parents: 'The sports day was spoiled a little bit, from the headmaster's point of view, by all the kids gathering around my father for his autograph. I realised then that he was a bit special.'

Even as England travelled further afield and games against other improving nations took on added significance, the Three Lions' annual match against Scotland remained, along with the FA Cup Final, the showpiece occasion of the footballing calendar. It was one of the few occasions that Lofty had failed to rise to, with one of his 'greatest ambitions' – scoring against the Scots – unfulfilled after two caps. Now, he had a chance to put that right. Nat had been dropped for two matches following his failure to find the net in England's first game after the World Cup against Northern Ireland, but his replacement Ronnie Allen couldn't capitalise on his opportunity and Nat was brought back into the fold for the 1955 meeting with the Old Enemy.

England's previous match had been a stirring 3-1 victory over the reigning World Cup holders West Germany – a result that reinvigorated the country's hopes that the national team were turning a corner after the humbling results of the previous two years. Helped by three debutants, including the youngest England player of the century, Manchester United's 18-year-old phenomenom Duncan Edwards, England's post-World Cup resurgence would continue in spectacular fashion as they didn't so much beat Scotland as annihilate them.

The tone was set straight from the referee's whistle as Nat's shot was saved and Dennis Wilshaw swept home the rebound within sixty seconds. The immediacy of England's goal stunned the Scots, and worse was to come as it became apparent that Stanley Matthews was in the mood to prove that age was just a number as only he could. Matthews so bewitched the Scottish players in the opening exchanges that they were more than happy to allow Don Revie space and time to loft a ball towards Nat. There appeared to be little danger thanks to some tight marking from Tommy Docherty, until Lofty performed a piece of skill that in many ways typified his greatest assets as a centre forward. Taking the ball on his chest, with one deft touch he was free of Docherty and surging into the box. While a less experienced player may have been tempted to hammer the ball in immediately, Nat knew he had the time to take another touch and, with Docherty sliding in and Scottish keeper Fred Martin rushing from his line, he powered the ball into the net. Lawrie Reilly pulled one back for the visitors, but even the Scottish players sensed this reduction in arrears wasn't likely to stem the tide. Lofthouse struck a post with a header and Revie scored his second in two caps to take the score to 3-1, before Nat made it four before half-time, the grateful recipient of a neat cut back from the rampant Matthews. Ten years later, in a newspaper piece, Matthews would describe the goal and Nat's overall performance with breathless admiration:

> Then came one of those goals that knock the stuffing out of a team … a goal that has the fans throbbing and stirs the hearts of even the most experienced players. Lofthouse was magnificent in the air, deadly with his right foot given half a chance anywhere in the box … and he tore the heart out of the Scots with this fourth goal. I can remember making my move down the right, bang up to the goal line. I pulled the ball back just inside the box. And there was Lofthouse the Lionheart – how aptly named he was – thundering in. He hit the ball with his right foot, and it went in like a thunderbolt.

The theme continued in the second half, with Wilshaw adding another three to his personal tally to become the first England player to net four in a single game against Scotland, before Docherty netted a free kick for the most meagre of consolations as the match finished 7-2. The final whistle had journalists flicking the pages of their almanacs all the way back to 1888 to find a game in which England had beaten Scotland by such a hefty margin.

As Bolton limped across the line to safety, Nat was virtually assured of his place in the England team for the post-season tour of continental Europe. The tour would lack the glamour of the trip to the Americas two years before or the prestige of the World Cup the previous summer, but nonetheless would prove to be a memorable one for those involved, and another chastening moment for the beleaguered Football Association. Nat flew out on twenty-five goals for his country, now one ahead of his great friend Tom Finney (who missed the entire tour through injury) and just four shy of the all-time record set by Vivian Woodward in 1911.[*] The tour ultimately proved a damp squib for Nat, who failed to score, and served as a reminder to England of the lessons of the past two years. Defeats to France and Portugal – two teams England had historically dominated – were a testament to the generally improving quality of European nations. The Portugal match was a particularly painful one for Nat. Nearing half-time, he challenged for a ball with all the bravery he had exhibited countless times throughout the years. This time, he came off worse than usual, receiving a Portuguese boot straight to the face, knocking him out cold. Groggy and bloodied, he wasn't able to continue, and without their focal point England faltered badly. Ironically, the game enhanced Nat's England credentials further, as it demonstrated the stark contrast between the team's abilities to form coherent attacks with him on the pitch and without him. However, Lofty knew as well as anyone that the FA were equally likely to find fault with him for being injured in the first place as they were to connect the dots between England's performance before Nat was injured and afterwards.

In between these two defeats was a trip to Madrid to face Spain and a game that Nat would describe as 'the hardest-earned draw I've ever played in', quipping 'there were times in that game when I wondered if they'd got our match mixed up with the tussle scheduled for later in the week in the nearby bullring'. Lofty's account of the game is characteristically humble, and fails to mention that he was stripped of the England

---

[*] Just as Nat's legend owed much to Austria, so too did Woodward's; of his twenty-nine goals for England, nine came in just three games against them.

number nine shirt – not by the FA but by an opposing player. Having bested his marker and begun his advance on goal, he found himself on the receiving end of a tackle so rudimentary and lacking in subtlety that even the most clogging lower league centre half would have cringed at the thought of it. Such was Nat's determination to keep going even in the face of such a crude attempt to stop him that his shirt was ripped to the point of worthlessness. He completed the game in a spare kit without a number on the back. Nat did deem it worthy to mention that such was the brutality exhibited by the Spanish that it was the 'first and only time the great Sir Stanley [Matthews] ever lost his cool on a football pitch'. Having been repeatedly fouled by Jesús Garay (who didn't make 'one genuine attempt to go for the ball all afternoon. It's a wonder Stanley didn't break both his legs'), Matthews told Roy Bentley that he 'could spit at [Garay]'. Bentley responded, 'Spit at him! Never mind spitting at him, Stan. Bloody well kick him back.' England refused 'to get involved in a kicking match … there was always national pride at stake' and were happy to get off the pitch relatively unscathed with a 1–1 draw, even though the scoreline flattered the Spanish.

The mood on the flight home didn't rival the despondency that had been felt in the England camp in recent times, but only because the players and Walter Winterbottom had, deep down, accepted that what was happening wasn't a blip. For all the personnel changes of recent times, they still had a team with an incredibly talented core; their performances and results were indicative of something more fundamentally wrong. What there was no doubting was the inevitability of the FA swinging the axe in their next team selection in a desperate attempt to find a formula that could restore the country to its former glory.

Over the previous months, England had resembled a small sailing boat caught in the eye of a ferocious storm – a helpless vessel hopelessly out of its depth. Ironically, given such uncertainty and flux, Nat was relatively sure of his position in the team, particularly compared to the previous season when his role had come under such scrutiny. He had been given a chance to prove himself at the World Cup and had grabbed it with both hands. There was no question now that, whether or not he was always the most in-form striker in the country at any one time, nobody had delivered as consistently as Lofty had.

The 1955/56 season brought wholesale changes at Burnden Park, as Bill Ridding effectively drew a line under the team that had come so close to FA Cup success in 1953 and forged on with a dramatic rebuilding process. Willie Moir, one of Burnden's great post-war heroes, departed the club soon after the start of the season, replaced at inside forward by another product of the Bolton youth academy, Dennis Stevens. Stan Hanson was phased out in favour of trialling some of the club's talented crop of goalkeepers. Roy Hartle, who had been cruelly denied a spot in the 1953 final team, finally made the right back spot his own and quickly became a fan favourite. Future Bolton chairman Phil Gartside recalled, 'It looked as if a runaway train wouldn't stop him and I almost, but not quite, felt sorry for the wingers whose duty it was to try to get round Roy and stay in one piece.'*

Whereas Nat had emerged from a core group in the early 1950s to become the team's talisman, for the new-look generation he would be focal point, elder statesman and, most notably, leader. With Moir's departure, Johnny Wheeler assumed the captaincy and Nat the vice-captaincy. He would eventually captain the side in Wheeler's absence for the first time against Huddersfield Town in the FA Cup third round. It was a role he took to with enormous pride, yet not without a tinge of sadness. The likes of Hanson, Moir and Barrass had all been mates, and although Nat would never be shy to join in with the dressing room banter with the revamped team, the younger plays recognised him as a role model first and a close friend second. Proactive leadership was never a role that sat particularly easily with Nat. He was at his best when leading through example, dragging the team through hard-fought games with his goals or, failing that, his perennial desire to hassle and harry every opposition player for the ball until he got a chance to stick it in the net. Actually leading a group simply wasn't in his DNA; although by no means shy, he was always more at ease when he was one of the lads, not trying to tell them what to

---

*   John Gradwell, *Legend: The Life of Roy 'Chopper' Hartle*, p. 7.

do. The captaincy, which he would ultimately win on a permanent basis, wasn't so formal an arrangement that he struggled with it – it was more an acknowledgement of his experience and his service to the club. However, in future endeavours, whether it was running his pub or managing the club, he would find this natural aversion to leading to be to his detriment.

Any worries about Wanderers' ongoing overhaul coming at the cost of another relegation battle in the 1955/56 season were dispelled by the team's start to the campaign. Having often begun seasons a touch off the pace in the goal-scoring stakes (invariably due to his involvement in taxing England tours or, in 1953, injury), Nat had bucked the trend of the previous season with six goals in the opening seven fixtures. In 1955, having had plenty of time to recuperate following the brief England tour, he came into the season fresh and simply exploded. In the first ten games he scored single goals against Charlton Athletic, Cardiff City and Tottenham, braces away at Portsmouth and Aston Villa, and a hat-trick against Arsenal. Though once again dogged by inconsistency (Wanderers beat reigning champions Chelsea 2-0 at Stamford Bridge, then lost at home to Charlton a week later), the Trotters were looking up the table rather than down as they had the season before.

Bolton had failed to break the habit of relying on Nat to fire them to victory. Of the eleven victories they secured in the opening half of the season, only two of them came despite Nat not scoring, and only one without him on the pitch, when he missed a home victory over Wolves to play for England against Denmark. Luckily for all concerned, Nat happened to be in exceptional form. Remarkably, between October and the end of December, he scored in seven games, but only netted a single goal in two of those matches. He scored his third, fourth and fifth braces of the season in a run of just four games against Luton Town, Manchester United (in a 3-1 win made all the more impressive as United ultimately won the title at a canter) and Sheffield United. A couple of weeks later, he enjoyed a remarkable home stand against Birmingham City and then Chelsea, netting four against the former and then a more modest hat-trick against the latter. At this stage, the Burnden Aces were in fifth, just three points shy of leaders United, and even the most cautious of Bolton fans were beginning to entertain the prospect that this could finally be the season where the stars aligned. Nat's form was scintillating, but given his age and his record across his career, it wasn't a huge surprise. The now 30-year-old's injury troubles had been limited, and he had yet to lose any of the explosiveness and precision with which he had made his name. The combination of a physically fit body with a seasoned knowledge of what to do with it was proving a deadly combination.

As Wanderers slipped back into the more familiar reaches of mid-table as winter turned to spring and their involvement in the FA Cup ended in the fourth round, Bolton fans would have had little to look forward to for the rest of the season were it not for one man. Lofthouse had won numerous England honours, as well as being named the 1953 FWA Footballer of the Year. One title that had eluded him, however, was that of being the First Division's top goal scorer. Since the war, the top scorer had needed an average of just over twenty-six goals to claim the title, with Dennis Westcott's total of thirty-seven in the first season after the cessation representing the high-water mark. Nat's key competition came from Sunderland's inside forward Charlie Fleming, whose final tally of twenty-nine would have been enough to see him finish top in five of the previous nine years. Unfortunately for 'Cannonball Charlie' it was another forward with thunder in his boots who denied him his chance at owning a piece of football history. A goal in a hard-fought loss to Arsenal at Highbury on New Year's Eve sparked a run where Nat found the net seven times in ten games. At this point, he was on an incredible thirty-one goals, well beyond the mean for being crowned the top scorer, having played just thirty-one games. A muscle strain forced him out of four games and then a rushed return brought his form back down to earth, but his final total of thirty-three league goals was comfortably enough to see him finish as the First Division's leading scorer. It was a triumphant end to the club season, but on the international stage, things had been anything but.

It had started well enough, with Nat starring in a 5-1 thrashing of Denmark in Copenhagen in October, netting twice to bring his record back to a goal a game on the occasion of his twenty-seventh cap. The victory was a tonic for the disappointing defeat to Portugal, and came despite the FA deciding to limit the squad to just one man from each club. The victory was to prove an exception in Nat's international season. The next three matches he competed in signalled the beginning of the end for his England career.

Despite now being agonisingly close to Vivian Woodward's status as his country's top scorer, Nat simply couldn't get over the line. Needing just two more goals to match Woodward (he'd score at least two in nine separate games for Bolton that year), Lofty endured the worst drought of his international career, going three full games without registering. Despite an extremely strong attack, England would lose their next game 2-1 to Wales, seventeen years to the day that their neighbours had last bested the Three Lions. In uncharacteristic fashion, perhaps with the England record in the back of his mind, Nat was guilty of squandering a glorious chance to equalise late on, badly scuffing a finish when one on one with goalkeeper Jack Kelsey.

Nat's punishment for his failure to find a way past the Welsh defence was being dropped for the next game, before being recalled for the year's mid-season showpiece, a return visit of Spain. The mist that shrouded Wembley before the match would have had the England players wondering if *La Roja*, after their brutal approach to the game in Madrid, had brought the literal fog of war with them, but their fears quickly abated once the game began. Spain, wary that they would be playing in front of more than 80,000 at Wembley and not the partisan fans of the Bernabeu, reigned in their more untoward tactics and, opting to try to go toe to toe with England on footballing merit alone, were pummelled. The 4-1 scoreline was flattering to the visitors, and should have been at least one more when Nat was denied his goal by a dubious offside decision.

The next match against Scotland, contested just over a year after the 7-2 mauling that would remain one of Nat's career highlights, promised to be a different proposition entirely. Played at the always-hostile Hampden Park and with Scotland desperate to restore some national pride, the opposition game plan centred around remaining compact and denying England the freedom to run riot again. The game was given some added spice by the situation in the Home Championships. The winner of the game would win the tournament, while a draw would result in a four-way tie. The Scottish tactics worked perfectly as they took the lead and looked to have won the game until a somewhat fortuitous last-minute equaliser from Johnny Haynes. Ever the team player, Nat, who had endured another frustrating match with limited service, rushed to celebrate with his teammates and congratulate Haynes, even with the knowledge that the game would be a third black mark against him in a row. Tommy Taylor had enjoyed a superb season leading the line for champions Manchester United. Having been previously deployed as an inside forward for England, the FA now had little recourse but to give the United man a shot at his favoured position. For Nat, it was the beginning of the end. He was under no illusions: 'I thought my international career was over.'

It's difficult to pinpoint quite what affected Nat during this period. Clearly, his form was not an issue, as he continued to score freely and dominate defences up and down the country for Bolton between his fruitless efforts for England. Nor was the quality of the opposition the root cause of trouble. Nat's fellow forwards punctured the Spanish defence on four occasions. The Wales and Scotland teams were well drilled and obstinate, but the same could be said of the other defences that Bolton pitted their wits against and that Nat routinely put to the sword. Of course, sheer dumb luck – or in this case an acute lack of – certainly played a part. Nat's record for his country was nothing short of prodigious. It was only because he was so prolific that a three-game drought deserves such microscopic attention. However, to merely dismiss this barren run as a fluke is to do an injustice to a career in which Nat was rarely less than the epitome of consistency.

What almost certainly factored into this run was a return of the familiar nerves that had dogged Nat throughout his career. The pressure of pursuing Woodward's record, of being one of England's main men, of the acute awareness of the fickleness of the FA all contributed to Nat's shaky, nervy showings. A further cause of worry was financial.

LOFTY

Playing for England was a privilege first and foremost, but it was relatively lucrative when compared to the wages doled out at Burnden Park, and there was no guarantee that it would continue much longer. The victory over Denmark was Nat's first England match since turning 30, a milestone that often spelled the end of international careers. The knowledge that every missed chance, every opportunity that went unfinished could be his last created a maelstrom of worries and gave his form for club and country that year a Jekyll and Hyde appearance.

It came as no surprise when he didn't receive the call to start England's next game, against Brazil. The FA signalled the beginning of a sea change in the team, debuting a much younger-looking side. The average age of the front five was 26, even with the 41-year-old Matthews in his familiar outside-right role. England earned a morale-boosting 4-2 win over the team considered by many the best in the world. The victory would, in the long term, prove to be to the detriment of the country, papering over the cracks that had been exposed by Hungary and Uruguay, but at the time it appeared to be a new dawn for the team, and the 24-year-old Taylor, who netted twice from centre forward, seemed to be the man to whom England could turn. If there had been any lingering hope that Nat may still have a role to play in the team following the win over the *Selecao*, the end-of-season tour extinguished it. Despite being a key member of the travelling party, Lofty's role on the pitch was far more marginal as England faced Sweden, Finland and finally world champions West Germany. Taylor started all three matches, and Nat wouldn't have got on the pitch at all were it not for an injury to the Manchester United man midway through the second game in Helsinki.

Freed of the expectations that normally went with the England number nine shirt by the knowledge that no matter what he did, he was unlikely to wrest the role from Taylor, Nat snapped from the paralysis in which he had played for England over recent months. His first goal, in the sixty-third minute, put the game beyond reach of Finland, who had been 3-0 down by the point when Taylor left the field. The match could well have fizzled out with the score now 4-1, but for one fact. Nat was now level with the legendary Steve Bloomer on twenty-eight goals,* in second place on the all-time England goal-scoring list and one solitary goal from tying Viv Woodward's record. If the achievement of matching Woodward, which Lofty finally managed with his second goal in the eighty-second minute, was apt for a season in which he'd secured his legacy as one of the best forwards in league football history, the manner in which he matched Woodward's tally was befitting of a season where very little had gone right for him on the international stage. Rather than a powerful strike or a trademark towering header beyond the reach of the goalkeeper, Lofty's record-equalling goal was a weakly headed effort from a corner. A Finnish defender and the goalkeeper both had ample opportunity to clear; both assumed the other would do so, and both watched in horror as the ball trickled over the line.

It was a moment of joy and celebration, with Nat seeing the funny side of his worst goal on the international stage being his record one and telling the British press it 'was blinking fantastic' to have reached the milestone. The moment was made bittersweet by the knowledge that his time as an England regular seemed to be coming to an end.

Despite Taylor's usurping of him, Nat never bore any ill will to a player for whom he was never short of praise. In later years, he'd freely admit that in his opinion, Taylor was destined to 'become the greatest centre forward of them all … I don't recall Tommy Taylor having any weaknesses at all.' Nat's assessment was more magnanimous than that found in some quarters of the media. The *Daily Herald*'s George Fellows, writing after a lacklustre 1-1 draw with Ireland in which Taylor failed to score, wrote that the United star 'changed his club style and tried to play like Nat Lofthouse. Nat is much better at that.'

---

* So famous was Bloomer's record that many newspapers paid closer attention to Nat's chase for that accolade than they did the overall record. Some newspapers even erroneously claimed that Bloomer's was still the overall record for the national team.

For Bolton Wanderers, the outlook was much brighter, even with Nat aware that the end of his time on the pitch was slowly creeping into view. He had had the good fortune to avoid any serious injuries – no mean feat given the no-holds-barred manner in which he still approached every game. Despite turning 31 at the beginning of the new season, he'd lost none of the physical prowess that made him such a formidable challenge for opposing defenders, to which West Bromwich Albion's centre half Joe Kennedy could all too readily attest. At the tail end of the previous campaign, 'Spring-Heeled Joe', so called because of his fantastic ability in the air, broke his collarbone when he attempted to meet Nat in an aerial duel. Harry Johnston, Blackpool's defensive stalwart, summed up just how critical this aspect of Nat's game was to Bolton's game plan: 'The whole depends on Nat Lofthouse's skill in getting up to the ball.'*

Even with Nat's abilities showing no signs of waning, Hassall's untimely retirement was still fresh in the minds of the Bolton Wanderers squad – a pertinent reminder of the fleeting nature of a football career. The maximum wage hadn't been raised from £15 a week since 1953, and even though it would receive a bump in two consecutive years, 1957 and 1958 (first to £17 a week during the season, then to £20), the money still wasn't close to being enough to live off for long after retiring. The average weekly wage at the time in the country hovered just under £10 (the real boon of a career in football remained not the money, but the jobs it kept the usually working-class players out of in the first place), and even with post-war austerity beginning to lift, it was still a time of scrimping, saving and making do. Nat was supplementing his income with his work as a paint salesman, and had begun speaking engagements around the country during the week. Tommy Banks remembers one of Nat's friends driving him the length and breadth of Britain each week, so much so that the Bolton players began referring to the driver as 'Mrs Lofthouse'. Even so, with his England appearance pay cheques apparently at an end, he knew he needed to start planning for his future, particularly with Jeff and Viv growing up and starting school. Fortuitously, a seemingly

* 'Bolton's non-stop brand of football pays dividends', *South China Morning Post*, 1955.

perfect opportunity would land in his lap within months of the new season beginning.

With the press, fans and even Nat himself in agreement that his time on the international stage was over, he was free for the first time since 1950 to focus solely on Bolton Wanderers. He had never been less than professional regarding his dual roles and was careful not to appear boastful to his Wanderers teammates about his international status. However, it would be naive to believe that there weren't times when he was giving his joints a pounding while running the Burnden Park gravel track in the rain that his mind didn't at least momentarily drift to thoughts of slightly more glamorous surroundings with England.

Bolton could also look forward to having a Lofty with a point to prove. He may not have been able to change the selection committee's mind about his future with the national team, but he could at least give fans up and down the country a timely reminder that he was still Lofty, the Lion of Vienna, while rankling the stuffed shirts at Lancaster Gate in the process.

As if he needed any further motivation, the 1956/57 campaign marked the point when Nat became the true leader of the Bolton Wanderers dressing room. Veteran Stan Hanson had played his last game the previous season, replaced by a 20-year-old stopper named Eddie Hopkinson who instantly made the position his own, with England honours following soon after. Club captain Johnny Wheeler was sold for £9,000 to Liverpool, with Ridding and George Taylor rightly confident in the abilities of Derek Hennin to take over at wing half. Another of Nat's great friends and a veteran of the Matthews Final, Mal Barrass, was too replaced by another product of the Burnden youth system, John Higgins. These departures of key men meant one thing: Nat Lofthouse was now Bolton Wanderers captain.

Nat bettered his scintillating start to the previous season, scoring in eight of the opening nine games, netting twelve goals in all. A hat-trick against Blackpool and Harry Johnston was evidence that although it wasn't difficult to identify how Bolton played, stopping them from putting their plan into action was another thing entirely. Despite his sensational run, it came as little surprise to anyone when Nat's anticipated omission from the England team was rubber-stamped by the release of the squad for the October internationals. Tommy Taylor continued at centre forward, but his failure to score against Ireland saw Tom Finney drafted in as a makeshift striker. The brave new dawn the England top brass had hoped they were ushering in by phasing out the likes of Lofthouse had got off to an inauspicious start.

Nat's superb run was ended not by a dip in form, but by injury, in late October, with inside forward Terry Allcock deputising for Nat for six matches; they would be the only games Lofty would miss for the entire campaign. His haul of twenty-eight goals (Bolton in total managed just sixty-five) wasn't enough to see him retain his First Division top goal scorer title, but was another chapter in an already incredible story. In one remarkable match against Wolves, Bolton had found themselves 3-0 down and with a goalkeeper nursing what looked an awful lot like a broken finger. Sure enough, Hopkinson was unable to continue and, with no possibility of bringing on a substitute goalkeeper for the second half, Ridding opted to avoid upsetting the team's structure as much as possible and put Nat in goal. Bolton clawed two goals back to give themselves a chance at the unlikeliest of draws, before Roy Hartle turned goalkeeper himself, stopping a shot with his hand after it had beaten the sprawling Lofty. It fell to young Wolves outside right Harry Hooper to take the resultant penalty, with the more experienced strikers in the team perhaps demurring on the grounds that if they missed, they would simply *never* live it down. Their reticence proved wise, as Hooper struck the penalty low and straight, only for Nat to plunge down and make the save. Even with the defeat, the remarkable turn of events allowed Nat to particularly enjoy that week's traditional Saturday evening beer.[*]

Despite Nat's marvellous form, however, the season had once again proved frustrating. Wanderers again looked capable of mounting a title challenge, beating champions-to-be Manchester United home and away,

---

[*] If this wasn't remarkable enough, Nat had also had to deputise between the sticks in the previous season's trip to Molineux as well, making a good save during an eight-minute spell while Joe Dean received treatment.

but fell foul of inconsistency and a lack of reliable scorers outside of Nat, eventually finishing ninth. 'They were definitely a top six team without any shadow of a doubt,' remembers Terry Allcock. Young stars such as Dennis Stevens and Ray Parry were displaying ability enough that it was hoped they could yet replace the Wanderers class of '53, but the mid-table finish was a huge disappointment. Whites fans were left pondering what might have been, as well as just what impact an extremely public spat between the club and their star man had had on the team's form.

Retirement plans were gradually occupying a larger part of Nat's mind, and the apparent end of his time with England served only as a reminder that there would come a point when he would no longer be the first name on the Bolton team sheet either. His work as a salesman and his speaking appearances were nice supplements to his income, but wouldn't bring in enough once his career was over. 'Alma and I had reached the stage where we were thinking long and hard about what we would do when I finally had to quit football,' recalled Nat, so it must have seemed like a blessing when what appeared an ideal solution materialised. Walker's brewery were on the hunt for someone to take over the running of their pub, the Castle. As the name suggests, the pub was located close to Nat's former school and was an easy drive from both his home on Temple Road and from Burnden Park. Lofty was a canny choice by Walker's, even if he had no prior experience of pulling pints. Much like how his paint selling was made easier by the fact that many were happy to part with a couple of shillings for paint they might never need if it meant they got to chat with Mr Bolton Wanderers himself, so too did Walker's bank on having the most famous man in town behind the bar guaranteeing a few extra punters through the door. Better yet, once the Lofthouse name had got them in, then the Lofty charm, wit and repartee would help keep them there – something that was more than could be said for many footballers-turned-publicans. For Nat and Alma, it would give them a steady income and was a way for Nat to leverage some of his fame to help continue to support his family.

With taking over as landlord of the Castle such a good fit for both Nat and Walker's, it seemed a match made in heaven. That was until, to Lofty's astonishment, Bolton Wanderers attempted to put the kibosh on matters. The club's directors felt that while contracted to Bolton, Nat's pay of £17 a week during the season was more than sufficient to keep him from taking a significant second occupation, and cited an old rule the club had that prohibited players from living on licensed premises. They told their star in no uncertain terms that he would not be permitted to take over the pub. A statement was issued, reading, 'The Board find no justification for relaxing the club rule, which they feel sure serves in the best interests of the club and player.' Despite Nat's protestations about the nature of the role – 'It wasn't as if I was rushing straight back from training to open the doors and pull pints. It was a big pub, with bar staff and a cellarman. I was more of a front man' – the directors would not be swayed, and put Ridding and Taylor in an invidious position by issuing the ultimatum that if Nat took the job, he would no longer feature in the team. These back and forths inevitably made their way into the press, first featuring in the pages of the *Bolton Evening News* before filtering into national coverage when it became apparent that the club may be seriously considering freezing Nat out or even, incredibly, selling him.

Newspapers reported that Bolton had made it known to other clubs that they would listen to offers of £12,000. The *Lancashire Evening Post* reported several clubs in the county were interested, but that Bolton's valuation of 'this fine player' had 'frightened most of them away'.* Haydn Berry in the *Bolton Evening News* came at the issue from the opposite direction, explaining that Bolton's problem would not be finding suitors for Nat, but 'replacing him'. Rather than feeling the 'chicken feed' asking price was too high, Berry, who was a personal friend of Lofty and had revelled in covering his progress from raw prospect to bona fide star, argued that 'any club quoting less than £20,000 would get a quick answer from me'. 'To limit his future to another season or so,' contended the venerable scribe, 'is the height of impertinence. He remains an England possible and is still a coveted match-winner.'**

Blackburn Rovers made an offer that was turned down as too low, while Ridding came out in the press with a somewhat uncharacteristic show of

★   *Lancashire Evening Post*, 15 March 1957.

★★ *Bolton Evening News*, 15 March 1957.

support for his player rather than the club, demonstrative of the strong bond between the two men. The manager acknowledged that, while it was 'a very difficult situation and so far as I am concerned there is much to be said for both club and player', Nat was only acting in order to 'safeguard his future'.*

It is possible to see some logic in the club's actions. After all, if the team's star was taking a second job as a publican, it was a tacit acknowledgement of footballers' wages being unfairly low – one that could come back to bite them should the whispers about the abolition of the maximum wage come to fruition. On the other hand, as soon as word was out that Wanderers were doing the unthinkable and entertaining the idea of selling the Lion of Vienna, their backs were to the wall, despite Nat's later assertion that 'I wasn't really in the driving seat. There was no freedom of contract in those days and if Wanderers had dug their heels in I would have been out in the cold.' The fans would never side with a group that, as football fans have immemorial, they always eyed with suspicion no matter how well run the club appeared. What effect this rigmarole had on the club's morale and form through the final lean months of the 1956/57 campaign is impossible to quantify. However, to see the team's talisman, captain and 'icon even then', in the words of Terry Allcock, treated so firmly by the club could not have done wonders for team spirit.

As Blackburn's interest continued, the fan reaction to the idea of their beloved hero turning out in the white and blue of their fierce rivals (in the Second Division, no less) killed any possibility of the club acting upon their strong words. 'I like to think that good sense prevailed,' said Nat, who took charge of the Castle soon after the season ended, signed his yearly playing contract in June and reported to pre-season training soon after with not so much as a shrug in the direction of the spurned directors. Bill Ridding's statement to the press merely read 'both parties have come to a satisfactory conclusion', while Nat's statement assured the fans that 'I am very pleased it is all over. I have been a one-club man all my career and want it to continue that way.' As Nat would later write, 'the twin roles couldn't have done much harm … we went on to win the FA Cup'.

★   *Star Green 'Un*, 9 March 1957.

11

WEMBLEY REDEMPTION

AS THE 1957/58 season dawned, Britain was on the up. The worst of the post-war malaise had been swept away, and the green shoots of prosperity were finally appearing. Emboldened by more spending power than they'd ever known, newly termed 'teenagers' were making their cultural impact on the country. In Liverpool, mere miles from Bolton, two young men by the names of Paul McCartney and George Harrison, not sufficiently tempted by Johnny Wheeler's arrival at Anfield from Burnden Park to abandon their instruments, joined a local skiffle outfit led by another local lad, John Lennon. The enthusiasm with which these young men threw themselves into their music was indicative of the growing prosperity in the country as a whole, as Britain cast off the shackles of austerity. Players who had been paid double the average industrial wage before the war now found themselves earning little more than labourers – a disparity they felt hardly justified their talents. Within three years, the country's growing wealth would trigger the collapse of the financial agreement that professional football had been built upon for more than half a century. Before that day of financial reckoning, however, Bolton Wanderers would write themselves into history with a team that cost a remarkable £110 to construct.

With the last remnants of a paid-for team gone from Bolton's ranks, Bill Ridding, by now officially operating in the dual role as manager–

secretary, was playing a potentially dangerous game. More and more clubs were throwing themselves heedlessly down the slippery slope of stumping up astronomical sums for players, bemoaning the need to spend while contributing directly to the issue. Ridding's decision to prevent Wanderers getting involved as much as he could avoid it was part thrifty, part courageous and perhaps part foolhardy. As the club set out in August 1957, he christened them the '£110 team' – because every member of the first-choice starting XI had only cost the club the sum of £10, the standard signing on fee. The previous two seasons had demonstrated that, despite some naivety and rawness, this group of players were capable of competing with the best of them. The team Ridding had built and George Taylor and George Hunt had moulded was defined by its physical strength ('Bolton had a tradition as a tough team,' remembers Doug Holden) and a willingness to fight to the end. 'We never lost until the 90th minute,' says Tommy Banks. 'All the players were workers.' Jimmy Greaves, who would emerge as a star at Chelsea that year, summed up the prevailing attitude to Bolton among opposition players: 'Bolton was a place where men were truly men. We feared their sheer brute force. For those of us who they regarded as Southern Softies there was no more daunting place to visit.'[*]

Unlike the previous two years in which they had started strongly, the 1957/58 campaign began badly. Two defeats – one a 6-1 reverse against Wolves – and an injury to Nat quickly put paid to any notions of a title challenge. A win and a draw without Nat led to Ridding taking an unprecedented decision when Lofty returned to fitness, with Terry Allcock, who had deputised in the centre forward role, retaining his spot. Allcock remembers:

> The players enjoyed the way I played there; I was less of a target man and more a link up player, different to the style Nat was. When he made his comeback, Nat was asked to play on the right wing. It only happened for one or two games but the players had requested it. It seems they thought we played more constructive football. He only played a couple of games on the wing, and you can understand his position.

[*]   Ian Seddon, *Ah'm Tellin' Thee: Tommy Banks, Bolton Wanderers and England*, p. 167.

If I was in his position I wouldn't have wanted to do that either. I'm sure he must have knocked on the manager's door!

It was the first time Nat had been asked to play out of position for club or country since 1949. The *Bolton Evening News*' Haydn Berry noted that Nat gave a 'fair' performance 'without looking very happy', as he scored and set up another in a 3-2 Wanderers win. Although his position as the leader of the players had been enshrined in the awarding of the captaincy, Nat had never been so aware of his footballing shelf life as when he saw another player's name by the number nine on the team sheet in the dressing room at Leicester's Filbert Street ground. As well as a reward for Allcock's fine form, the decision may have been encouraged by the board as retribution for the Castle pub disagreement. Whatever the reason, the inescapable truth was that in past years, it would have been nigh on impossible to justify not placing the Lion of Vienna at the heart of the forward line. Perhaps encouraged by Nat's shunting to the wing, Blackburn Rovers returned to bid for the striker, as they had when tensions over the Castle were at their height. While they had been politely turned down before, Bill Ridding was this time more bullish in his rebuttal, informing the press that 'Blackburn Rovers have as much chance of signing Nat as we have of persuading them to part with Bryan Douglas – and Douglas would be very welcome on our staff'.*

Playing out of position wasn't the only thing that had Nat looking around with a sense of the game beginning to change. The gravel track and sand pit in front of the Burnden Stand were left dormant as the club moved their training sessions to a pitch on Bromwich Street – a move that enabled George Taylor to implement some more innovative training methods (Banks remembers Taylor was 'in his element', while his fullback partner Hartle recalls, 'he had a lot of good ideas'). Floodlights had been erected at Burnden Park over the summer and, in October, the first night game in the ground's history was contested between Wanderers and Hearts. It goes without saying that the Lancashire weather did its best to spoil the occasion by rolling in a thick fog that made seeing the far side of the pitch impossible anyway.

*   *Birmingham Daily Post*, 3 December 1957.

It wasn't just in Bolton that there were signs reminding Lofty of his footballing mortality. He had received a surprise recall to the Three Lions squad for the three World Cup preliminaries in the May of 1957, although his role was chiefly to share some of his wisdom and knowledge with the younger players. He never set foot on the pitch, with Tommy Taylor firmly cemented as first choice. If this significantly reduced role wasn't reminder enough that the end of his time as a professional footballer was looming, Nat also had the bittersweet pleasure of seeing one of the young Bolton forwards whom he had mentored receive the call. Although Dennis Stevens would never receive a full cap, his call-up was a cause for celebration for the club and the town, just as Nat's had been, and very much had the feeling of the torch being passed. Nat, as always, took it in his stride, happily posing for the *Bolton Evening News* cameras shaking Stevens' hand and telling the reporter that 'If any lad deserves an honour, Dennis does for his play this season,' before quipping, 'I think I've only also been picked to daddy little Dennis. I think I'm there to keep an eye on him'* – a joke rooted in reality a little more than Nat would have liked to admit.

Away from the limelight, Nat had taken on the challenge of the Castle with all the gusto he applied on a Saturday afternoon on the pitch. Sometimes he loved it. The punters wasted no time in engaging in repartee once they learned that Nat's reputation as an easy-going chap who was all too happy to give as good as he got was justified: 'Life was never easy if I'd had a bad day. I had to take my fair share of stick. But the regulars enjoyed telling their mates that the landlord wouldn't be behind the bar on Saturday … he'd be away at Wembley on important business for Bolton Wanderers!' Nat's teammates broke their unwritten rule about avoiding drinking in Bolton's pubs ('We daren't have a drink down Bolton,' recalls Banks, for fear of word reaching the directors) to indulge in ordering Nat about behind the bar. A particular highlight for Nat was when the pub was visited by the *Daily Express*' Henry Rose, one of the most renowned football writers of the era. Nat recalled Rose striding into the pub, ordering a round for the

---

*   Leslie Gent, *Making Headlines: The History of Bolton Wanderers Football Club as Seen Through the Eyes the Pages of the Bolton Evening News*, p. 87.

regulars at the bar before loudly discussing 'the ability, or otherwise, of their landlord as a centre forward'. However, it was becoming clear to Nat and Alma, who was having to work long hours when Nat was away, that their future did not lie at the Castle. 'We were not cut out for the business,' Nat found. 'It was just not our lifestyle and I was never happy about bringing up our two kids in a pub environment.' Club promotions manager Andrew Dean remembers Nat telling him that he 'knew it was time to get out when a guy walked up to the bar, drunk, and said [to Alma] "Come here Blondie and give me another pint"'. Less than two years after putting his future with the club he loved in serious jeopardy to go into the pub trade, Nat would take the decision he felt best for his family and left the Castle.

By the time January arrived and introduced the season's edition of the FA Cup, Wanderers' league form had settled into the wearily familiar pattern of fantastic victories and bewildering, frustrating defeats. The Trotters had at least continued their hoodoo of recent years over Manchester United. Wanderers' comprehensive, clinical 4-0 win in front of more than 48,000 – Burnden's biggest league crowd for three years – put an end to United's rampant start to the season, where they had been unbeaten and scored twenty-two in six matches. Victory over the side that had won the previous two league titles was encouragement enough that a Cup run was possible, and with the league season destined for mid-table mediocrity, Bolton could afford to focus solely on their Cup adventures. The run threatened to be over before it began when Wanderers were handed a tough tie away to Tom Finney's Preston, but Nat ensured that his close friendship with North End's mercurial winger didn't affect his bulldozing performance, with Wanderers running out 3-0 winners. After beating Third Division York City in the next round, more than 56,000 crammed into Burnden (despite Bolton not having won a league game for well over a month) to see Lofthouse, Stevens and Ray Parry all net in a 3-1 win over Stoke City in the fifth round.

So comfortable had Bolton's passage been thus far that the fans began to believe like they hadn't since the 1953 run. No matter if it was in the local pubs (not least the Castle, where the landlord's mere presence drummed up plenty of additional interest) or the collieries and the factories or the Saturday night dances, Wanderers were once again the talk of the town. That talk quickly turned to worried murmurs, however, as Bolton's sixth round draw threw up the team that nobody wanted to face. Wolves, a direct side that aimed to simply overwhelm their opponents, were on their way to the first of two successive league titles and were utterly dominant. By the time the two sides met, Wolves had netted over twenty league goals more than Bolton and conceded a remarkable thirty fewer. The only silver lining could be found in the fact that the match would be played at Burnden Park, which was in a sorry state after a week of snow and freezing conditions.

Another near-capacity crowd of 56,000 (with an estimated 15,000 of those from Wolverhampton) filled Burnden, and the game they would witness on a foggy evening would rival the epic Everton semi-final of five years earlier in terms of drama. Jeff Lofthouse remembers the game specifically as one of the most memorable he witnessed of his father's playing career. The game started at a roaring pace, with the battle between Nat and his long-time England captain Billy Wright setting the tone for a truly titanic contest. Dennis Stevens poked Wanderers in front from Brian Birch's floated cross just before the half-hour point, but Wolves hit back within two minutes through Bobby Mason. The toing and froing continued into the second half, with Wolves exerting more and more pressure before a Bolton counter drew Malcolm Finlayson out of his area, where he handled to give Bolton a free kick and a rare sight of goal. Ray Parry made sure it counted by curling the ball home. The stands were so packed that as Parry's shot hit the net, some of the jubilant crowd spilled on to the pitch, but any thoughts of a full-scale pitch invasion were put on hold as it became clear what sort of mood Wolves were in. As the Burnden pitch – never good at letting the rain filter through – began to resemble a bog, Wolves turned the screw. The Bolton defence were forced deeper and deeper, on more than one occasion resorting to Keystone Cops-esque scrambles to get the ball clear. When the efforts of Hartle, Banks, Higgins and company failed, the frame of the goal came to Bolton's rescue, attracting the ball with magnetic precision (some accounts reported no fewer than six occasions where Wolves were denied by the woodwork). Both sets of players were disbelieving that, as the referee blew for full-time, the score remained 2-1 in Bolton's favour. Writing in the *Bolton Evening News,* Haydn Berry echoed what many of the players were privately thinking: 'They have come through their Cup crisis at the gateway to Wembley and go forward without fear to the end of this journey.'

The league was by now a distant second in terms of importance compared to the Cup, which was good considering how abject the Whites were. Bolton would play ten league fixtures between the Cup victory over Wolves and the end of the season and conspire to win only two. A significant factor in Bolton's downturn, in contrast to earlier in the season when his absence had helped the team find some form, was an injury to Nat. A dislocated collarbone sustained in a loss to Spurs at White Hart Lane in March caused him to miss the majority of the rest of the season. So bad was the injury that Lofty was hospitalised for two days and 'drugged to relieve the pain',[*] according to the press. Iconic images of Nat celebrating later in the year would bear witness to the gruesome nature of the injury, with a large, railway track style scar displayed prominently on his shoulder. With the Cup semi-final, pitting Wanderers against Blackburn, looming, an ashen-faced Bill Ridding solemnly informed the press outside the hospital that Nat would miss the match.

Though neither of Blackburn's bids for Nat had much chance for success, the draw had posited a fascinating 'what if?' scenario in which Nat Lofthouse, the greatest icon in the history of the club, could have actually played *against* Bolton. Contested at Maine Road, as their legendary semi-final against Everton in 1953 had been, the biggest obstacle Wanderers had to overcome was one of selection. Six hours before Nat sustained his shoulder injury, the club's go-to replacement Allcock had been sold to Norwich City. After shuffling the pepper pots and salt shakers around a table, as Ridding did to demonstrate some rudimentary tactical ideas, he and Taylor settled on Ralph Gubbins as the best option they had. Gubbins had lost his place on the wing that year following the

[*]   *Daily Herald,* 13 March 1958.

emergence of Brian Birch, and had managed only two goals all season in a utility role. Although he had never played centre forward before, Taylor and Ridding gave him an audition against Sheffield Wednesday, who would end the season bottom of the table with almost 100 goals conceded. The clean sheet that Wednesday recorded that day did little to instil confidence that Gubbins had missed his true calling.

Still, Taylor and Ridding were pragmatists. They understood that not to play Gubbins would mean displacing one of their regular forwards from their favoured positions, and they ultimately determined that to do so would risk upsetting the balance more than Nat's absence already had. Gubbins was handed the number nine shirt of Bolton's red change strip and emerged from the Maine Road tunnel into torrential rain in front of 74,000 Lancastrians with the reassuring words of Lofty in his ear.

Immediately, Bolton's recent deficiencies in their league play surfaced. Their forward play looked disjointed and demonstrated ably just what an impact Nat had beyond his goals in terms of giving the attack a tangible focal point. Rovers, on their way to winning promotion from the Second Division, began on the front foot, using the torn up pitch to their advantage by launching balls into the box from the channels and throwing men forward in the hope of a slip or a mistake granting them a chance at goal. It wasn't long before their tactic paid dividends, as Peter Dobing rose to meet a corner and bury the ball past Eddie Hopkinson with a header that would have made Nat proud. It appeared Blackburn were well on their way to becoming the first side from outside the First Division in nearly a decade to reach the FA Cup Final. However, the hand of fate had other plans. A quick break saw the ball slid to Gubbins, the man who had spent most of the season contemplating life away from Burnden Park. While the Blackburn defence turned to the referee and linesman to appeal for offside, Gubbins decided that he had no intention of hanging around to find out whether he was or not. Harry Leyland rushed from his goal and Gubbins took a touch before slipping the ball past the advancing Leyland and into the net. Bolton fans mingling with the Blackburn faithful in the packed terraces celebrated wildly, but at 1-1 Rovers were still the dominant team. If Gubbins' first was a sucker punch, however, then less than sixty seconds later he delivered the knockout blow, latching on to a whipped cross from Tommy Banks, skipping past the exposed Leyland and tapping the ball into the empty net with such calmness that some onlookers may have wondered whether Lofty had passed a late fitness test and was playing after all. The *Bolton Evening News* would lead with the headline 'Nat-trick Gubbins!' Nat later admitted (with a characteristic touch of excess modesty) that had he been on the pitch in Gubbins' place, 'I wouldn't have scored either of them. Both came from inside the penalty box and for both he needed close control and good footwork. Never my strong points.' Rovers fought back manfully in the second half, determined to put Hopkinson to the test, but the newest Bolton Wanderers England international stood firm and the Trotters booked their place in the world's most prestigious Cup final for the seventh time.

At the same time as Bolton were defeating their historic rivals, the British public's attention was firmly on the other semi-final between Manchester United and Fulham. In January, United had got revenge for Bolton's 4-0 win at Burnden Park, crushing the Whites 7-2 at Old Trafford to dramatically underline their credentials for a third title in a row. It was United's biggest win over the Trotters in almost fifty years – a potent reminder of the sheer brilliance of the team that manager Matt Busby had constructed so meticulously. 'Beat us? No, they annihilated us,' Nat recalled. Over a customary drink in the dressing rooms after the match, Lofty and the rest of the players from both sides were able to see the funny side of the lopsided result. 'We had you going in the last ten minutes … I could tell you were worried!' Nat joked. One of Bolton's crumbs of comfort that day had come courtesy of a Lofty goal in which he launched himself at the ball, as only he could, and sent both it and United keeper Harry Gregg into the net. With that distinctive Lofty cheek, he asked readers of his second autobiography if the goal sounded familiar.

Within a matter of days, that result would take on a different hue entirely. On 6 February, as the Manchester United team travelled home from a European Cup away tie in Belgrade, their plane failed to take off in snowy conditions in Munich, sliding into first a fence and then a house. Twenty-three people died, among them eight players. The match played between United and Bolton on 18 January 1958 will forever remain as one of the final reminders of just what the 'Busby Babes' were capable of as a team, and of the potential they were tragically to never fully realise.

Since the Munich Air Disaster, United had been stumbling through their now seemingly inconsequential matches in a daze. Geoff Bent, Eddie Colman, Billy Whelan, Mark Jones, David Pegg and England international and club captain Roger Byrne all died in the crash, as did Nat's replacement in the national centre forward berth, Tommy Taylor. The team's outstanding talent and England's newest star, Duncan Edwards, died fifteen days later in hospital. Two more players, Johnny Berry and Jackie Blanchflower, survived but never played again. Busby, so gravely injured that he twice received the last rites, was hospitalised for two months. Bill Ridding, who was close to the United manager having played with him briefly at Manchester City, was one of the first at Busby's home upon hearing the news, taking it upon himself to help field calls from the press. With Busby incapacitated, it fell to assistant manager Jimmy Murphy to cobble together a side with the available survivors from Munich. Reserve and youth teamers were brought in, as were veterans Ernie Taylor and Stan Crowther. United even turned to non-league Bishop Auckland for reinforcements.

Predictably, United's form in the league collapsed, even after the return of Bobby Charlton upon his recovery from his injuries. In the FA Cup, however, perhaps encouraged by the 'one game at a time' mindset it allowed the team to adopt, they advanced valiantly, seeing off Sheffield Wednesday in the fifth round in their first game just thirteen days after the crash. They then beat West Bromwich Albion in a replay in front of 60,000 at Old Trafford. On the day Bolton overcame Blackburn, national attention was focused on whether United could defy all the odds and give themselves a chance of silverware in the most trying of circumstances by beating Fulham. Britain was forced to hold its breath for four days longer, after the game at Villa Park was drawn 2-2, before United produced a Herculean effort to win the replay 5-3 at Highbury and continue to write one of the most improbable stories football had seen. In Nat's words, 'Their fight stirred the emotions of the whole nation. Their battles against adversity to the gates of Wembley was an epic journey … the dream had come true.'

Once again, Bolton Wanderers found themselves at odds with national sentiment. In 1953, it had been the supposedly-on-the-verge-of-retirement Stanley Matthews that had captured the hearts of the public. Now, five years on, it was an altogether different situation. Bolton Wanderers wouldn't be playing a team spurred by a collective sentimentality but by a grim tragedy that completely transcended the sport. Everyone in the country was willing United to win and 'deep down', Nat later admitted, 'I probably thought that myself sometimes'. Lofty echoed the thoughts of the Wanderers camp when he explained, 'We simply dare not let sentiment and our personal feelings about Munich creep into it. We had a job to do. For ourselves. For our fans.'

For Bolton Wanderers, the final represented an immensely difficult proposition. In a footballing sense, even allowing for complacency, they were clear favourites. Nat remembered, 'United worked a miracle even to get a team together, let alone to reach the Cup final. We were a strong, experienced First Division side. This was a match we knew we should win.' His conviction was echoed by Tommy Banks, who recalled, 'I was never as confident of winning a game as I was then. If I had been a betting man, I would have had money on us.' However, on a personal level, the idea of beating United so soon after Munich introduced an emotional element to the game that was difficult to overcome. Winning was something they *had* to do, but would not be something they'd necessarily be able to take pleasure in. They had to focus on the joy of winning the Cup, not who they'd be winning it against.

George Taylor had the unpleasant task of picking apart United's make-shift team for particular weaknesses. On the left, United would be playing Ian Greaves* and newly signed Stan Crowther. Greaves was firmly an understudy to the late Byrne, while Crowther was only a couple of years shy of a voluntary early retirement after finding himself falling down the league ladder. The wings were always a potent attacking option for Bolton given Nat's uncanny knack of making something of even the weakest, most misguided of crosses, and it was drummed into Dougie

---

* Greaves would go on to manage the Trotters during the 1970s.

Holden and Brian Birch that Bolton's best chance of victory depended on them beating their men.

Although Holden and Birch were especially aware of their role in Bolton's route to success, the spirit and desire for victory ran through Bill Ridding's proudly named '£110 team', described in the Wolves match day programme that year as a side 'with an adventurous approach to the game and a workmanlike team to apply it'. Roy Hartle had been dropped for the 1953 Final and was determined to make amends in his first game under Wembley's famous twin towers. Opposite Hartle was Banks, who'd seen his brother suffer heartache from the same position five years earlier and had absolutely no intention of allowing the same thing to happen to him. By this stage, Hartle and Banks were at the very peak of their powers; indeed, Banks would receive his first England call immediately after the final, and would go on to play every match in the World Cup finals that summer. The fullback combination was, after Lofty, the defining aspect of Bolton Wanderers during the era. Both were fine players in their own right, and their reputations put the fear of God into the opposition before they even set foot on the pitch. Even the fearless Lion of Vienna professed his relief that he played with the pair, not against them, joking, 'I used to wear shin pads at the backs of my legs and I was on their side.' In between them was centre half John Higgins ('a stopper pure and simple. And he stopped 'em'), and if anyone got past those three, they still had the most promising young goalkeeper in the country to beat. Eddie Hopkinson, despite his tender years, had made the transition from Stan Hanson smoother than anyone would have dreamed possible, and was now England's number one as well as Bolton's. The midfield pairing of Bryan Edwards ('He never had a bad game') and Derek Hennin was highly reliable and equally comfortable in stopping opposition attacks and starting Bolton's. At inside forward, Ray Parry and Dennis Stevens offered skill and tenacity to knit with Nat's raw power. Stevens had become one of the team's most important players ('one of the most underrated players of them all … a real tiger, an old-fashioned inside forward'), netting thirteen league goals in the 1957/58 campaign. The 24-year-old found the circumstances around the final more testing than most, as Duncan Edwards was his cousin.*

Then, of course, there was Nat. Along with the dependable Holden, Nat was the only remaining member of the 1953 Final team. His unshakeable determination, described by Terry Allcock as an immense 'perseverance to do something better than anyone else', was bolstered further by the desire to right the wrongs of the Matthews final: 'We were there to win the Cup. This time we didn't intend to fail.' Nat's recall to the side upon his recovery from his shoulder injury was never in doubt despite Ralph Gubbins' heroics in the semi-final. Ridding had made it clear, with his spell on the wing earlier that season, that they didn't consider Lofty completely untouchable. However, for such a big occasion, there was simply no one else Bolton would have wanted at centre forward. Nat offered a typically understated (to the point of untruthfulness) assessment of his role in the team at the time of the final – 'still in the middle, still running, shooting and heading – just like George Taylor had told me after that first game for England back in 1950' – but even he had to acknowledge how critical he was to the team. He was the player that his teammates not only looked up to, but looked to when they needed bailing out, the one man they knew that could haul them back into a game no matter how bleak the team's prospects looked. As always, he never gave a hint of nerves in front of his teammates, regardless of what he felt inside. The only slight deviation from the assertive, confident Nat everybody knew came the night before the final, when he confided in his roommate Hopkinson just how desperate he was to win. 'We've got to win tomorrow, Hoppy,' Nat told his keeper. 'It could be my last chance to get that medal.'** His

---

*   Stevens and Parry, who played with Edwards at England schoolboys, had both been enlisted by Bill Ridding to try to tempt Edwards to join Wanderers instead of United, with Stevens commenting, 'Bolton were very confident of signing Duncan, and naturally, being part of the family and knowing what a player he was going to develop into, I was quite looking forward to him joining me at Bolton.' Another Wanderers connection to Edwards came from the team's former star Ray Westwood, Edwards' uncle.

**   John Gradwell, *Legend: The Life of Roy 'Chopper' Hartle*, p. 90.

status as one of, if not the, single greatest player in the club's history was already assured, even if his total number of league goals still sat some thirty-one behind that of record holder Joe Smith. Had the Munich Disaster not taken all precedence, it's likely that the national mood would have swung in Nat's favour just as it had Matthews' in 1953.

Guarding against complacency was the first item on the agenda for Ridding and Taylor as Bolton arrived at their hotel in Hendon, the same in which they'd stayed prior to the Matthews final. Not only did United have the public support and momentum gleaned from the sheer improbability of their Cup run, but they still had a group of players who no doubt felt capable of winning the game for the Red Devils. Bobby Charlton had already established himself as a player set apart from most, with his natural goal-scoring ability and all-round play shining through from his teenage years. Charlton, in the pages of the *Daily Herald*, offered a confident prediction for the game, citing his 'sincere belief that United are a better footballing side than Bolton' and forecasting that United would win by two clear goals. Inside forward Dennis Violett was more seasoned and could consider himself unfortunate to have not yet received a call from the England selectors. Although United's defensive record had taken a hammering post-Munich, in Harry Gregg, who had helped pull survivors from the wreckage, they still had one of the best keepers in the First Division. Even one of the emergency replacements drafted in to fill the void left in the wake of the disaster gave the more superstitious Bolton fans something to worry about. Ernie Taylor's career had been winding down after some stellar years at Blackpool before United signed him. It had been Taylor's presence that many, including Nat, believed had been the key to Matthews finding the space and time he needed to put Bolton to the sword in the final five years before.

Unlike Bolton's traditional model, with Taylor in charge of coaching and Ridding secretarial duties, Matt Busby was one of the first truly modern managers, ruling Old Trafford with near autonomy, picking the team and the tactics as well as negotiating contracts and scouting – roles that were usually entirely separate. United were given a late boost when they learned their inspirational figurehead would return for the final, albeit only in a symbolic capacity. Jimmy Murphy was entrusted to continue his outstanding managerial work in the competition. The day before the final, the *Manchester Evening News* encapsulated the mood of the nation, writing, 'the Red Devils have not merely survived, they have added yet another chapter of success and the club is gloriously alive again.' It was Bolton's unfortunate task to try to puncture the hopes of a fairy-tale ending to the nightmare.

The day of the final broke with a familiar mix of anticipation and nerves. Some in the Wanderers camp had been chomping at the bit to get to Wembley. Banks was confident; Hopkinson remembered approaching the match as 'the pinnacle … all that matters is winning'. Lofty would never profess to have had the same ironclad faith in Bolton's success that day, but his steely determination left his teammates in no doubt as to who they should turn to should they find themselves with their backs against the wall. Others were less relaxed, although they did their best to mask their emotions. Hartle, having not even made it to the pitch for his first shot at Wembley glory, was entitled to feel the nerves more than most: 'I remember being in the tunnel and everybody is trying to kid on that there isn't a problem and they are quite relaxed.' Hartle struggled particularly with the emotion of the occasion, remembering tears on the coach as he and his teammates prepared to face an unrecognisable United team for the first time.* Out in the stands, the travelling mass of Trotters fans were experiencing the same potent cocktail of excitement and trepidation. A paltry 15,000 tickets had been allocated to each side, and just as in 1953, Wanderers' meagre quota was comprehensively oversubscribed. Thousands of regular match-goers missed out, but despite the game being televised, thousands of ticketless fans made the long journey down to London determined to join the legions of fans lending their voices in support of the team.

In living rooms and pubs up and down the country, people crowded around televisions to watch the BBC coverage of the game. As usual, Kenneth Wolstenholme was doing the honours on commentary, the

---

★   John Gradwell, *Legend: The Life of Roy 'Chopper' Hartle*, p. 91.

boyhood Bolton fan ensuring that any private desire to see Lofty lift the Cup remained comprehensively hidden from the British public.* Wolstenholme's pre-match preamble spent more time discussing the 1953 final and Nat's shoulder injury than Munich, perhaps in the knowledge that everything that could be said about the tragic situation already had been. There was nothing more to do than wait to see whether United could add a fitting final chapter to what had already been an extraordinary tale.

As club captain, Lofty led the Bolton side out into the sunshine to be greeted with the roar of the crowd. It was the moment that every preco-cious, football-mad youth dreams of, just as Nat had the day he stole into Burnden to first watch the Whites in the Cup twenty-five years before. In some ways, his entire career had been building to this moment, and he was well aware it was likely his final shot at silverware. Nat exchanged niceties with Prince Philip before introducing him to his team, who were clad in cotton kits after the satin silk fiasco of 1953. As the royal turned his attentions to United, Bolton minds were able to focus once again on the matter at hand. They knew that, given their superior quality, the worst thing that they could do would be to allow their opponents to get a foothold in the game and gain some belief that perhaps fate intended for them to succeed against all the odds. Wanderers needed to burst out of the blocks, just as they had done against Blackpool when Nat scored within the opening two minutes.

What ensued was a blood-and-thunder opening that made it clear to the millions watching that United had no intention of settling for simply having reached the final. Bolton, meanwhile, demonstrated that they'd be offering their opponents no additional respect. Tackles flew in from the first whistle, with Stevens taking a nasty blow to the midriff that brought Bolton's trainer, Bert Sproston, on to the pitch within seconds. The first

---

* Later that year, Wolstenholme would find himself embroiled in a minor controversy after coming out in support of Nat's candidacy for the BBC's annual 'Sportsview Personality of the Year' award. The resulting uproar that a BBC employee would publicly back a candidate likely did more harm than good to Nat's chances of win-ning, and he eventually finished third in the voting, behind Bobby Charlton and the winner, Scottish swimmer Ian Black.

clear sight of goal came moments later, when Gregg, put off by the sight of Lofthouse steaming towards him, dropped a routine cross, only for it to be bundled behind. From the corner, first Holden and then Parry flicked crosses into the box, which United defended in increasingly ragged style, before the ball dropped to Edwards. It's unclear whether Edwards was attempting a shot or a cross as he spun and volleyed the ball back into the area. What Nat did with the ball as it arrived at his feet was absolutely certain. With Gregg springing from his line and spreading himself, Lofty took a touch and poked the ball home. The Bolton fans went berserk as Nat led his teammates back towards the halfway line, cheering and celebrating every step of the way. 'You never really remember the exact feeling when you've scored a goal. I just recall racing back to the halfway line and getting ready to start again. We were one up in the Cup final.' It took him precisely forty-five seconds longer to find the net than it had in his last final.

Bolton had United exactly where they wanted them. As if to prove that their goal, while a touch fortuitous, hadn't been a fluke, Wanderers assumed a stranglehold on the match, reducing United to ineffectual counter-attacks while the Whites launched concerted forays forward. Lofthouse and his fellow forwards, inspired by his earlier moment of shaky handling, attempted to put Gregg under pressure whenever possible, although a superb save from Nat after fifteen minutes settled the Irishman's nerves somewhat. Lofty was revelling in his first time on the big stage since his England exile, demonstrating not only the fearlessness, hold-up and shooting skills for which he was renowned, but the aspects of the game he often claimed he lacked, spraying passes out to Birch and Holden with finesse and accuracy. United's few attacks generally went through Violett, but Hopkinson was equal to everything, making two fine saves in quick succession, first from Taylor and then Charlton, who was dropping deeper and deeper as he sought to impose some sort of influence on the game. As referee Jack Sherlock blew for half-time and the players retreated from the scene of continuous, cacophonous noise, it was the Bolton players who were more frustrated that they hadn't been able to make their dominance reflect in the scoreline. As it had been in the first, the game plan for the second half was to come out all guns blazing and put the game beyond the reach of their great rivals. They would do just that, but rather than bringing closure to the contest, it would instead ignite a debate that still rumbles on over six decades later.

From the off, United found a rare moment of attacking understanding, ending with Charlton's shot coming back off the post and into Hopkinson's grateful arms (he was, in Wolstenholme's words, 'as lucky as a man with half a dozen tickets for *My Fair Lady*'). Seconds later, Bolton swarmed forward again with Stevens, who wrought havoc throughout the afternoon, testing Gregg from 25 yards out. The shot, while almost straight at the Red Devils' custodian, was driven hard towards the roof of the net, and it was all Gregg could do to parry it skyward. What happened next has become one of the immortal FA Cup Final moments. As the ball began to fall, Gregg turned and took two quick steps back towards his own goal-line. With blood-hound instincts, Lofty sensed his chance, bursting from the edge of the area in an attempt to meet the dropping ball. Just as the ball fell into Gregg's arms, he was met by a mighty shoulder charge from Nat and crashed into the net along with the ball. The Bolton players appeared to have no doubts over the strike's legitimacy, all joining Nat as he raced away, arms above his head, for the second time. Some United players briefly appealed to the referee by pointing at the prostrate Gregg, face down in his goal. As the referee checked on Gregg, more United players arrived to join in the protests to try to persuade Sherlock that there was simply no way a blow of such force could have resulted in a legitimate goal.

The idea that the goal was par for the course for the times has been exaggerated for modern uses: it was controversial even then, although certainly less clear cut as a foul. Describing the incident years later, Nat himself said:

> I was following in at top speed. I saw Gregg turn to catch the ball and then I hit him, the ball, the lot into the back of the net. A foul? Looking back, yes. Today [1989] I would probably have been sent off. But in those days you could challenge the keeper. That's what I did. I didn't go in to hurt Gregg. I went for the ball. And that's how the referee saw it. When I looked round he was pointing to the centre circle. Goal. I don't argue with referees.

Wanderers' promotions manager Andrew Dean remembers Nat would often say he was extremely grateful for having won 'two-none', reducing the significance of the strike. The reaction of the United players, while far more measured and gentlemanly than modern 'discussions' between players and officials, was still unusual for the age when the done thing was to accept the referee's decision as sacrosanct and move on with the game. United fans booed the decision to award the goal. From the commentary booth Wolstenholme remained objective, although even he noted, as Sproston and Jimmy Murphy both jogged on to aid Gregg, that the 'consensus of people is that Gregg was charged in the back, but it doesn't matter what many people think, there's only one man who counts, Mr Sherlock, he's given a goal'. Banks, when interviewed for this book, chuckled and remembered, 'Lofty having a slight knock with the goalkeeper.' Gregg himself, in the newspapers the following week, pointed out that 'the middle of the back isn't recognised as a normal place for a shoulder charge'.* At the other end of the pitch, Gregg's opposite number, Hopkinson, felt the goal should have been ruled out, but he too would echo Nat's point about the goal not ultimately influencing the final result. As for the travelling Wanderers fans, while sympathetic towards the groggy United keeper, it mattered little. Future player and head of the PFA Gordon Taylor, watching from home after failing to get a ticket, summed up the feelings of most Bolton fans, saying, 'Of course, I felt it was a fair challenge. It was Gregg's own fault for trying to hold the ball while turning his back on the line. In those days shoulder charges were part of the game.' Haydn Berry, the long-time *Bolton Evening News* Wanderers scribe, allowed his biases to perhaps get the better of him in his match report, noting only that 'some mild attempt to make capital out of the incident by a small section of the crowd quickly died away for lack of support, especially as Gregg appeared to be unaffected by the fall'.

The remaining forty minutes proceeded without any danger of a Matthews-esque comeback. Higgins, Hennin and Edwards demonstrated a masterclass in teamwork, hounding United's forwards and frequently

---

* John Gradwell, *Legend: The Life of Roy 'Chopper' Hartle*, p. 95.

making timely interceptions to break up attacks. Hartle and Banks went long stretches without much involvement as United wingers Colin Webster and Alex Dawson interchanged and drifted inside in the vain hope of making a greater impact upon proceedings. After Nat's second goal, the result was never really in doubt. So complete was Bolton's dominance that, for the Wanderers players, the only blemish was that they had been denied the opportunity to prove what they could have done against the pre-Munich United side. Nat would later say that 'It would have been very different if we'd been playing the Busby Babes. We MIGHT have won that one. We might not! But what a final that would have been!' His feelings were mirrored by those of Banks, who would state, 'To be honest I think we would have had a good game even if it was their full team.' The 7-2 hammering Busby's team had dished out just days before the tragedy is often held up as proof that United would have without question won the Cup had the team made it home from Munich. However, Bolton's stellar record against United – Wanderers lost just a single game to United between the start of 1953 and the 7-2, a run of ten matches that included the memorable 5-1 win at Old Trafford in 1954 and the 4-0 success earlier in the 1957/58 season – suggests Wanderers would have more than held their own.

The match meandered to a conclusion, as United's comparative disorganisation saw them fatigue markedly (Wolstenholme noted towards the end that Bolton appeared to have 'fourteen or fifteen' players on the pitch, such was their superiority in stamina). Birch almost added a third only to be denied by a goal-line clearance by Greaves, and then it was all over. Nat, who had been on the ball as Sherlock blew his whistle, spun around in celebration and found himself almost immediately in the arms of Ridding. The focus of the BBC cameras and the rest of the Bolton team left nobody in any doubt as to who the man of the moment was. Wolstenholme, in a repeat of the eulogy he'd delivered for Matthews immediately after the 1953 final, told viewers, 'No man deserves the Cup winner's medal for such a fine career as Nat Lofthouse.' Gregg suggested no hard feelings by way of a firm handshake.[*] Some months later, Gregg would walk into the Castle for a pint, which Nat insisted was on the house. When Gregg thanked him, Nat wryly replied, 'We don't charge goalkeepers here.' Lofty's next well-wisher was England manager Walter Winterbottom, who made a beeline for the man of the moment to give him some personal congratulations. Wolstenholme suggested that the England manager may well have been convinced to restore Nat's England career on the basis of his performance, much as the 1953 final had revived Matthews'. In all the chaos immediately following the whistle, one key feature of the match was missing – the ball. It had been booted into the stands and simply hadn't returned. Some days later, Nat appealed for this key memento, offering whoever delivered it to him 'a pint of beer every night for the rest of [the fan's] life'.[**] The fan who did end up bringing the ball to Lofty, either out of altruism or fear for the health of their liver, opted not to take Nat up on the offer of the beer.

Then there was the small matter of collecting the trophy that had eluded Bolton Wanderers for twenty-nine years. Nat's trip leading his team up the famous thirty-nine steps was made slower by numerous fans, who ranged from giving his hair a quick tousle to those who practically had to be pried from his muscular frame. As he emerged from the crowd on to the level with the royal box, a roar from the Bolton fans erupted that almost equalled that which had greeted the goals. Nat's second meeting with Prince Philip that day was to accept first the Cup, then his winner's medal. As the royal handed Nat the most prestigious and famous piece of silverware in world football, it was all Nat could do but shake his head in disbelief, before planting a quick kiss on the lid and lifting it skyward

---

[*]   Despite the exchange of best wishes, Nat would field questions about his relationship with Gregg for years to come. 'People often ask me if Harry and I speak to one another these days,' said Nat over thirty years after the match. 'Of course. We were speaking to one another after that Cup final, sharing a drink. He was a guest at my testimonial dinner. I see Harry three or four times a year and the one thing we never talk about in any detail is the 1958 Cup final. That's in the past.'

[**] *Bolton Evening News*, 5 May 1958.

to another roar from the thousands of Boltonians below: 'I honestly can't recall my emotions as I received the trophy from Prince Philip and held it aloft. I just recall holding that precious piece of silver and handing it to the rest of the lads in turn so that they could do the same.'

The jubilation was tempered somewhat as the Bolton team returned to the pitch and turned to see the despondent United players following down the steps having collected their runners-up medals. Roy Hartle remembered that he was heading straight back to the dressing room:

> When Bert Sproston, the trainer, came over and told us: 'You must do the lap of honour. It will be the biggest thing in your career and you will remember it all your life.' He was right as it turned out, but at the time we just couldn't see what all the fuss was about. After Munich the match was a bit meaningless I suppose.*

Although Nat never offered such a damning indictment of the situation, the numerous mentions of the Munich Disaster in his 1989 autobiography are testament to the conflicting emotions he felt over what was, after all, the crowning achievement of his career.

To underline the bittersweet nature of the victory, after the team and coaches were done lapping up the adulation of the crowd (Nat himself was paraded some of the way on the shoulders of Higgins and Hopkinson) and had headed back to the dressing room, there came a knock at the door. In walked Jimmy Murphy and, supported by the Welshman as well as a cane, Matt Busby. No jokes were exchanged between members of the two camps, no cheeky banter or promises to avenge the result next year. Instead, Busby told the room that 'the better team had won' before slowly walking around the players and individually congratulating the Bolton stars. Though Bolton had gone about the final in a business-like fashion and deserved to feel pride in their achievement, Busby's visit was a sobering reminder of what could have been one of the all-time great

---

★   Versions of this story appear in both Ian Seddon's *Ah'm Tellin' Thee* and John Gradwell's *The Life of Roy 'Choppter' Hartle*.

finals. Nat recalled, 'Something – something very special – made that man come into our dressing room in what must have been one of the saddest moments of his career to congratulate us on beating his team. Tommy Banks summed it up for us all when he said, after Matt had hobbled quietly away: "That's the finest sportsman you'll ever see."'

After some moments of reflection, the Bolton celebrations continued in earnest. The team's traditional post-match celebratory drink of choice was Double Diamond (incidentally Prince Philip's favourite tipple, too) and this was enjoyed alongside some champagne swigged straight from the trophy. The scrupulous Bill Ridding had never been so happy to part with money as he was when he handed Nat a £1 note. Lofty had bet Ridding that he'd recover from his shoulder injury in time to play for the final, and the manager was relieved to have lost the wager. As the jubilant Bolton fans spilled out from the stadium on to Olympic Way, the players finished their drinks, enjoyed a customary sing-song, led as they often were by George Taylor, and eventually stumbled out into the late-spring afternoon for the coach ride back to the team hotel.

The official banquet, held at the Café Royal, proved a raucous affair with the Bolton players, now joined by wives and girlfriends, as well as the club's directors and various associates, in no mood to take it easy. Tommy Banks had rather presumptuously arranged (after Bolton's away fixture at Chelsea in early April) for the party to continue at a London nightclub, but when the players arrived, they found the club to be packed to the rafters with Bolton fans who'd gotten wind of their heroes' impending arrival. Nat took charge of the situation, suggesting the group return to their hotel to continue the party there instead. The night turned into a predictably riotous one. Banks ended up drinking champagne from his wife's shoe. George Taylor, who'd declined the invitation to the nightclub, was persuaded to stay up for a bit and was soon playing master of ceremonies, leading the group through the standards and more contemporary pop tunes they'd sung together in dank, dark, cold dressing rooms for years. Now, in somewhat more salubrious surroundings and with a conspicuous piece of silverware sat proudly in the centre of the room, suddenly all those Saturdays spent slogging away felt completely worth it. Several players made it through to dawn, when they were the first ones down to breakfast, served by some sleep-deprived hotel staff who'd spent half the night apologising to other guests for the noise.

The sore heads were made considerably worse when Bill Ridding learned that the players had exceeded their celebration pot of £50 by another £20 – an overspend that effectively equated to what Bolton had paid for two of their eleven Cup-winning players. Lofty, who'd slipped off to bed a few hours before the most dedicated drinkers, was found eating his breakfast in the foyer of the hotel rather than the restaurant. When Banks asked him why, Nat responded that it was so he could meet and greet any and all the fans who ventured to the hotel that morning to congratulate the team. 'It was out of character for him,' Banks remembered, 'but he was so elated at winning the Cup. I think of those of us there, he had been the most disappointed when we lost in 1953 and winning had meant so much to him.' Going out of his way to speak with fans wasn't unusual for Nat, but what was 'out of character' was Nat acknowledging that people might want to meet him. Even now, as an FA Cup-winning captain, he scorned the idea that he was any different from the average man on the streets of Bolton, and the notion that he'd even need to give fans the 'chance' of meeting him would have been faintly ridiculous to him.

The more hungover players roused and the entire team changed into their Cup Final suits, the group began the long journey back to Bolton. The trip was, by all accounts, a bit of a continuation of the night before, with the only blip coming when the coach travelled through Salford, where it was duly pelted with tomatoes by disgruntled United fans. A window by Alma was shattered, with broken glass narrowly missing her. The players who still had the shadow of Munich cast across their minds may well have secretly welcomed the barrage as a step back towards normality. Nat, in typically playful fashion, told the newspapers that Mancunians needn't worry, for the team would again 'come through Manchester next year if we win the Cup'.* After stopping at both Kearsley and Farnworth town halls, the bus made its way into Bolton among thronging crowds,

★   *Daily Herald*, 6 May 1958.

an exhilarated, joyous mass, reportedly around 90,000 strong. Such was the excitement that, after the players disembarked and made their way up the town hall steps, the public address system simply couldn't compete against the volume of noise being generated. Unsurprisingly, the bulk of the songs being sung, including 'For he's a Jolly Good Fellow', were aimed squarely at Nat, and the *Bolton Evening News* reported groups of Bolton fans competitively trading songs exalting their hero Lofty. Nat, who the paper said appeared 'overwhelmed' by the reception, attempted to keep his speech short and sweet. He elicited boos when he told of the reception the coach had received on its way through Manchester, before recounting the last time the team had been on the town hall steps, after losing in 1953. As soon as he uttered the words 'this time, we have –' he was completely drowned out by cheers. He concluded by simply saying, 'On behalf of the lads and myself, thanks a lot, thank you!' Wanderers' celebrations continued into the evening at the Palais de Danse.

While Lofty could laugh off the antics of the 'hooligans' along the parade route, the same could not be said of the more sinister developments over the course of the next week. As Alma worked through the piles of post praising and thanking Nat, she came across some more unsavoury pieces of correspondence, eight of them in all (six with Manchester postmarks, two from Salford). One writer spoke of their wish that Nat would 'meet his Munich', while another hoped that the plane taking Wanderers on their post-season tour would succumb to the same fate as had befallen United's aircraft in Germany. When the story hit the press, Nat refused to comment and subsequently never mentioned the incident in his autobiography. Instead, it was Alma who delivered the damning verdict, telling the papers, 'I feel sorry for the people of Manchester that they have such awful people among them.'* It was a highly distasteful postscript to one of Lofty's greatest moments, but he chose to move himself and his family swiftly past it.

The brutal physical and financial realities of football in the 1950s meant that for many of the great stars of the day, an idyllic swansong end to their

---

* *Daily Herald*, 8 May 1958.

career was simply not on the cards. The tales of great players dropping down the divisions, battling agonising aches and pains, far outnumber those of players gloriously ending their careers with the clubs they'd made their names with. Even those First Division players lucky enough not to be cut adrift when their team deemed them too old tended to go with a whimper rather than a bang, scarcely afforded an opportunity to say goodbye to the fans who still adored them and sang their names. With his time in the England set-up appearing well and truly over and his first forays into post-retirement planning at the Castle floundering, Nat Lofthouse was faced with two major questions: how would the end of his playing career come, and what would he do when it did?

12

THE FINAL CURTAIN

IN THE SUMMER of 1958, Boltonians felt on top of the world. Their club had returned to true prominence in the English game, and even those who'd never set foot inside Burnden Park were hard pressed not to get swept up in the infectious celebratory atmosphere of the town. One milkman had got so carried away in the wake of the FA Cup victory that he gave every family on his round a free pint. Worrying events elsewhere in the country, such as the Notting Hill race riots, failed to puncture the mood of optimism in Lancashire, which was continuing to enjoy growing prosperity as the spectre of post-war austerity receded. Mosley Common, where Nat had worked when enlisted as a Bevin Boy, was in the process of a multi-million pound redevelopment to make it one of the most modern collieries in the country. It sometimes seemed that the most pressing thing on the minds of those in the town was what showing of the first film in the *Carry On* series they should take in at the cinema.

Even the England national side's recent poor form could not dent the spirit of Bolton. Two of the victorious Bolton XI were not on the town hall steps to celebrate the Cup win. Eddie Hopkinson had stayed behind in London for England duty, with the Three Lions playing Portugal at Wembley three days later in preparation for the summer's World Cup in Sweden. Tommy Banks only got halfway back to Bolton before the word arrived that he'd been called up, at which point he hopped off the coach and got a train back to the capital. When he joined up with the squad, the uncapped fullback told Walter Winterbottom that the call had meant he'd missed out on a big day back in Bolton and that the England manager had 'a lot to answer for'.

Despite Kenneth Wolstenholme's speculation at the end of the final that Nat's heroics could see him break back into the team, the FA saw fit to cull Nat from the original forty-man World Cup squad, citing a lack of fitness after his injury and opting to select just one recognised centre forward, Derek Kevan. Tommy Taylor's death had left a void at the centre forward position, and though Lofty was never less than grateful and humbled by the opportunities afforded him in an England shirt, he could feel justifiably aggrieved to have missed out on his second World Cup. One of Winterbottom's obituaries even saw fit to mention it as one of his gravest errors. In the tournament itself, with England facing a winner-takes-all play-off against the USSR, Winterbottom elected to give two players debuts yet omit Bobby Charlton. Charlton had scored both goals against Portugal in May but was never called upon at the World Cup for fear of the pressure being too great – a laughable notion given what the young forward had lived through in recent months. Charlton's snub was so glaring that, after England's 1-0 defeat, Winterbottom's young son met him at the airport and immediately asked why Charlton hadn't played.

Following England's exit, the presiding mood in Bolton and beyond was that with Winterbottom so unwilling to play Charlton, England should have taken the Lion of Vienna. To rub salt into the wounds of those indignant about Nat's omission, in England's first game with the USSR at the tournament, Tom Finney netted from the penalty spot and tied Nat and Vivian Woodward for the record as England's top goal scorer. The news likely took some time to reach Nat, as he was enjoying a summer of relaxation and recuperation (with a bit of football thrown in for good measure) on tour with Bolton in South Africa. Syd Farrimond remembers one overnight train ride on the tour when a slightly tipsy Nat took great pleasure in waking his teammates up by impersonating a ticket inspector. It was a welcome break from the stresses of running the Castle (although one that Alma suffered for as a result), where the honeymoon period was definitely over. The Lofthouses were already discussing when they'd be best to leave the pub, and what they'd do with Nat's one potential retirement plan having gone up in smoke. For Lofty, given the fuss that had been kicked up by his taking over at the Castle, the most sensible decision seemed to be focus on family and, while he still could, football.

The 1958/59 season was somewhat confounding for Bill Ridding and George Taylor. The FA Cup had been the shining beacon they'd been aiming for throughout Ridding's tenure. Now it had been achieved, what was next for Bolton Wanderers? Their fifteenth place finish in the First Division the season before told little of the story of a remarkable year, and had been heavily influenced by their lackadaisical finish to the league when focus had shifted entirely to their march toward the Empire Stadium. Now they wondered if their small, tightly knit squad could translate their Cup heroics to the league, or whether they'd be best continuing to look to the Cup for success. History was against them: back-to-back victories in the Cup had only happened once since the final had first shifted to Wembley more than thirty years before.

The £110 core would play a critical and consistent role in the team all year, a credit to Ridding's instincts for which players should be hung on to and to Taylor's ability to get them working together. With no clear direction on which avenue would represent their best chance of success, Bolton had no choice but to start playing and see how the season revealed itself before them.

An opening day crowd of under 26,000 at Burnden Park was a slight disappointment given the magnitudes of Trotters fans who'd attempted to make the journey to London months earlier. Once it became clear, however, via a brace in a comprehensive 4-0 victory over Leeds United that Nat was in no mind to let age dim his now customary hot start to the year, the next home fixture, against Manchester City, saw almost 40,000 cram into Burnden Park. The multitudes were rewarded with a 4-1 victory. A 6-1 humbling at Highbury brought the club back to earth with a thud, but steady progress throughout the rest of September left the team in third, with Nat having netted nine times in nine appearances.

October was to be a showpiece month. Four league fixtures promised to be highly instructive of just how strongly the Wanderers could compete, with trips to league leaders Preston North End, Chelsea and Aston Villa around a home tie against Blackpool. However, it was two additional games that truly caught the eye. One saw the Whites play host to a special England XI, with Billy Wright pulling on the shirt of the 'other' Wanderers rather than his typical Wolverhampton one. Before that game was the other odd fixture of the month: the Charity Shield, the one-off annual game that pitted the league champions against the FA Cup winners. Although boasting nowhere near the prestige of either of the qualifying criteria for reaching the game, the Shield was nothing to be sniffed at, having been contested since 1908. That Wanderers had never won it was an added incentive for Ridding's charges. In fact, by a remarkable fluke of timing, Bolton had never even been given the opportunity to contest the Shield, despite having won the FA Cup three times during the 1920s. During that decade, with the Shield still new enough to be unprotected by tradition and history, the format had switched to Professionals v Amateurs in the years in which Wanderers would have contested the match. Taylor had been on the club's books for the Cup wins in 1926 and 1929 as an amateur, and now, three decades later, he finally had a chance to bring the Shield to the Burnden Park trophy room as coach.

The scenes before kick-off on Monday, 6 October didn't quite bring the town of Bolton to a standstill as the celebrations for the Cup win had, but the 15,500 in attendance were determined to make as much noise as they had at Wembley to help their boys bring home another piece of silverware under Burnden's still-novel floodlights. Both Bolton and opponents Wolves fielded strong sides and a tense opening ensued. Wolves appeared to take the upper hand when Joe Dean, deputising between the posts for Eddie Hopkinson that night, suffered a dislocated shoulder, forcing Nat into the third emergency goalkeeper appearance of his career (all of which, incredibly, had come against Wolves). This time there were no penalty-saving heroics, and Hopkinson was eventually given special dispensation to appear as substitute. Just before the half was up, the complexion of the match changed entirely when Fred Hill and Neville Bannister, filling in for the injured Ray Parry and Brian Birch, scored twice in two minutes to give the Wanderers in white a significant advantage. The youngsters may have got the ball rolling, but it was the veteran who put the matter to bed. Nat had actually played in the Charity Shield before (the unusual 1950 edition had seen England's World Cup squad take on the Canada touring squad he'd been a part of) and had scored, and now he took his record in the competition to three goals in two games to make the score 4-0. A late Wolves goal did nothing to stop Bolton from adding another piece of silverware to their trophy cabinet.

Two days before the Charity Shield, Wanderers had come through their first league test of the month with a creditable 0-0 draw at Deepdale against Preston. They had done so without Tommy Banks, who was on England duty as the Three Lions toiled to a 3-3 draw with Northern Ireland – hardly the tonic the country needed after the chastening World Cup. After his inexplicable omission from the World Cup teams, Bobby Charlton had been given his opportunity at centre forward and had taken it with two thumping goals. Tom Finney had netted the other with his thirtieth international strike that gave him sole ownership of the England record and relegated Nat to second place. Had Lofty been the sort inclined to gripe and moan – he instead congratulated his close friend on achieving the mark – he would have found many a willing ear to hear how the incompetence of the suits in the FA had robbed him of the chance to put together an even greater tally of international goals. However, unbeknownst to him as he scored his twelfth in twelve in the league as Wanderers won at Stamford Bridge, he was about to be on the receiving end of some good luck courtesy of the men at Lancaster Gate.

Charlton's two goals against Northern Ireland had brought the selectors and Walter Winterbottom under fresh scrutiny. The decision not to play him in the World Cup had been believed, at the time, to be foolish; now, there was concrete proof. The FA could have swallowed their pride and admitted that their decision to exclude Charlton from the World Cup team was a hopelessly misguided one. However, the prospect of being harangued every time Charlton performed or – God forbid – scored for England was none too attractive to the FA. It was this, twinned with Lofty's apparently ageless goal-scoring knack, which led to Nat getting his unlikely recall to the England team.

He had missed twenty-two games since his last England appearance and although his predatory instincts remained intact, niggling injuries and age had cost him a yard of pace and a touch of his Herculean stamina since he'd last donned a shirt emblazoned with the Three Lions. Derek Kevan, a striker very much in the Lofthouse mould, had been criticised in the press for his style, reflecting the dawning realisation across English football that the sun was setting on the age of the classic centre forward at the heart of the WM. More than ever, and in spite of his excellent record in the league that season, the Lion of Vienna's battering ram boisterousness appeared a relic of a version of football that was being replaced with a faster, less physical, more fluid sport. Some writers praised the decision to recall Nat. Peter Lorenzo of the *Daily Herald* approved of England's selectors abandoning their 'clever boy' passing forward line strategy in favour of a return to the 'tried, trusted and orthodox strength-through-power policy personified by the recall of Lionheart Nat, Bolton's dashing, crashing two-goal Cup Final hero'. Others were less convinced. Undoubtedly aware of some of the criticism in the press box at the news of his recall, Nat determined to do exactly as he had six years earlier in Vienna after journalists hadn't been shy in their declarations that Jackie Milburn should have his spot.

Having wondered if he'd ever set foot in Wembley again as a player just months before, Nat emerged in the white number nine shirt of his country on an overcast October day already hinting at the coming of winter. His first match back was against the USSR, who England had faced in a pre-World Cup friendly and then twice at the finals themselves. The England team that day reflected the lack of direction and identity within the national squad following the Munich Disaster, with two distinct age groups making up the side. Optimistic fans hoped that the blend – with five players born in 1934 or later, and four, including Nat, Billy Wright and Finney born in 1927 or earlier – would provide an effective balance, stamina and agility paired with wisdom. In reality, the team selection was really an exercise in making do and trying to fit pieces into a jigsaw that had seemed so close to completion before the loss of the departed Busby Babes.

Nat never felt nerveless when representing his club and the sensation was always exacerbated when playing in front of a roaring crowd 100,000 strong as well as the TV cameras, but the pressure was magnified by the prospect of this potentially being his final appearance for his country. A cagey opening half-hour reflected the narrow matches the two nations had contested at the World Cup, before an injury to Lev Yashin, the Russian goalkeeper already regarded as the best in the world, shifted the balance of the match. Without the 'Black Cat' in goal, England dared to try more audacious efforts in the hopes of catching his replacement, Vladimir Belyayev, off guard. Nat was having a larger influence off the ball than on it, his commanding presence drawing the Soviet defenders magnetically towards him and away from his teammates. With the half headed toward a stalemate, Johnny Haynes burst through a couple of challenges and slammed the ball home. England came out of the gates quickly after the restart and, after Nat's header was blocked, Haynes fired home the loose ball for his second. Now the floodgates opened. Haynes completed his hat-trick with a highly speculative strike from outside the box before a foul on Blackburn's tricky winger Bryan Douglas gave England a penalty – and a conundrum. Tom Finney, who had scored from the spot at the World Cup, had the opportunity to take the kick and extend his lead as England's all-time top goal scorer to two. Nat, if he scored, would match Finney's record. Perhaps out of deference to their close personal friendship, or perhaps wanting to put another nail in the coffin of the notion that young Bobby Charlton lacked the bottle for the big stage, they elected to give the opportunity to the young Manchester United star, which he duly seized.

The match all but decided, the majority within Wembley were in good spirits, although the BBC cameras did pick up a couple of punters, boasting large CCCP rosettes pinned to their coats, looking dejected. The crowd would have been more attentive and uproarious had they known that this was to be the last of Tom Finney in an England shirt. Beyond his record-setting goals tally, he had been capped seventy-six times, a number only bettered by his teammate Billy Wright, and few were able to remember a single time when he'd pulled on the England shirt and not delivered. Injury would take him out of contention in the short term, and by the time he'd recovered, the FA had deemed it unwise to welcome a 37-year-old back into the fold, even for a celebratory swansong. Finney's final bow wasn't to be the only landmark the crowd were to witness. Having been carefully marshalled throughout, the USSR defence were taken by surprise by a sudden burst of strength and speed from Nat's ageing legs so late in the match. With all the power and purpose of the goal he'd made his name with in Vienna six years earlier, Lofty charged into the box under close inspection from two defenders. Then, as Belyayev advanced, his markers converged on his run and the window of opportunity to get his shot away appeared to shut, the Lion of Vienna unleashed a thunderbolt that was the equal of any he'd hit before, beyond the Soviet keeper and into the top corner. The sheer force of the shot was such that it left Nat, already losing his balance as he struck it, flat on the floor, able to celebrate only by punching the air triumphantly. The improbability of the goal seemed to catch the crowd off guard, with many taking a moment to process the sight of the ball nestling in the net and Nat sprawled on the floor, arms aloft, before exploding into rapturous applause.

The goal not only re-established Nat as England's joint all-time top goal scorer[*] with thirty but gave him the closure that he'd been denied when he'd lost his place in the England team back in 1956. The newspapers generally noted the record, but were more preoccupied with praising Nat as one of England's greatest footballing heroes. Lofty himself was well aware that his recall was a temporary measure and perhaps, as he lay sprawled on the Wembley turf, the crowd's cheers washing over him,

---

[*]   For years, the apocryphal retelling of Nat's goal had the man he equalled, Finney, supplying the through pass for Nat to tie the record. However, it was actually Bobby Charlton's pass that set up Nat.

he knew this would be the last time he'd experience such a moment on the international stage. His final game for his country came the following month in a 2-2 draw with Wales at Villa Park in which he failed to score, leaving him with a quite remarkable record of thirty-three caps and thirty goals. No player has ever scored more for the Three Lions at such a remarkable rate, something which Jeff remembers his father being particularly proud of. England didn't play again until April, by which point Bobby Charlton had made it all but impossible for the FA to ignore his credentials, and, behind him, Jimmy Greaves was patiently waiting in line to show the world what he was capable of. Nat's time had come. In assessing his England career, he simply said, 'I'd had a good run.'

Stan Matthews' curtain call had arrived the year before; Tom Finney's, just one game earlier. Billy Wright would bow out after his 105th cap in 1959. One by one, the names without which the post-war game would have been unrecognisable were fading from view and with them the very fabric of their era of football.

It wasn't for a lack of trying on Nat's part that he was never to represent his country again. In fact, the 1958/59 season proved to be most productive of his career overall, with a remarkable thirty-five goals spread across the league, Cup and Charity Shield. Dougie Holden summed up the general dynamic between Lofty and Bolton, saying that 'when he was in the team, we played to him. Find him, you got a winner. When he wasn't on form, neither was the team,' and his words would never ring truer than in the final full season of the 1950s. Nat's final England cap meant he missed the first meeting between Bolton and Manchester United since the Cup Final, but the Whites executed an attacking masterclass without their talisman, running out 6-3 winners. Upon his return, Bolton secured their second triumph of the season over Wolves, this time at Molineux, with Nat netting the winner and, to his relief, not being asked to stand in as goalkeeper. The two wins kept Bolton in the title hunt, two points behind leaders Arsenal, before indifferent form led to them slipping to fifth at the turn of the year (although still only three points off the top). January proved to be a banner month for Nat, even by his enormously high standards, as he netted a brace and a hat-trick in Bolton's only two league matches, at home to West Bromwich Albion and Luton Town. In the midst of those victories came the start of the team's FA Cup defence. Scunthorpe United were despatched comfortably before Wanderers again got the better of Wolves in the next round.

As they had the year before, Bolton saw off Tom Finney and Preston in the next round, before their Cup defence finally succumbed to Nottingham Forest in a second replay. With the Cup gone, the Trotters were free to focus their efforts on the league campaign. They rallied following the Forest game, hitting Chelsea for six at Burnden Park and moving up to fourth. Although Fred Hill's treble was the story of the match, what nobody at the time realised was that the two goals Nat had managed were to prove his final league brace. The win over Chelsea firmly established Wanderers' title challenge, and set them up perfectly to begin their assault on the First Division summit and attempt to claim the title that had eluded the club for so long.

Unfortunately, it wasn't to be. The momentum gathered by the rout of Chelsea was halted when, just three days later, Blackpool comprehensively took the Whites apart 4-0 at Bloomfield Road. Defeat at home to an average Aston Villa team eleven days later was even tougher to swallow. Three days after that, the team conspired to score three times at West Ham, yet still took nothing from the game after an unusually lax defensive effort saw them finish on the wrong end of a 4-3 scoreline. Another defensive aberration followed, this time at home to Leicester City. Goals from Nat, Dennis Stevens and a slice of luck in the form of an own goal at least salvaged a point in a 3-3 draw, but Bolton's title run was over. Bill Ridding had been able to call on a largely unchanged side throughout the season, but the number of games was quickly mounting up,[*] and what the team gained in terms of synergy, their small squad – 'we never had a lot of reserves,' explains Banks – sacrificed in fatigue. Nat echoed Banks, saying, 'We had the ideal side for the FA Cup. We were

---

[*] Although they only reached the fifth round, Wanderers had played just one fewer game in the FA Cup than their victorious campaign the year before.

always a good league side, finishing in the top ten in the First Division, but we were never really in with a serious shout for the Championship.' Bolton's failure to capture the league championship in this period certainly owed something to a lack of consistency and squad depth, but they were also unfortunate to have peaked at the precise moment that two of the greatest sides in English football's history – Matt Busby's Babes and Stan Cullis' Wolves – were at their respective zeniths.

Bolton ultimately finished fourth, missing out on third place to Arsenal on goal average. Despite boasting the joint-third best defensive record in the league, the thinning crowds that attended the final few games (the final home fixture, a local derby with Blackburn, drew under 19,000, by some distance the lowest of the campaign) had their attention firmly fixed on the other end of the field, where Nat was still turning back the clock. Lofty never quite lost touch with the league's leading goal scorer that year, his eventual long-term replacement for England, Jimmy Greaves. Nat scored in five of Bolton's final six fixtures, bringing his total in the league to twenty-nine. One of those games, a 1–0 win at Portsmouth's Fratton Park, saw him finally usurp Joe Smith's mark of 277 league and cup goals for Bolton; he now stood alone as the club's greatest ever goal scorer. Despite the ultimately disappointing finishes to the league and Cup campaigns, Bolton and Nat had plenty of reasons for optimism. If the team, with its experienced core, could eke another season from their talismanic captain like the one he'd just had, the sky was the limit. The elusive First Division championship was tangible, in reach. Little did Bill Ridding, George Taylor, the players, the fans or Nat himself know that he had already made his final significant contribution as a player.

Having come to terms with leaving the Castle and the prospect of long-term future security behind them, the Lofthouses, who had waved goodbye to the publican life in March 1959, were content to see what the future held while Nat saw out his playing days. Within five months of leaving the pub, they 'had to start giving the matter serious consideration'. The problems began in July, when the players returned from a post-season tour of South Africa. Having trained at Burnden Park for so many years, it was a moment tinged with irony when Nat went down during a training match after twisting his ankle not on the muddy, rutted pitch or unforgiving grit track, but on the club's much more well-appointed Bromwich Street training ground. In those days, with diagnostic procedures far more rudimentary, a rolled ankle could keep a player out for a stretch of time ranging from just a couple of days to untold months. Nat himself said, 'It seemed like just another injury. I'd had plenty of those over the years, though thankfully nothing serious, and always bounced back as good as new.' Both Lofty and the club can't have been overly concerned about the injury, as no attempt to transfer a replacement in was made, although Bill Ridding's oft-mentioned pride in the club's policy of youth over expensive signings may have influenced the decision not to sign another player. Such was their confidence in Nat's recovery that when utility forward Ralph Gubbins, who had performed so heroically in Nat's stead in the 1958 semi-final, failed to find the net in two appearances as a stand-in centre forward, he was transferred to Hull City. As August turned to September and then October, however, Nat had still to make an appearance. Fred Hill, Dennis Stevens, Malcolm Edwards and even Derek Hennin were trialled in the position that had given Bolton so few problems over the years that Ridding may have taken Nat's reliability for granted. Stevens had the most success, although what he provided in terms of goals through the middle, the team lost in creativity and drive from his preferred inside forward role. Nat did gradually show signs of recovery, appearing in 'A' team reserve matches and scoring the winner in one. However, it was now apparent that when he did return, expecting him to match the same level of production he'd provided the season before was a huge ask. Further setbacks led to Lofty undergoing surgery in late October, but the operation did little to improve the situation. Nat was still trying to work through the injury in December, although it appeared inevitable that he'd miss the congested festive period. On Christmas Day, for the first time since Jeff and Viv had been born, Nat was to have a greater influence on the present unwrapping and turkey eating than he was to have on Bolton

Wanderers. The team were relatively stable without him, but if it hadn't been before, it was now clear just how critical he had been to Wanderers, and not just in terms of his goals. Even while he attempted to stay close to the team while he rehabilitated, Nat's geeing up of his teammates, the experience he brought to managing close games and his easy way with players that helped disarm them and expel their nerves before matches were all sorely missed.

It was almost certainly over Christmas, surrounded by his loving wife and his two kids who were, by now, in school and growing up before his eyes, that Nat made perhaps the hardest decision of his life. Many of the other milestone moments he'd faced in his thirty-four years – defying the conventional wisdom of finding a trade in favour of trying to make it in football, marrying Alma – had been matters of the heart. They were easy decisions for a man who, beneath a hardy, humble, typically Lancastrian exterior, was in possession of an intuitive, emotional intelligence. It was this emotion that helped elevate him from being just another player to one who could draw on apparently bottomless wells of bravery, courage and grit, inspired by an intrinsic empathy and understanding with the fans who thrilled in his play for so many years. This decision, on the other hand, was one he had to make based on not only his health, but his pride. Dropping down the divisions to stave off the inevitable was out of the question:

> I had already decided that I would go out at the top. I had no intention
> of fading quietly away in the lower divisions. I had only ever played for
> Bolton Wanderers in the First Division. That's how I wanted it to stay.
> I sometimes used to look at players and wonder what they were doing
> there. I suppose they just didn't want to stop.

Wanderers had been drawn away to Bury in the FA Cup third round, the sort of local derby that Nat had always thrived in, in the competition he had become synonymous with. But he wouldn't be there on 9 January. Two days before, Nat Lofthouse, already enshrined as Bolton's greatest ever player, had announced his retirement from the professional game:

'The end was in sight. It seems odd to say it but I just sort of fizzled out. I carried that ankle injury until January 1960, but it was no good. So I quit.'

For both player and club, the months following Nat's retirement felt something like a science-fiction movie. On the face of it, little had changed. The crowds still poured into Burnden Park to see the vaunted Whites take on First Division opposition, with varying results. Nat still made the journey by bus to the ground, was still recognised and warmly greeted by all. And yet something was decisively different. Without his presence on the pitch, both the man and the club had lost something intrinsic to their respective souls.

The Lofthouses' financial position was secured for the immediate future after his retirement, with his Wanderers contract seeing him through to May. Taking the summer off, a full year after his ankle injury, any monetary concerns were eased further when Wanderers offered him a position as reserve team manager. As well as helping to refine the gems in the club's youth system in an attempt to find the next First Division star, the role came with some less glamorous aspects, including mopping the changing room floors, scrubbing the toilets and even cleaning the boots of those players who hadn't been assigned an apprentice to do theirs:

I'll be honest. I didn't fancy cleaning out the dressing room and all that sort of thing. I had, after all, been club captain and an international player. But when I took a step back and thought it over, there was never much chance of me turning the job down. It meant I could stay with Bolton Wanderers. And that, basically, was all I wanted to do. All I'd ever wanted to do.

The months off had given his injured ankle a well-needed rest, and without the pressure of getting fit as quickly as possible, he had taken a more measured approach to his rehabilitation. The result was the joint finally showing signs of significant recovery, so much so that he felt capable of making one final go of it. 'Fizzling out' was, after all, no way for the great Lion of Vienna to go. 'Like a prize fighter always thinks he's got another fight in him, I believed I might just be able to give it one more season,' Nat said. He re-signed for the club as a player in July, more out of hope than expectation, even though doing so meant he had to forfeit the compensation he'd received due to his injury-enforced retirement. Throughout the autumn, he was able to get more and more involved with the training sessions he was coaching.

He certainly had no need to worry about his potential return to the fold causing any selection headaches for Ridding. Bolton had ended the previous season in sixth, a quite frankly incredible achievement given that as well as losing Nat, Eddie Hopkinson, Tommy Banks and Bryan Edwards had all missed significant chunks of the season in what was truly an *annus horribilis* in terms of injuries. Nat's absence had manifested itself in the Wanderers recording the third-fewest goals in the top division, twenty fewer than they'd scored the year before. Bolton's respectable final position in the table was owed entirely to their stoic defence, which was the second best in the league. However, the 1960/61 campaign had begun badly, with the Whites still impotent in attack but now looking shaky at the back as well. Having wondered – fancifully at first – since the start of the pre-season, Nat began seriously entertaining the possibility of a comeback in September. His ankle was giving him fewer problems, and he had kept himself in shape through his training of the reserves. In mid-September, he netted a hat-trick in the testimonial for his best friend Tom Finney. By the end of the month, Wanderers had won just two of their opening ten matches and were sat second to bottom. If ever a moment had a sense of 'cometh the hour, cometh the man' in Bolton Wanderers' history, this was it. With their First Division status under serious threat, there was no doubting who the man was.

More than 39,000 bore witness to a sight that most had assumed would never be seen again when Nat emerged from the Burnden Park tunnel to face Manchester United, displacing his £15,000 replacement (a fee that underlined just how critical the higher ups at the club felt the situation was becoming) at centre forward, Billy McAdams. After six goals in seven reserve team games, Ridding had been convinced the time had come to give Lofty one last try. Wanderers earned a spirited 1-1 draw that could so easily have been a fairy-tale return for Nat had Roy Hartle not missed a penalty and a chance to claim a much-needed win. Nat's return was a painful one for McAdams, who Harry Gregg mistook for Nat and, seeking revenge for 1958, 'clattered into this white shirt and took everything', leaving his fellow Irishman in a heap. The *Bolton Evening News* found Nat to be 'a less mobile Lofthouse, rarely able to elude the close and unceremonious marking of Bill Foulkes', but noted he 'nevertheless commanded the Manchester defenders' constant attention and thereby left others a little freer'.

With Ridding convinced by the added attacking threat that the rejigged front line had posed against United, Nat kept his spot for the home match against West Bromwich. The Baggies were also struggling, but what Bolton hoped would be the game to kick-start their season ended in a demoralising 1-0 loss. Nat retained his place – and scored the first goal since his return – in an absolutely critical match away to Cardiff City but with his fitness still not quite there and the Bolton directors' desire to see their considerable investment in McAdams pay dividends, he was dropped for the next two games, both of which Wanderers lost without scoring a goal. With the Lofty-less trial a complete bust, Nat played the next couple of fixtures at inside forward, with the thinking being he could perhaps use his experience and nous to help orchestrate the attacks without the same physicality required for the number nine role. Nat scored in a 3-1 victory over Manchester City in which another scorer was 16-year-old winger Franny Lee. Despite his goal, which Nat scored from one of several bullet crosses from Lee ('head high. You only needed a touch'), the promising starlet had no problem letting the veteran Lofthouse know what he thought of his goal, as Nat remembered:

'Well done, Franny, nice ball,' I said waiting for the congratulations. 'About bloody time, Lofty, the number of crosses I've put over,' came the reply. There I was, over 20 years in the game, 33 England caps and a few goals to go with them, being put firmly in my place by a 16-year-old kid just starting out. I knew it was time to go!

Another goal in the next game sparked hope anew that Nat could still rediscover his old form, but despite his performances, it was becoming clear that his days were numbered. Just two years before, Nat had been the one who had dragged the team up by their bootlaces. Now, he was being accommodated in an unfamiliar position, his remaining on-field attributes diluted by greater baggage and drawbacks. He did manage to achieve several landmarks that he would have otherwise missed. The most significant by far was his finally surpassing of Joe Smith's league goal-scoring record for Wanderers. He equalled Smith's total of 254 in the City match, before moving one ahead a week later away at Nottingham Forest.* He made his first appearance, and netted the final hat-trick of his illustrious career, in the newly introduced League Cup competition against Grimsby Town. Another, less welcome, milestone was also achieved. As was demonstrated multiple times over the course of Nat's career, there was an incredible physicality to the game at the time. This was never better summarised than by Nat himself, whose most famous and enduring maxim was that players of his era would 'kick your bollocks off. The difference was that at the end of the match, they'd shake your hand and help you look for them.' However, the gentlemanly nature of the game alluded to in Nat's words played a significant role in referees taking a typically lenient view of many incidents, including what warranted a yellow card or – heaven forbid – a sending off. 'Bookings in my day were generally few and far between,' remembered Lofty, and he wasn't wrong. Some players, among them perhaps most famously Nat's former England teammate Jimmy Dickinson, avoided mention in the referee's notebook for their entire career. Nat was able to proudly call himself a member of this exclusive club until the City match, when he finally received a blemish on his record for sarcastically throwing the ball at a linesman for disallowing a goal. Nat called it a 'black mark on my career' without a shred of insincerity.**

---

* Nat had surpassed Smith's total of 277 goals in all competitions for the club in his third-to-last game before his first retirement in 1959; he would ultimately record 285 goals.

** Lofty would receive an autograph request on a beach that summer from a young fan; as he signed, he realised the boy's father was none other than the same linesman.

Extending the analogy of his return being like that of a boxer, Nat said of his comeback (which he jokingly referred to in inverted commas in his 1989 biography) 'they always say fighters never come back [to the same level] and I should have known the same applies to footballers'. He had promised himself that he wouldn't fade away, whether it be at Burnden Park or in the lower leagues. He may have already made up his mind that the time finally had come to call it quits as he travelled down to Birmingham's St Andrews ground on a foggy, wintery morning a week before Christmas. Within a couple of hours, the decision would be made for him. Challenging the goalkeeper for a loose ball in classic Lofthouse style, he twisted his knee, tearing the ligaments. When asked what the family would say when he got home, he grinned and said the kids would probably greet him with 'Hello, daddy's done it again'.[*] The initial diagnosis was that he could return within six weeks, but when the injury failed to respond to treatment, Lofty knew his time had come. He would announce his retirement shortly afterwards. As his wry anecdote about his admonishment from Franny Lee suggested, he was under no illusions about the possibility of ever returning to his former glory. The stop-start nature of the end of his playing days didn't befit a career that had never been played at less than 100mph, but it did at least give him a chance to say goodbye, not just to the fans but to his livelihood and a vital part of his life. Just as his England career had appeared to end abruptly in 1956, only for him to be given something of a proper send-off two years later, so too did his brief emergence from retirement allow him a more tangible farewell to his life as a player.

[*] *Bolton Evening News*, 19 December 1958.

13

MANAGERIAL MISERY

NAT LOFTHOUSE SIGNED his first contract the day after Britain declared war on Germany, when players were paid a maximum of £7 a week during the season, cars were still something of a novelty, and Stan Matthews had been playing for *just* seven years. By the time Nat had played his final game, on 17 December 1960, the conflict that had ultimately become the most destructive in world history had been over for more than a decade and a half, men had been into space – and Stan Matthews had been playing for twenty-nine years. One thing that hadn't changed much was players' pay, but it soon would. As Nat, Tom Finney and Billy Wright all retired within a matter of months of each other, the complexion of English football was changing markedly. A proposed player strike over wages, which would have forced the first halt in the regular footballing calendar since the war, could not have been more symbolically timed, slated for two weeks into 1961, just days after Nat had confirmed his retirement. Nat's era has been enshrined as one in which players asked for nothing more than an honest day's pay and could truly consider their lot in life to be on a par with that of many of those in the stands. This idyllic view of players' contentment in the 1950s is, of course, an oversimplification. Several high-profile players had moved abroad, first to Colombia and then to Italy, lured by wages that dwarfed those on offer in the UK. For the majority that remained, the grumbling about wages was far more frequent than the sepia-toned images painted by modern commentators would have you believe. As post-war prosperity began picking up pace and the wage cap's gradual upward creep was outpaced by the growth in the average wage across the country, even First Division players found they were little better off than they would have been as semi-skilled labourers.

The proposed strike, organised by a hundreds-strong group of footballers among whom Tommy Banks was a vociferous member,[*] was the greatest threat to the footballing status quo in years. With the date drawing nearer, club owners finally caved, abolishing the maximum wage. It was a watershed moment. Almost overnight, wages exploded. Johnny Haynes became the game's first £100 a week player, dwarfing the £20 Lofty was earning when he retired. Two years later, the 'retain and transfer' system that meant players had no freedom of movement was ended, granting players much stronger negotiating positions. The game had undergone an irrevocable powershift; money was now king.

Nat would later join the cavalcade of former stars who linked many of the ills of the modern game – the dominance of richer clubs, the win-at-all-costs mentality, a lack of loyalty – to the rapid increase of money in the game, although he would always remain humble about his lot and would never bemoan the fact that, but for a few years, he could have earned enough money to have retired on. It would have saved him and Alma plenty of worry and sleepless nights, and from their brief, unhappy stint at the Castle. Banks put voice to what many players of that era felt about the disparity in earnings in his day and the stars of the late 1960s:

That [during the mid-to-late 1950s] was when they should have sorted this contract business out, when the players had the upper hand and there were large crowds generating the money. Not just at Bolton but throughout the league. That was when we should have universally gone for better money.

---

[*]   Banks rebuffed the suggestion that footballers shouldn't earn significantly more than miners by pointing out he'd worked in a mine and that his colleagues there, while good men, wouldn't have been able to mark Stanley Matthews.

Nat's biggest gripe in later years regarding the money situation had nothing to do with himself and everything to do with what happened to his beloved Bolton Wanderers and their neighbouring teams. In 1989 he bemoaned that 'in my playing days we had Bolton, Blackburn, Preston, Blackpool and Burnley all within 30 miles of one another, all in the First Division and all doing well. Small-town clubs with a reputation for building their own sides. Look at them now.'

Of the clubs Nat cited, Preston were the first to go, symbolically relegated just one year after the club's greatest son – and Nat's best mate – Tom Finney had retired. Theirs is perhaps the most instructive example of the havoc wreaked by the abolition of the maximum wage; they have never returned to the top flight. Blackpool, Burnley and Blackburn would all spend more time outside the top division than in it after the 1960s, and only Rovers would again enjoy anything like the sort of success that they had back in football's earlier eras. But it was, of course, Bolton's fate that Nat felt most passionately about, and more than watching the day's stars flitting around in designer clothing and fast sports cars, what really stung the Lion of Vienna was watching the gradual demise of the club he'd done so much to make great.

The writing had been on the wall for Wanderers when it became clear just how much the club missed Lofty in the months before his brief attempt at a return. Now, with the club no longer able to compete with the wages being offered by other teams to their next crop of stars, which included Franny Lee, Warwick Rimmer, Gordon Taylor and Freddie Hill,[*] everyone involved with the club was about to have their worst fears realised. Having finished fourth and sixth the previous years, the 1960/61 season, in which Nat had made his ill-fated comeback attempt, saw the team slump to eighteenth. A brief rally saw the Trotters return to the safer climes of mid-table the next season, but in truth, it was a case of prolonging the inevitable. The 1962/63 season saw another battle against relegation. The Bolton squad, so recently an ebullient mix of celebrated,

---

[*]   The club also released Alan Ball, who would go on to be immortalised as a World Cup winner with England.

experienced heads and youthful vigour, now took on a different hue entirely. The seasoned veterans appeared increasingly slow and tired, the youngsters were raw and shoved in at the deep end more often out of necessity than the genuine belief that they were ready for the rigours of the First Division. The hole left at centre forward was the most glaring; Dougie Holden remembers the club were desperate 'to get someone to fill the centre forward position at Bolton who was as good as [Nat], but there wasn't anybody'.

In the 1963/64 campaign, things at Burnden Park came to a head. The loss of key members of the team of the late 1950s – Dennis Stevens had been sold to Everton in 1962 – and the ageing of others with no clear plan to replace them gave the team sheets a wildly varied look, and the lack of consistency and chemistry translated to disastrous results on the pitch. In the 1958 Cup-winning season, only thirteen players were called upon more than ten times in the league. In 1963/64 that number was eighteen. Only Lee reached double figures on the goals front, and Wanderers scored the fewest in the league. By Christmas, the Trotters found themselves six points adrift of safety after just three wins. A brief rally did put Bolton one point above the relegation zone and their fate in their own hands going into the final game of the season, but a 4-0 hammering by Wolves and a victory for Birmingham City brought the curtain down on their twenty-three-season stay in the top flight – their longest ever unbroken sequence in the First Division. The emotional distress of relegation always fades with time, but even now, the 1963/64 campaign feels like a nadir for Bolton Wanderers. Never again, even with the subsequent returns to the top flight and their immense success during the mid-2000s, would the club be considered among the country's elite. The days of routinely playing before home crowds well in excess of 30,000 were over, too. Three home matches during the relegation season were played out in front of a sparse attendances of fewer than 10,000, and over the following years smaller gates became emblematic of the club's fall from grace.

Nat's retirement precipitated the end of the club's heyday, and his continued presence at the club as reserve team coach served as a nagging reminder of past glories. He'd only been gone for a couple of years, but already the rougher edges of his ability and the bad games were scrubbed from fans' minds. Instead, they remembered all the joy he'd brought them and the goals he'd scored and made 'If only we still had Lofty …' the most popular refrain in Lancashire. He was a frustrated – and horrified – spectator of the car crash that was the 1963/64 season, but, like the rest of the officials at the club, he had no remedy for the club's ills. Throwing vast quantities of money at the wage bill and transfer fees may have provided a short-term fix, but was also potentially ruinous for the club in the long run. Indeed, when the club did dip into the transfer market, the returns rarely matched the outlay, as had been the case with Ridding's few forays into the market in the early 1950s. When Franny Lee was sold to Manchester City in 1967, having firmly established himself as the team's star, the club reinvested the money, spending £50,000 on Gareth Williams and £70,000 on Terry Wharton, neither of whom truly hit the heights required to justify such hefty fees.

By the time Lee left Burnden Park, Wanderers had spent three seasons out of the top flight and seemed to be getting further away instead of vying for promotion. As is so often the case with lower-league sides, the team was in a constant state of flux, and behind the scenes there was change, too. George Taylor, having dedicated such an extraordinary period of his life to the club, retired from coaching duties and became a scout on a part-time basis. His testimonial in 1967 was a star-studded affair, with big names of the day including George Best playing alongside those from yesteryear, with Nat, Tom Finney and Stan Matthews all participating. George Hunt took up the reigns from Taylor as head coach before calling time on his equally impressive tenure at Burnden Park in 1968. The net result of these movements was Nat rising up the ranks and his influence at the club growing.

Although the fact he was no longer playing still panged, particularly as he was reminded on a daily basis by passers-by that the team could really use a bit of that old Lofty battering ram brute force, Nat found himself enjoying life as a coach. As he first took over from Taylor as assistant coach and then from Hunt as Bill Ridding's number two, he found the passions he'd had as a player – fine tuning his fitness ('nobody fitter than me ever played football'), working relentlessly to improve his all-round game, rousing the rest of the dressing room before big games – translated well to helping coach the young crop of players coming through. One particular success was the development of Wyn Davies, who in the words of Andrew Dean, arrived 'as a raw centre for-ward from Wrexham'. By the time Davies was sold to Newcastle, he'd earned the nickname 'Wyn the Leap' thanks to an incredible heading ability that Nat had done much to nurture. Though many players of the 1950s adopted a suspicious view of any tactics beyond those with which they'd been familiar, Nat's time with the international team, and in particular Alf Ramsey, gave him a more enlightened outlook on the possibilities beyond the WM, which was finally falling out of favour. In Nat's own words, he was an:

> ideal number two. I could have been the Malcolm Allison to Joe Mercer … the man who trained the players, worked with them day in and out, shared the dressing-room banter … I knew what made players tick, how to keep them happy on the training ground, how to build them up for matches and so on. Team spirit was always a crucial part of Bolton Wanderers' success.

Given the tenures of the managers he'd played under (by the late 1960s, only Matt Busby had served as a single team's manager longer than Bill Ridding; Walter Rowley had the job for six years before him, and his predecessor Charles Foweraker had racked up a quarter century), Nat could be forgiven for expecting his time as head coach to be relatively long lasting. Instead, he was to be thrust into the club's premier position far sooner than anyone expected in 1968.

The previous season had been a continuation of the club's stagnation. The team had performed well enough to be only six points adrift of second placed Portsmouth on New Year's Day 1968, but the sale of Lee, who scored eight in nine before leaving Burnden Park, ultimately proved disastrous. Even with the expensive additions of Wharton and Williams, the team combusted, winning two of their final fifteen matches and finishing twelfth – their worst ever league finish. It would prove a season too far for Ridding. Despite being only 57, the veteran manager-secretary decided that his time had come and resigned as manager on 18 July, citing his dual role as being 'too demanding'.[*] He then resigned the secretarial role a month later. Ridding was naturally desperate to repair his legacy by leading the club back to the top flight. However, the apparent abandonment of the youth policy with the sale of Lee and the two big-money transfers into the club made it clear that although he still had the support of the board, he and they had very different opinions on the best route to take to lead the club back to the head table of English football.

Wanderers began ultimately fruitless pursuits of Malcolm Allison and Frank O'Farrell to succeed Ridding. Meanwhile, Lofty, never one to shirk a challenge, fended off competition from former teammates Harold Hassall, now an FA coach, and Roy Hartle to win the job on an interim basis just before the beginning of the 1968/69 season. In the pages of the *Bolton Evening News*, he promised Bolton fans 'no lack of effort', 'a new spirit' and even 'entertaining football' – a bold and perhaps naive goal given the team's precipitous decline.

The job of manager of a Second Division football club had none of the glamour of the modern-day equivalent. Granted, Nat wouldn't be scrubbing the changing room floors and cleaning the players' boots as he had when he first moved to the coaching side of the operation, but the idea of treating his team to mini-breaks in Dubai would have got him laughed down the Burnden Park corridors. The secretary's role, which he would have acknowledged even then was far outside his comfort zone, had been given to former winger Ted Rothwell, so he had no need to worry about that. Nonetheless, making the move from head coach to manager was a daunting one.

Nat was trading the tracksuit to which he'd grown accustomed, that enabled him to take a seat in the dressing room beside the players and

[*] *Bolton Evening News*, 18 July 1968.

have a laugh and that tied him intrinsically to the parts of the game that he knew best, for a stifling, suffocating suit. Instead of man management and drilling his players, his priorities now lay with overarching plans, scheming a way to get the club back where it belonged without breaking the bank. The head coach's role he'd so enjoyed would go to Jimmy McIlroy, a stalwart for Burnley against whom Nat had played many times. The initially temporary nature of the role gave Lofty a period in which he'd be able to discern whether he had any true aptitude for management. The position was by far the most alien to his natural skillset that he'd ever held. Being a Bevin Boy down the mine at Mosley during the war had been a million miles from playing football, but it had at least lent itself to Nat's powerful physique and outstanding levels of fitness. For the directors, the trial period avoided any potentially costly payoffs that the club could scarcely afford should Lofty prove such a bust that they had to do the unthinkable and relieve him of his duties.

From the start, the omens seemed good. Nat had established himself as a hugely popular coach among the reserves and youth teams. Dougie Holden, who played under Nat a couple of times for the reserves, remembers thinking that 'he was such a good player, you respected him'. Gordon Taylor, who emerged from the youth ranks under Nat, was glowing in his assessment of his hero: 'It was brilliant playing for him in the youth team. He'd be leading the singing when we won, and he'd always tell you how well you'd played.'

Wanderers had finished the previous campaign with two wins in fourteen games; now they began with two in four, drawing the other pair. The players weren't the only ones to respond to the Lion of Vienna's appointment. Fewer than 10,000 had come through the turnstiles for the curtain raiser at Burnden Park in Ridding's final year in charge. For Nat, over 16,000 turned up as they comfortably beat Bury in the second game of the season. A combination of his fresh take on the club's stewardship and the fact that his young side, many of whom were Lancashire-born, were enthused by their manager being a player they had grown up admiring and idolising was responsible for Nat's strong start. However, the honeymoon period soon ended. A series of close games saw the Trotters lose more than they won. The team were dogged by inexperience on the field – a trait that Nat may well have struggled to empathise with, given he'd never been without a group of steadying senior pros in the team before graduating to that status himself. A 7-2 exit from the League Cup at the hands of First Division West Ham United was demonstrative of just what a task the rookie manager had on his hands should he defy the odds and get Bolton promoted. The following month, a 4-0 drubbing at home to a pedestrian Millwall team cast significant doubt on the prospect of Lofty leading Bolton back to the promised land on his first attempt.

The old adage goes that timing is everything in football, and so it proved for the great misstep of Lofty's career. Following the hammering by Millwall, Wanderers were fifteenth, five points off the top of the table, five points from the bottom, having scored and conceded the exact same number of goals. The season was thirteen fixtures old, mature enough to provide a decent barometer of how things were going. Bolton were bang average under Nat's stewardship, and he was already finding the stresses of the job were equalling any of those he'd experienced as a player. It's not hard to envision him on the sidelines during the training sessions he had time to attend, gazing wistfully out on to the pitch as McIlroy put the players through their paces and wishing for nothing more than to stick on a pair of old boots and run out there to join in. If there was ever a point to exercise the freedom of his temporary contract and let the club know the role wasn't for him, this was it.

But Nat didn't. Two successive victories, with clean sheets to go with them, over strong Charlton Athletic and Cardiff City sides revived hopes that Wanderers could demonstrate progress with the Lion of Vienna at the helm, if not actually achieve promotion. Between the middle of November and December, Nat oversaw a six-match unbeaten run that included a superb 4-1 victory at Deepdale over Preston that lifted the Trotters to eleventh and kept them just about in touch with the leaders. While the Bolton attack was often anaemic, the Whites had improved markedly as a defensive unit – a not uncommon by-product of managers who had been forwards. These ex-strikers invariably struggled to elucidate what made them effective in front of goal, but often had a wealth of experience when it came to what defenders did right and wrong.[*] This bright run of form was what convinced Nat to sign a permanent contract as manager on 18 December 1968, with club chairman Harry Tyldesley anointing him the 'Lion of Bolton'.

What Nat called a 'wonderful Christmas present from the directors'[**] almost immediately took a southward turn. A 2-1 defeat in front of a scant Burnden Park crowd of below 9,000 to Cardiff served as notice of a sea change in Bolton's season and was followed up by an embarrassing 1-0 reverse at home to Carlisle United on Boxing Day. The team selections, which had been consistent at the start of the term – nine league games had come and gone before Lofty had been forced into changing his XI – took on a scattergun look as injuries and desperation to change the team's fortunes set in. The effect was emotionally draining on Nat. Every decision to drop someone from the team or – worse yet – the thought of having to let some players go at the end of the season cast his mind back to the stomach-churning fits of worry he was subjected to in his early days as he wondered if each game would prove his last. His demeanour was far more suited to an arm around the shoulder, not the cold shoulder. He simply lacked the necessary ruthless pragmatism and was too senti-mental to make the hard choices: 'I'd learned all about life on the training ground from George Taylor and George Hunt at Burnden Park. I knew all about man management from Walter Winterbottom. I'd talked tactics and training methods with men like Billy Wright, Tom Finney and Alf Ramsey. But what I'd never done was take the big decisions.'

It took until mid-March, ten games since Nat had taken the reins on a permanent basis, for the team to finally break out of their funk and record a victory. Before the 3-2 success over lowly Fulham, Nat's men

---

[*] That season's Second Division champions were Derby County, managed by another striker and one who had joined Nat in the preliminary 1958 World Cup squad, Brian Clough. The explanation for Bolton's strong defensive showing is borne out in Derby's statistics for the season; three teams outscored them, but they won the league at a canter thanks to their superb defence.

[**] *Bolton Evening News*, 19 December 1968.

had slid from their place in the chasing pack down to eighteenth, now well adrift of the top sides and more likely to slip toward the relegation zone than produce a late surge toward promotion. Four successive defeats followed, in which they shipped nineteen goals. With Wanderers now balanced precariously just one place above an unfathomable relegation to the Third Division, Nat resorted to appealing to his status as a club legend to try to draw a performance from the players not out of fear, but of pride. 'He led,' remembers Gordon Taylor, 'by example; with a great will to win.' It worked, as three wins and two draws in the final five fixtures (one of which, against Hull City, was watched by just over 5,000 people, the smallest crowd Burnden Park had seen since 1947) lifted Wanderers to safety but still their lowest ever league finish.

The next season began promisingly. One of Nat's signings, John Byrom, had struggled in his first season at Burnden, but began paying back his £25,000 fee, netting twenty goals. Though Bolton had begun well enough to suggest that last season's struggles were behind them, Nat was slowly coming to the realisation that the job was not for him. His worrisome side, which had lain largely dormant since the early years of his career, was now troubling him more than ever:

> Your head is on the block. The buck stops in the manager's chair. You HAVE to make decisions that you know will hurt someone. I used to worry all night about how I would tell a player I was dropping him. If we won I'd go home and worry about whether we'd win again the next time out. If we lost I'd go home and go straight to bed.

The long hours and amount of work ('Often there's only Thursday night and Sunday night at home. And even then there's always the telephone waiting to ring') posed little problem for Lofthouse, whose pride in hard work had been drilled into him by his parents and would never desert him. Instead, it was the strain that the constant pressures of the job put on him that wore him down. He fretted not just about the prospect of losing his job and livelihood, but about what he'd do if he decided once and for all that life as a manager wasn't for him. He was already well aware that his having been 'one of the lads' for such a long time was counting against him. ('Everyone knew me at Burnden Park ... but not as the boss. It was hard for the players to accept me.') Now he had the added concern of whether it would even be possible for him to return to the coaching role in which he'd felt so much more comfortable.

The club's ultimate survival in the 1969/70 season did little to ease Nat's worries. So bad was Bolton's form at one stage that Lancashire-based hypnotist Mirza offered his services in order to break the team from their malaise. Anticipating a PR opportunity or, at worst, a cheeky rebuttal from Nat, the hypnotist may well have been taken aback when he read the Bolton's managers thoughts in the paper, where he called Mirza's approach 'an insult' and indicated he wouldn't even be bothering to reply to the request. Any fans labouring under the belief that the team would survive based on name and illustrious history alone had that illusion shattered by taking a look further down the table and finding the name of Preston North End at the very bottom.

Nat never truly felt suited to the job, and would never miss an opportunity to tell people in later years about his poor aptitude for it. The chapter of his 1989 autobiography dedicated to his managerial tenure opens with the optimistic line: 'To this day I don't know why Bolton Wanderers wanted me to be their manager ... I must go down as just about the worst manager in the world.' However, there were mitigating factors beyond his control that hindered him, not least the club's financial situation. Burnden Park suddenly lacked the lustre now present at the likes of Anfield, Elland Road and Old Trafford, where the wages offered to players were far beyond the means of the Bolton directors. When he was able to operate in the transfer market, he actually performed relatively well. The aforementioned Byrom would be Bolton's most prolific forward for several years. Veterans like Charlie 'The King' Hurley and Liverpool's legendary striker Roger Hunt were coaxed by Lofty to join the club and played their part in helping the club stabilise somewhat. Hunt was a particular coup, given the role he'd played in England's World Cup success, and there was no doubt as to why he'd made the decision to come to Burnden. Andrew Dean recalls that, on the day the annual squad photo was to be taken, Hunt made it absolutely clear that there was 'no way he was sitting next to anybody but Nat'.

The 1970/71 season began with the same weary pattern, with Bolton losing more than they won but generally doing just enough to stay out of harm's way. The stress of the job led to the usually genial Nat publicly exhibiting some irritability. As well as the Mirza incident the year before, he argued in the press that, just two months into the season, Wanderers had already been denied 'nine legitimate goals' due to the fact that 'Roger [Hunt]'s reactions are too quick for many referees and linesmen. He times his runs so well that he is clearly in an offside position when he collects the ball, but onside at the vital time when the ball was played.'* October found them situated in mid-table, with a porous defence being mitigated by a relatively productive attack, a reversal of the trend exhibited when Nat had first taken charge. It was the belief that, by changing a few of the losses into wins, Bolton could be contenders for the division that then spurred the board into the decision that was to set off a devastating chain reaction.

Firstly, Nat was removed as the club's manager, moving to the somewhat vague and woollily defined general manager's role. On the one hand, Nat was happy to have the burden of overseeing the day-to-day running of the team lifted from his shoulders: 'I was glad. I was relieved to be out of the job. And if anything Alma was even more pleased about it than I was. If being a manager had been hard for me, it hadn't been much fun for her either.' On the other hand, the change did mean that Nat was now further away than ever from the footballing side of things that he longed to be back involved with. 'I haven't been able to get across to Bromwich Street for training sessions recently,' Nat explained at the time, 'because of the amount of work here and I will now be able to devote my time purely to this.'** The club's statement to the *Bolton Evening News* that Nat was 'happy with the new arrangement' can only be interpreted as Nat putting a brave face on developments. The role of general manager entailed looking after the club as a whole, rather than focusing specifically

★   *Sports Argus*, 26 September 1970.
★★ *Bolton Evening News*, 2 November 1970.

on footballing matters, a task for which he was patently ill-suited. This fact wasn't lost on the man himself: 'I'm the first to admit this wasn't my kind of job either. As I've said, I was always a players' man. I could have been out there on the training ground and joining in the dressing room banter. Instead I was office-bound. It just wasn't me.'

In Nat's place came McIlroy, who graduated to the hot seat from the lead coaching role. With the length of Nat's managerial tenure paling in comparison to Ridding's, the board were desperately hopeful that McIlroy was there to stay. The opposite proved to be the case. With just seventeen days and two games under his belt – both losses – McIlroy quit, citing broken promises over the amount of money that would be made available to him for transfers. Nat, having just found time to catch his breath after escaping the suffocating pressure of the manager's job, was asked to return while the club started their search from scratch. He agreed, overseeing a single win and two draws in seven games while the club frantically searched throughout Christmas and the New Year to find a suitable replacement, their bargaining positioning worsening with each bad result. By the time Jimmy Meadows, who had played alongside Nat for England in the famous 7-2 rout of Scotland in 1955, was recruited, on 15 January, Bolton weren't so much hoping for a new manager as they were a miracle worker. The team were now just three points off the bottom of the table and showing no signs of moving in the right direction, with the fire sale of Terry Wharton, Gordon Taylor and Paul Fletcher necessitated by the club's deepening financial woes.

As with McIlroy, Meadows' appointment was a false dawn. Eighty-one days later, one week into April, the directors were hunting for their fourth permanent manager of the season; the four before them had lasted a combined fifty-one years. The club were staring down the barrel in a manner never before seen in Bolton's long history. Meadows had scored a 2-1 victory over Sheffield United, who would end the season as runners-up, in his first match, but it was his only victory. By the time Nat stepped in for the third time, Wanderers were bottom, despite having played more games than their nearest rivals. Nat's first three games of his third stint in charge all ended in defeat, effectively condemning Wanderers to a three-team mini-league consisting of themselves, Blackburn Rovers and Charlton, with the winner escaping the drop. Bolton's next two opponents just so happened to be their closest rivals, with a trip to the capital to face the Addicks up first. Nat steeled himself, hoping to instil the same spirit in the players as he had at the end of his first season in charge, but it wasn't enough. A 4-1 loss in London meant Bolton's failure to beat Blackburn the next weekend was irrelevant. For the first time in almost 100 years of history, Bolton Wanderers would be playing in the Third Division.

'I've been associated with Bolton Wanderers for fifty years. Forty-eight of them have been happy. The other two,' Nat would later quip, 'I was manager.'

14

WANDERERS' SAVIOUR

ALTHOUGH STILL ONLY 45, the 1970/71 season was to mark the end of Nat Lofthouse's career on the front lines of football. The rigours and stresses of the manager's role had proved far too great, and after several unhappy months stuck behind a desk as general manager, Nat again changed jobs, this time becoming the club's chief scout. It was, on the face of things, a good match. The club's economic model had changed drastically in light of their relegation to the Third Division. Now, rather than attempting to keep the youngsters they brought through their youth teams, they recognised that developing the stars of the future and helping them to catch the eye of First Division sides was an ideal way of bringing in some much-needed funds as gate receipts dwindled. For Nat, it gave him the opportunity to get outside and get back involved in the rough and tumble of proper football.

The fact that Lofty was taking a step back from the spotlight did little to diminish his status in footballing circles. Ever since he had retired, and particularly as the Whites had begun their inexorable downward spiral, his name had never been far from the lips of the people of Bolton. They bemoaned his absence not only when the club's current crop of forwards were firing blanks, but whenever a player appeared to not be giving his all, or limped off the field to be replaced by a substitute ('If that were Lofty, he wouldn't have even gone down!'). They weren't the only ones. In 1966,

England had won the World Cup, but the famous victory had been far from plain sailing, with a particular headache coming at centre forward.

Although Alf Ramsey's much-critiqued 'wingless wonders' system was radically different to what he and his contemporaries had played in, it still benefited greatly from a centre forward that possessed the skills that those of yesteryear had needed: courage, strength, aerial ability, and of course, the ability to put the ball in the net more often than not. Though Nat would later state, 'I'm certain that I could never have been part of Alf's England set-up. I needed wingers … just ask Tom Finney and Stanley Matthews!', this was self-effacing to say the least. Ramsey's system would certainly have required adaptation on Nat's part, but he hardly would have been left behind, even if the manager's innovation did spell 'the beginning of the end for the domestic game as I had known it'.

Even as Bobby Charlton and Jimmy Greaves surpassed Nat's record for England, neither ever quite made the centre forward berth their sole dominion as he had. Geoff Hurst, England's hero in the final, had only made his debut five months before the 4-2 victory over West Germany. In fact, as late as 1965, the void left by Nat was still a topic of popular discourse. In a retrospective he wrote to celebrate the tenth anniversary of the 1955 7-2 romp over Scotland that both he and Nat had starred in, Stan Matthews put voice to the feelings of many fans when he bemoaned the lack of a striker of Lofthouse's creed and calibre in the squad: 'How we could use a centre forward like him in the England side today!'[*]

Despite wishing he could have been part of similar success as the 1966 team were, Nat was still delighted by his fellow countrymen's victory. The World Cup was 'the best thing that happened to our game … Our standing in the world game has never been higher.'

Hurst's legendary appearance in the World Cup Final in place of Jimmy Greaves, who was injured earlier in the tournament, offers a telling reminder of the fleeting and unforgiving nature of football and the

---

[*]   'With Lofthouse at his best we slammed the Scots 7-2', *South China Sunday Post Herald*, 1965.

glory it can bestow. Records fall, apparently immortal heroes are quickly forgotten, dynastic teams crumble. Though Nat Lofthouse had little concern for his own legacy (not that he had any cause for worry in Bolton, where he would struggle to go five minutes without having his hand shaken for the rest of his life), he continued to agonise over the sight of the once-great Bolton Wanderers receding from prominence. The achievements of the teams he'd been a part of were now remembered with a rueful air, as his torically smaller clubs surpassed Wanderers' league standing. Thanks to the rate at which money was expanding in the game, the new status quo would prove harder to upset than that of old, when the distinctions between teams in one division and those below were far less pronounced. In 1971, Bolton's first ever campaign outside of the top two tiers, the game suddenly seemed very different from that which hadn't changed a great amount between Bolton's first FA Cup win in 1923 and their most recent in 1958. Transfer fees were now making a mockery of those that had grabbed headlines during the 1950s. Players in the Fourth Division were typically earning a better basic wage than the entire pay packet, including bonuses, that Nat finished his career on. When Liverpool, then in the First Division, bought a 20-year-old named Kevin Keegan from Scunthorpe United, they agreed to pay him a basic wage of £50 a week that, when combined with various add-ons, regularly saw the youngster collect a wage slip over £100. The number of footballers grumbling about the proximity between their wages and the national industrial average was reduced to nil.

All of this would have reduced some men to a life of bitterness and recriminations, but Nat remained eternally grateful for merely having the opportunity to continue his involvement with Bolton Wanderers. However, the influx of money in the sport was not only helping to make some clubs richer, but also serving to cripple some of those who were now spending beyond their means to try to keep up. Lofty's final season as manager had seen the likes of Terry Wharton, Gordon Taylor and Paul Fletcher all sold to bolster the club's coffers, with none of their combined transfer value of roughly £90,000 being made available for transfers into the club. Jimmy Meadows had quit as manager after his proposed transfer plan to the board was rejected on the basis that it represented, according to

Chairman Jack Banks, 'a financial commitment'* that risked the future of the club. In December of 1970, the board of directors resorted to giving personal guarantees that they had the finances to keep the club going. The severity of Bolton's crisis, and the speed with which it engulfed the club, took everyone by surprise. However, nobody could have predicted the club's next move to attempt to keep the wolves from the door.

On 8 June 1972 (Nat recalled the exact date in his autobiography with a degree of specificity often lacking in other passages, demonstrating the sheer impact the event had upon him), Lofty was summoned to the Burnden Park boardroom. Wanderers had finished seventh in their first season under the guidance of new manager Jimmy Armfield – a campaign that stopped the rot but that also quashed the hope that Bolton could return to the Second Division at the first time of asking. Wanderers had once again been let down by a faltering attack. Yet as Bolton fans were sighing and yearning for a striker of Nat's ability, he was about to become further away from the club than he'd been since signing his amateur papers in 1939.

A call to the boardroom was always likely to stir the butterflies in the stomach, but Nat never feared the meeting would be anything more than a state of the union discussion with Banks about the direction of Bolton Wanderers. Instead, Nat found himself in the meeting that ended his thirty-three-year association with the club that 'I thought I would always have a place at':

> The Chairman, Jack Banks, was there with other directors. He was in tears. A big strong man, a builder, Jack was crying.
>
> He just told me that the club had decided not to keep me on as Chief Scout. I had been relieved when they sacked me as manager. But this was different. This hurt. It came out of the blue and to this day I don't really know the background.
>
> I was devastated. I don't really remember my reaction but I can recall walking out of Burnden Park, across the car park and down Manchester Road wondering how it could have happened to me. It was just a bad

---

★   *Bolton Evening News*, 6 April 1971.

dream. Bolton Wanderers had been my life. Now I was no longer part of the furniture. It didn't seem true.

Lofty put on a brave face, telling the papers that the move was 'a complete surprise'* but avoiding letting on just how upset he was: 'I have taken some hard knocks in football, but believe me, this is the hardest.' His son, Jeff, recalls the period as 'a sad time': 'I remember him phoning me, he was absolutely devastated.' The reasons behind the dramatic decision were, in the words of the directors, 'economic'. The *Bolton Evening News* called the move 'the end of an era'. The board were 'gambling' on the reaction they'd get from a public that had 'turned its back on the present-day Wanderers to a great extent but who will carry memories of Nat and his whole-hearted battlers with them for ever'. At least one board member considered the move so unpalatable that he offered his resignation. To no one's surprise, Nat wouldn't hear of it.

Wanderers were now operating on a shoestring budget, scarcely able to afford a single transfer fee while doing what they could to ship their top assets out of the club to help keep the cash flowing. Although Nat's role as chief scout did encompass keeping an eye out for promising youngsters, his remit would ordinarily have had a greater emphasis on finding first-team-ready players who could come in and help out immediately. However, even during his managerial reign he had told the *Bolton Evening News* that several players he'd spotted had been beyond Bolton's financial reach, and had subsequently gone for sums far more than they could hope to afford. 'It was after this,' Nat told the paper, 'I decided my youth policy was the only salvation.' With the transfer coffers now even further diminished, Nat's quest to find players had become an all but redundant role.

A Bolton Wanderers without Nat Lofthouse was scarcely imaginable, not least for the man himself. The tremendous hurt created by his departure from the club was somewhat assuaged as, in Armfield's second season in charge, Wanderers surged to the Third Division title and dispersed the

---

* *Birmingham Daily Post*, 9 June 1972.

clouds that had hung over the club ever since their relegation from the top flight. Although tempted to keep his distance, Nat couldn't resist the lure of Burnden Park and quietly enjoyed taking in the games from the terraces as a fan, without the worry about who he'd have to drop for the next match or any of the other umpteen duties he'd been tasked with over the previous few years. He also, once again, enhanced his legacy as a man who never put himself first, steadfastly refusing to utter a word against the club in public: 'There were things I could have said about the club. But I didn't. I never wanted to dig the dirt.' Nat would spend the next six years solely as a spectator of Bolton Wanderers, enjoying rubbing shoulders with the same fans who had spent so many years cheering him as a hero.

As much as Nat enjoyed watching from the stands, the next few years were strange ones. Jeff said of the time that 'he was a bit lost without football' and the life that came with it that he hadn't been without for more than three decades. His wages as coach and manager had surpassed those he'd earned as a player and had put the family in a financially stable situation. Alma, who had trained as a hairdresser after school and had been working as one when she and Nat began courting, opened her own salon, Mrs Nat Lofthouse Hair Fashions, and with Jeff and Viv leaving home, Nat's financial obligations were less of a concern than they had been when his playing days were coming to an end. He was still able to bring in money through public relations work for local businesses and by appearing at events, remaining one of the region's most recognisable faces and trusted voices. Speaking engagements and charity matches gave him the opportunity to keep in touch with his old mates. Tom Finney fondly recalled one testimonial they played together in Grimsby, after which they were presented, as per local custom, with some fish: Finney plaice and Nat cod. When Nat queried, tongue-in-cheek, why Finney had received the better fish, the man presenting it told Lofty that his best mate had been the better player. Regular work as a PR figure for a local supermarket kept him busy and, in Jeff's words, 'saved his pride'. For a time he worked as Lancashire scout for Arsenal, in the first and only time he'd be employed by a club other than Wanderers. Beyond that, he was largely free, for the first time in his life, to do as he pleased, taking long walks and busying himself with involvement in community projects. Several offers came in for his coaching services from abroad, but the prospect of leaving all he had behind in Bolton made such a move a non-starter. He remained firmly out of the picture at Burnden Park, cheering the team on as they continued to recover, spending four years in the Second Division before finishing the 1977/78 season as champions, powered by youth team graduate Neil Whatmore's goals, and finally, after almost a decade and a half, returning to the First Division.

Not only did Wanderers' promotion bring the crowds surging back, but it also brought Lofty back into the fold. Emboldened by their new-found financial stability (several big-money signings were made in an attempt to establish Bolton as a top-flight fixture for years to come) and armed with a touch more nous than they'd had when football had suddenly seemed to leave them behind in the mid-1960s, Wanderers fitted Burnden Park with a new executive club. It was felt among the Bolton directors, chief among them Derek Warburton, that to truly cap off the experience for visitors to the new function area there needed to be a host who'd be able to enjoy a laugh with the guests as well as, of course, being Bolton Wanderers through and through. There was only one logical choice. For Nat it was, in many ways, the ideal role. His efforts to work on the playing side of the game, even with his vast experience, had been hamstrung by his own ability. His footballing talent had been a combination of natural skill twinned with a fearlessness and bravery few players even of his era could replicate. Yes, he'd worked hard to refine his ability, but having the ability and psychological make-up in the first place was what set him apart from most. Unfortunately, that made him ill-suited to management, as he struggled to teach players what came to him so instinctively. Here, however, he would be free from the pressures of team performance and would be able to indulge in two of his favourite things: meeting fellow Bolton Wanderers fans and Bolton Wanderers itself.

Nat took to his new role like a duck to water, and had the pleasure of entertaining the 100 regular club members over the course of a successful return to English football's top table as the Whites avoided the drop. A particular highlight of the season was the club's first double over Manchester United since the 1956/57 season. Ian Greaves, who had appeared for United against Bolton in the 1958 Cup Final, was now Whites manager, and Nat felt he was the man under whom Wanderers could rebuild their status as a First Division mainstay. Lofty noted that unlike his own time as manager, the relationship Greaves had with his players meant 'they could share a joke and a laugh with him but there was never any doubt who was in charge'.

However, as had happened a wearying number of times since Nat's retirement, just when things were looking up, they fell apart. Several expensive signings failed to live up to their billing, and Frank Worthington, who had in 1978/79 become the first Wanderers player since Nat to top the First Division goal-scoring charts, was sold. Greaves was sacked midway through the following campaign and Wanderers were relegated with five games left to play. A familiar pattern of selling to cover costs − costly renovations made to Burnden during the club's brief stay in the top flight had added further strain on the club's creaking coffers − ensued, and a swift return to the top division never looked likely. With the crowds dwindling to worrying lows again, Wanderers had to find a way of making more money from those that did attend. However, significantly raising ticket prices for fans watching increasingly poorer football was simply not on the cards. Instead, Nat would now play a new role for Wanderers, as the club's saviour.

On 11 December 1982, Nat walked out onto the Burnden pitch. It was a walk he'd made hundreds of times as a player, but rarely had his stride carried more purpose than it did at the half-time break in a relegation six-pointer against Charlton Athletic. Though his playing days had seen the stands packed with magnitudes more than the 5,645 scattered around the ground that day, Lofty was not about to be deterred. Microphone in hand, he called on the crowd of diehard Wanderers fans to dig deep; the club had reached financial breaking point, and without their support, things would soon come to a head. Lofty's solution had been masterminded by the club's commercial manager, Alf Davies, and chairman,

Terry Edge, and was appropriately called the Lifeline programme: a lottery, in which half the money earned from ticket sales would be used as the prizes for entrants, with the other half going to the club. The day after Nat's impassioned plea, Wanderers staff arrived at Burnden to a scene like a child opening their curtains on Christmas morning to a fresh layer of snow. A queue, hundreds strong, was snaking down the Manchester Road, each person waiting patiently to play their part in saving their club. Andrew Dean, now in charge of Lifeline, believes the initiative could easily have failed but for Nat's role as spokesperson. 'People came down to save the club,' explains Dean, 'because Nat asked them to.'

Within six years, the fund, which Nat would endlessly champion and promote wherever he saw an opportunity, had raised in excess of £1.5 million. Although it hadn't helped the club turn its fortunes around on the field, it had staved off the threat posed by mounting debts and had been instrumental in keeping Bolton Wanderers afloat. Dean offers a summary echoed by many involved with the club at the time: 'Without Nat, in that era Bolton Wanderers would have folded.' For years, he and Nat would make the rounds on Monday, personally delivering prizes to the winners throughout the Bolton area. Pubs notified ahead of time that Lofty would be there would inevitably be packed to the rafters, with Nat all too happy to meet yet more adoring fans. 'Nat used to say it was his favourite night because he just used to get free drinks all night!' remembers Dean. While the Lifeline scheme lacked the glory of scoring goals in front of a packed Embankment, Nat's role in making it a success was perhaps his greatest contribution of all to Bolton.

Even as Lifeline pumped in desperately needed funds, things on the pitch were going from bad to worse. By 1986, the club were back in the third tier and were in the process of recording their worst-ever league finish of eighteenth. Things were looking bleak. Nat certainly had fewer punters to entertain on match days, but that was the least of the club's troubles. The playing squad was threadbare, with the majority of the clubs around them (to say nothing of those in the divisions above) able to comfortably outbid Wanderers for players and pick the bones of the Bolton team in the knowledge that the board couldn't afford to turn down a transfer fee when the opportunity arose. Operating constantly from the back foot, the rare occasions when the Bolton board were persuaded to part with some cash rarely yielded results, such as when £10,000 was splashed on forward Wayne Entwistle, who was unable to find the net once.

Unlike some of his contemporaries, and despite Wanderers spiralling towards the bottom rung of professional football (they would hit rock bottom with relegation to the Fourth Division in 1987), Nat never fell out of love with the game. Rather, he took to his role as club president, which was awarded to him in October 1986, with aplomb. '[Being president] is a great honour but I see the job as much more than a title at the top of the club's letter headings. I'm still working flat out for Wanderers in any capacity,' he said. His dedication was demonstrated when, the year before he became president, he did what he probably swore he'd never do again, becoming interim manager in December 1985 and guiding the team to a victory before Phil Neal took charge of the team. Rather than sitting back, he took his new title with the understanding that it carried a responsibility for him to act not only a spokesman for the club, but as a crusader for the sport as a whole against the ills he now felt were befalling it.

He became a vociferous opponent of the growing strain of hooliganism on the terraces and never failed to tell people that the gradual rewriting of his era as being a solely masculine football experience was false, reminding readers of his autobiography that 'thirty years ago the football match was a day out'. Eventually, Nat was moved to appear before a game shortly after he was awarded the presidency to deliver another passionate on-pitch speech, as he had with the launch of Lifeline. Those in the stands who had personally contributed to the recent crowd trouble at Bolton matches expected little more than a mild ticking off from the now 61-year-old icon. Instead, what they got amounted to a quite significant bollocking; 'The manager and the team don't need you,' he roared, fist aloft, 'and the rest of us don't want you!' He was, however, still very much on the side of those he deemed real football fans, not the hooligans who simply 'use the game [as an excuse] to create trouble'. Along with Tom Finney, John Charles and Ivor Allchurch, Nat visited the

House of Lords in 1989 to oppose the proposal to force football fans to carry ID cards, something he felt would do little to curb hooliganism but could dent the casual fan's enthusiasm for attending games. He dedicated a chapter of his autobiography to discussing the recent Hillsborough Disaster, expressing his horror at what had occurred and his disbelief that events like Hillsborough could still happen even after the Burnden Disaster and similar episodes such as the deaths at Ibrox and Bradford City. He strongly advocated for the introduction of all-seater stadiums,* contending that safety was vastly more important than any potential loss of atmosphere. 'We know now how lethal those vast standing areas can become. Lives come first. If we can save lives by having all-seater stadiums we must have them,' argued Lofty.

For an outsider, the idea that someone in their 60s, rapidly nearing retirement age, would work themselves relentlessly day and night for such an ailing cause as Bolton Wanderers would have been baffling. For anyone who knew Nat, it wasn't a surprise in the slightest. Dean, who worked closely with Nat for years, remembers a man with extraordinary work ethic and professionalism: 'He always made time for the sponsors, never hid away.' On match days, scarcely five minutes would pass between requests for the Lion of Vienna, and he never failed to answer the call: 'I don't think I can ever say I saw him lose his professionalism with someone.' Even if the office got a bit too noisy for his liking, his rebuke was laced with some trademark dry wit, as he declared, 'I could have sworn I heard a train coming!'

Without consistent work during the week with Wanderers, he dedicated himself to aiding community causes and charities. However, there was a tragic reason behind his eagerness to throw himself into his work. The year before he was given the role of president, 1985, Nat had lost Alma, his wife of thirty-nine years, to cancer. As anyone with a spouse who had provided such loving care and staunch support would be, Nat was heartbroken. Four years later, in his autobiography *The Lion of Vienna*,

---

* The Taylor Report, published a year after Hillsborough and Nat's book, moved to make all major football stadia all-seater.

the brevity of his account of her death speaks volumes for the tremendous sense of loss he still felt: 'I was totally devastated. I will never get over it.' His book, which is peppered with references to his family, contains not a single mention of Alma that is less than glowing with warmth and love, and despite the number of influences that Nat could thank for his career, he was unequivocal about Alma's pivotal role. 'From the start,' he explained, 'she wanted me to reach the top and was willing to sacrifice anything to help me get there. I would not be where I am today without her.' After her death, he continued many of the family rituals that had started in recent times, going to Viv's home for Sunday dinner and holidaying in Antibes in the south of France where Jeff now lived. Nat became such a regular visitor to the historic Riviera town that he was recognised almost every time he took his morning stroll, sometimes for footballing reasons, sometimes simply as the genial, friendly man that was always willing to stop and have a chat.

Though Nat's first years as club president had been marred by the club's descent into the Fourth Division, his testimonial year in 1989, celebrating fifty years since his association with the club began, provided great cause for celebration. The club put on gala events, including a presentation featuring some of his greatest moments, a testimonial dinner and a star-studded match. It wasn't just the club that were getting in on the act of celebrating the town's favourite son. Bolton-based folk group Houghton Weavers released a celebratory single called 'The Lion of Vienna' ('There'll be other centre forwards/and other football teams/ but the Lion of Vienna/is the best there's ever been'), while the same name had been bestowed upon a pub on the outskirts of the town centre. Later, the name would also be emblazoned upon, appropriately given Nat's playing style, a train. 1989 also saw Nat made a Freeman of Bolton, and five years later in the New Year's Honours list, he was awarded an OBE. Appearances on *This is your Life* and *Through the Keyhole* served as a reminder, to Lofty himself more than anybody else, of just how beloved his personality and his achievements had made him. Even as the English game entered a new age, his name was never too far from the minds of fans. The emergence of Mark Hughes and Alan Shearer drew inevitable comparisons, and introduced another generation of fans to Lofty. At Burnden, a new mascot design in 1995 saw the creation of 'Lofty the Lion'. The real Lofty was over the moon ('so proud,' recalls Andrew Dean) at such a fun preservation of his remarkable legacy.

When football wasn't keeping him busy, Nat could be found spending time with a new companion, Mildred Clayton, who had been introduced to him by his former captain, Willie Moir, at a function at Burnden. Mildred, who only vaguely recognised the face of Wanderers' greatest having never been to a match herself despite living in the area her whole life, vividly recalls the moment they met: 'Nat came over and said, "What are you doing with him [Moir]? You should be with me!" Some of the other players were going "ohh" and rolling their eyes. He pulled the chair out and whispered in my ear, "You will be one day, you know."' From that moment until Nat's death more than two decades later, he and Mildred enjoyed a loving relationship, filled with laughter, fun with Mildred's grandchildren and even the odd impromptu singing performance from Nat. No matter if they were vacationing abroad or simply enjoying a curry at Farnworth's Royal Balti House, they were almost inseparable.

Even as the face of Burnden Park changed dramatically – the railway signal box had been destroyed by fire in 1971, while half the iconic Embankment had been sold to the Normid supermarket group for them to build a new superstore in 1986 – gradual progress once again imbued the club with a feel-good attitude. One of the key turning points, Nat felt, was Wanderers enjoying their first taste of success at Wembley since 1958 with victory in the Sherpa Vans Tournament in 1989, the season after they'd been promoted back to the third flight. Under the stewardship of Bruce Rioch, Wanderers finally returned to the Second Division (now known as Division One following the rebranding of the top tier as the Premier League) in 1993/94, ten years after they'd last played at that level. Rioch then needed just a single season to guide the club to a long-awaited return to the top of English football. Amidst their phoenix-like rise through the leagues, Wanderers enjoyed a succession of stirring FA Cup performances, knocking out Liverpool and Arsenal, previous Cup holders, in successive seasons. These years were a true thrill for Nat, who could not help but be reminded of his glory days of wreaking havoc in the Cup against more fancied sides. They also saw the emergence of one of the very few players since Nat's time who was able to command something like the same devotion and fanaticism amongst Wanderers supporters. John McGinlay joined the club as a prolific lower-league goal scorer, but with Bolton his record of more than a league goal every other game in the top three divisions earned him legendary status. Fittingly, it was McGinlay who scored the final home goal of Wanderers' 1996/97 season that was a landmark for several reasons. Not only did the Whites return to the Premier League with gusto, winning a league for the first time in almost twenty years, but it was to be the final year in which the club played at Burnden Park. With the old ground no longer matching the club's ambitions in the increasingly commercialised world of English football, a state-of-the-art stadium was being constructed on the outskirts of town in order to replace the ground that had enjoyed so many historic moments, not least Nat's entire career.

Those fearing that the links to the past would be broken as Bolton left their historic home behind were appeased by Nat's presence front and centre of the club's PR around the opening of the Reebok Stadium. Lofty posed for photos as the massive structure was taking form and pulled strings to have former Prime Minister John Major, who he had got to know thanks to his involvement in England's bid for the 2006 World Cup, visit the stadium when it opened. Further historical connections were ensured by two honours for Lofty. The first, a hospitality room named the Lion of Vienna Suite, was a nod to his tireless hospitality work at the club, where his efforts to bring in money any way he could had saved Wanderers from oblivion. The second was the greatest tribute. Beneath the enormous curve of the Reebok's roof, with the iconic floodlights looming above it, his name was emblazoned on the ground's eastward-facing side, enshrining it forever as The Nat Lofthouse Stand. 'At Burnden, I've only ever seen my name go up on the team sheet,' he said. 'To see it on the side of a stand will give me a real thrill.'* Nat had never failed to be humbled when given any sort of

★   *Bolton Evening News*, 10 January 1997.

honour over the years – Alma carefully packed away various mementos of his playing career, with a commemorative lion statuette he was given by the Earlestown FC Supporters Association one of his 'most treasured possessions' – and these two celebrations of him were some of the greatest of all. A dedicated campaign to see Lofty knighted garnered much support, and though it never came to fruition,* Mildred recalls Nat being extremely touched by the lengths people went to try to help him achieve the accolade. In a classic display of Lancastrian obstinance, many fans simply took to referring to Lofty as 'Sir Nat' anyway. In their eyes, nobody was more deserving.

★ Roy Hartle: 'Tom Finney was the best opponent I ever played against and fully deserved his knighthood. But Nat was the best player I ever played with and it would have been nice for him to get one, too. Why he was not knighted I'll never know.' John Gradwell, *Legend: The Life of Roy 'Chopper' Hartle*, p. 207.

15

FULL TIME

ON A CRISP winter's morning in 2011, Bolton witnessed scenes the likes of which hadn't been seen for years, perhaps since the town's beloved football club returned home triumphant with the FA Cup in hand in 1958. On that day, there had been jubilation amongst the thronging crowds, the only break in the hubbub and the cheers coming when one man had appeared on the steps of the town hall to bid thanks to all the well-wishers. Nat Lofthouse never saw himself as any different from the people he addressed that day – after all, he thought he could only really 'run, shoot and head' – but it was precisely that sense of equality that made him so unique. As a club, Bolton Wanderers has played host to a legion of superb footballers before and after Lofty's time, players who have been admired, idolised, adored. But none has ever been loved as Nat was, and none could have relied on their mere presence to command such a vociferous crowd as Nat did on that day. On 26 January 2011, the crowds were just as large, but the atmosphere was almost (there were still cries of 'there's only one Nat Lofthouse!') unanimously different. The applause was that of sorrowful appreciation rather than joy for the man who had, after dedicating what seemed to be every waking moment of his entire life to Bolton Wanderers, passed away eleven days before at the age of 85. His final words were a beautiful evocation of the game that had defined his life and that he'd done so much to define: 'I've got the ball now. It's a bit worn, but I've got it.'

Up until the mid-2000s, Nat had remained a regular presence at the Reebok Stadium, delighting in the team's return to prominence in the English game.* He had led the team on to the pitch alongside 'best buddy' (in Jeff's words) Tom Finney, with whom he still enjoyed an indefatigably close friendship, as Wanderers faced Preston in the 2001 Play-Off Final. Bolton's victory was the springboard for success the likes of which hadn't been seen since Nat's day. Four consecutive top-half finishes under former player Sam Allardyce (who Nat had originally signed as an apprentice) firmly established the team as the country's premier over-achievers, and even ushered in two separate campaigns of European football for the first time. Lofty was still rarely able to step outside for longer than five minutes before being recognised and asked for an autograph or a photo, something that he still took great joy in, particularly if the request came from a fan decades too young to have seen him play. Nat's natural aversion to the spotlight meant that when he did begin to display signs of illness, the details were largely kept from the public eye. Mildred made a great effort to visit him every single day, bringing him enormous comfort. Sometime after his death, his name was added to the tragic roll call of players from his era who had suffered from dementia in later life, likely as a result of repeatedly heading the weighty leather balls of the 1950s.

Nat would have scarcely believed the outpouring of grief upon his passing. As Phil Gartside, the club's chairman at the time, remarked during his eulogy, 'He'd probably look me in the eye and say, "Don't be daft cocker, you'll be alright."' Nat scored 285 goals for Wanderers in league and cup, ending his career as the club's all-time record holder with a total that is unlikely to ever be threatened; since his retirement, no one has scored half as many. He was the FWA's Footballer of the Year and the First Division top goal scorer. In

---

* In 2001, he proudly boasted to have not missed a home game for sixty-two years (allowing, with some poetic licence, for the few he missed as a player while on England duty).

between his remarkable service for Bolton, he also became England's record scorer, with a goals-to-games ratio that is unmatched in the post-war era. Yet somehow, none of these superlative achievements come close to detailing who Nat Lofthouse was as a man, or what he meant to so many people.

His funeral procession was attended by thousands, most of them fans, many others just Boltonians who recognised what he'd done for the town and wanted to say goodbye to one of their own. Footballing luminaries including Finney, Sir Bobby Charlton and Sir Alex Ferguson were all in attendance. Four managers from the club's past – Jimmy Armfield, Bruce Rioch, Colin Todd and Sam Allardyce – bid farewell to their counterpart. Bolton's manager at the time and former striker Owen Coyle was a pallbearer, as was Kevin Davies, who had led the Bolton forward line for several years, and Dave Whelan, chairman of Wigan Athletic. As expected, tributes were plentiful and glowing. Charlton, the man who took up the mantle as England's centre forward from Nat, said of his predecessor, 'He was a leader, he had fantastic ability in the air and he was strong. He was a talisman.' Roy Hartle said simply, 'He was a great man and a great friend to me.' Don Howe, with whom Nat played for England, recalled not only his ability, but his spirit and innate talents as a teammate, saying:

> He was not only a great player, he was a great character. On the pitch – wonderful, powerful, put the ball in the box and he will do the job for you. Off the pitch, I was one of the young caps then, he would come up to you and say 'hello son, how are you doing?' He would give you a real gee up, that's how he was. I was one of the young lads of the group then and wherever he was in the hotel, he would be around everybody picking people up.

Armfield said, 'He was probably one of the best centre forwards England ever had, very aggressive and combative with great speed. He was everything a centre forward should be and was a great one-club man. The two words Lofthouse and Bolton go together.' Some months later, with Wanderers readying themselves for their first trip to the new Wembley Stadium for an FA Cup semi-final, Doug Holden, the only surviving member of the 1953 final team after Nat's passing, remarked, 'He was a dominant fellow, ruled the dressing room, a good-looking man, a good-living man. His funeral brought the town to a standstill. I'm not surprised."*

There are few professional football clubs of such stature that owe so much to a single person, player or otherwise. As a player, he simply dominated the team for well over a decade, and deserves the lion's share of credit for what remains one of the crowning achievements of one of the most famous teams in England, the 1958 FA Cup win. The trophy remains the last major honour won by the team, a barren run of more than fifty years that has tortured Trotters fans but has also acted, in an odd way, as a comforting reminder of the past, of the fact the last time the club achieved national glory they did so thanks to truly the greatest player the team has ever known. The day Bolton Wanderers win major honours again will be a source of great joy, but one tinged with sadness, as it will truly draw a line under the legacy of Lofty.

Although his time as manager never threatened to match his storied impact as a player, the sense that he never truly courted the managerial role yet answered the call when the club needed him again speaks volumes about his loyalty to the team. His tireless work later helped to first save the club from financial doom and then to revitalise it, aiding Bolton in reaching heights that scarcely seemed possible when the club dipped to the fourth flight in the late 1980s.

In the final years before his full retirement, Nat had the pleasure of watching one of the great Wanderers teams under Allardyce, brimming with international-calibre players. Yet none of those players – not Kevin Davies, the boisterous, barrel-chested centre forward who reminded so many older fans of their days in the Burnden paddocks watching Nat; not Jay-Jay Okocha, the majestic magician; not Nicolas Anelka, the world-renowned marksman; not Fernando Hierro, the bona fide Real Madrid and Spain legend – ever truly came close to usurping Nat. Lofty was a one-club man, but he made Bolton a one-man club. Bolton Wanderers Football Club is now nearing 150 years of age. It's impossible to imagine the next 150 yielding anyone who comes close to matching Lofty.

---

*   John Gradwell, *Legend: The Life of Roy 'Chopper' Hartle*, p. 207.

APPENDIX

CAREER STATISTICS

CLUB

| Season | LEAGUE | | | CUP | | |
	Division	Apps	Goals	Competition	Apps	Goals
1940/41	Football League North (Wartime)	11	11	--	--	--
1941/42	Football League North (Wartime)	12	7	--	--	--
1942/43	Football League North (Wartime)	25	14	--	--	--
1943/44	Football League North (Wartime)	24	16	--	--	--

Season	Competition			Competition		
1944/45	Football League North (Wartime)	31	30	---	---	---
1945/46	Football League North (Wartime)	34	20	FA Cup	6	2
1946/47	Division One	40	18	FA Cup	3	3
1947/48	Division One	34	18	FA Cup	1	0
1948/49	Division One	22	7	FA Cup	3	1
1949/50	Division One	35	10	FA Cup	3	3
1950/51	Division One	38	21	FA Cup	2	1
				Charity Shield	1	1
1951/52	Division One	38	18	FA Cup	1	0
1952/53	Division One	36	22	FA Cup	8	8
1953/54	Division One	32	17	FA Cup	6	1
1954/55	Division One	31	15	FA Cup	2	0
1955/56	Division One	36	32	FA Cup	2	1
1956/57	Division One	36	28	FA Cup	1	0
1957/58	Division One	31	17	FA Cup	5	3
1958/59	Division One	37	29	FA Cup	6	4
				Charity Shield	1	2
1959/60	Division One	0	0	FA Cup	0	0
1960/61	Division One	6	3	FA Cup	0	0
				League Cup	2	3

INTERNATIONAL

Season	Apps	Goals
1950/51	1	2
1951/52	7	7
1952/53	8	8
1953/54	5	6
1954/55	5	2
1955/56	5	4
1956/57	0	0
1957/58	2	1

BIBLIOGRAPHY

In my attempts to be as thorough as possible, I consulted a wide range of sources. I made extensive use of several newspaper archives, particularly that of *Bolton Evening News*, as well as *The Guardian*, *The Times*, *Daily Herald*, *Daily Dispatch*, *Lancashire Evening Post* and numerous other local and regional newspapers. I also referenced the following on multiple occasions:

Sir Bobby Charlton, *My Life in Football* (Headline, 2009)

Tom Finney, *Tom Finney: My Autobiography* (Headline, 2004)

Leslie Gent, *Making Headlines: The History of Bolton Wanderers Football Club as Seen Through the Eyes the Pages of the Bolton Evening News* (Sports Programme Publishing Ltd, 2004)

John Gradwell, *Legend: The Life of Roy 'Chopper' Hartle* (Paragon Publishing Rothersthorpe, 2014)

Sean Hedges-Quinn, *I've got the Ball Now: The Making of the Nat Lofthouse Statue* (Penultimate Creative, 2013)

Jon Henderson, *The Wizard: The Life of Stanley Matthews* (Yellow Jersey, 2013)

Douglas Lamming, *An English Football Internationalists' Who's Who* (Hutton Press, 1990)

James Leighton, *Duncan Edwards: The Greatest* (Simon & Schuster, 2012)

Nat Lofthouse, *Goals Galore* (Stanley Paul, 1954)

Nat Lofthouse & Andrew Collomosse, *Nat Lofthouse: The Lion of Vienna* (Sportsprint, 1989)

Simon Marland, *Bolton Wanderers: The Complete Record* (DB Publishing, 2011)

Simon Marland, *Bolton Wanderers FC: The Official History, 1877–2002* (Yore Publications, 2002)

Stanley Matthews, *The Way it Was: My Autobiography* (Headline, 2001)

Dave McVay & Andy Smith, *The Complete Centre Forward: The Authorised Biography of Tommy Lawton* (SportsBooks Ltd, 2003)

George Orwell, *The Road to Wigan Pier* (Penguin Classics, 2001)

Tim Purcell & Mike Gething, *Wartime Wanderers* (Mainstream Publishing, 1996)

Ian Seddon, *Ah'm Tellin' Thee: Tommy Banks, Bolton Wanderers and England* (Paragon Publishing Rothersthorpe, 2014)

Rory Smith, *Mister* (Simon & Schuster, 2016)

David Tossell, *The Great English Final: 1953: Cup, Coronation & Stanley Matthews* (Pitch Publishing, 2013)

John K. Walton, *Lancashire: A Social History, 1558–1939* (Manchester University Press, 2003)

Percy M. Young, *Bolton Wanderers* (Stanley Paul, 1961)

ACKNOWLEDGEMENTS

When I began researching Nat's life in early 2015, I never dreamed that I would one day be publishing a book detailing everything I found. I couldn't have done it without the following people.

Firstly, thank you to everyone at Bolton Wanderers Football Club, without whom none of this would have been possible. Particular thanks to Paul Holliday and Andrew Dean, who have done so much in helping arrange interviews and field what I'm sure must have been an incredible quantity of stupid questions from me.

Thank you to all those who graciously gave up their time to be interviewed, including Tommy Banks, Doug Holden, Terry Allcock, Gordon Taylor, Jeff Lofthouse and Mildred Clayton. Additional thanks to Tommy's wife Rita, who helped put me in touch with various people. The closest player to Nat's heir that there's ever been (both on and off the pitch), John McGinlay, graciously gave up his time to contribute a glowing tribute to the man as the foreword for this book.

Thank you to all those who have helped bring the book attention, including Tom George, Marc Iles and Jeremy Fullam, as well as many Bolton fans on social media. I'm also extremely grateful to everyone who has got in touch with personal anecdotes about Nat and has generally helped spread the word about the book.

Huge thanks to Clare Bate, whose late father Peter Stafford had accumulated possibly the most extensive private library of Bolton Wanderers literature in existence. Clare generously passed these books to me, and they formed the backbone of my research.

Thank you to my commissioning editor Christine McMorris and everyone at The History Press who believed in the book and brought it to life.

I owe an enormous debt of gratitude to my intrepid team of proofreaders. My grandma Carolyn who has reassured me that what I've written resembles the Bolton she grew up in. My fiancée Charli, who's not only read several versions of the book, but has also put up with me relating every conversation we've had for the past four years back to the 1954 World Cup. My mum, who spent an inordinate amount of time searching for stray apostrophes and has always supported my writing, and my dad, who has done the same, as well as spending countless hours ferrying us up and down the country to watch some very good Bolton performances, and a lot of not so good ones.

Finally, thank you to Nat Lofthouse, for living such an extraordinary life. I hope this book has done some justice to it.

INDEX